Deleuze's *Difference and Repetition*

T0322490

Edinburgh Philosophical Guides Series

Titles in the series include:

Kant's *Critique of Pure Reason*
Douglas Burnham with Harvey Young

Derrida's *Of Grammatology*
Arthur Bradley

Heidegger's *Being and Time*
William Large

Plato's *Republic*
D. J. Sheppard

Spinoza's *Ethics*
Beth Lord

Descartes' *Meditations on First Philosophy*
Kurt Brandhorst

Nietzsche's *Thus Spoke Zarathustra*
Douglas Burnham and Martin Jesinghausen

Deleuze's *Difference and Repetition*
Henry Somers-Hall

Foucault's *History of Sexuality Volume I, The Will to Knowledge*
Mark Kelly

Kant's *Groundwork of the Metaphysics of Morals*
John Callanan

Visit the Edinburgh Philosophical Guides Series website at
www.euppublishing.com/series/edpg

Deleuze's *Difference and Repetition*

An Edinburgh Philosophical Guide

Henry Somers-Hall

EDINBURGH
University Press

© Henry Somers-Hall, 2013

Edinburgh University Press Ltd
22 George Square, Edinburgh EH8 9LF

www.euppublishing.com

Typeset in 10.5/13pt Monotype Baskerville by
Servis Filmsetting Ltd, Stockport, Cheshire, and
printed and bound in Great Britain by
CPI Group (UK) Ltd, Croydon CR0 4YY

A CIP record for this book is available from the British Library

ISBN 978 0 7486 4678 4 (hardback)
ISBN 978 0 7486 4677 7 (paperback)
ISBN 978 0 7486 6967 7 (webready PDF)
ISBN 978 0 7486 6968 4 (epub)
ISBN 978 0 7486 6969 1 (Amazon ebook)

The right of Henry Somers-Hall
to be identified as author of this work
has been asserted in accordance with
the Copyright, Designs and Patents Act 1988.

Contents

Series Editor's Preface

To us, the principle of this series of books is clear and simple: what readers new to philosophical classics need first and foremost is help with *reading* these key texts. That is to say, help with the often antique or artificial style, the twists and turns of arguments on the page, as well as the vocabulary found in many philosophical works. New readers also need help with those first few daunting and disorienting sections of these books, the point of which are not at all obvious. The books in this series take you through each text step-by-step, explaining complex key terms and difficult passages which help to illustrate the way a philosopher thinks in prose.

We have designed each volume in the series to correspond to the way the texts are actually taught at universities around the world, and have included helpful guidance on writing university-level essays or examination answers. Designed to be read alongside the text, our aim is to enable you to *read* philosophical texts with confidence and perception. This will enable you to make your own judgements on the texts, and on the variety of opinions to be found concerning them. We want you to feel able to join the great dialogue of philosophy, rather than remain a well-informed eavesdropper.

Douglas Burnham

Acknowledgements

This book has its origins in an MA course on *Difference and Repetition* taught at Manchester Metropolitan University in 2010 and 2011. I would like to thank the students who took that course, Matt Barnard, Leda Channer, August Crook, Billy Griffiths, Georgina Hemstritch-Johnston, Simon Jones, Maxime Lallement, Alan Stowell, Paul Wren and Ashley Wyatt, for making it such a vibrant and fruitful experience, and for putting up with the various missteps and revisions of my account of *Difference and Repetition*. I owe special thanks to David Deamer and Rob Lapsley, who attended the course in both years, and did much to make the course a genuinely collaborative endeavour. Thanks are also due to the series editor, Douglas Burnham, and to Jenny Daly and Carol MacDonald at EUP, for their advice throughout the project. David Deamer, Helen Darby, Katrina Mitcheson and Nathan Widder all read various drafts of the book, and I am very grateful for their invaluable questions, comments and suggestions. The book has also benefited from discussions with Beth Lord, Daniel Smith, Daniela Voss, Nathan Widder and James Williams about various aspects of Deleuze's philosophy. I would also like to thank Seb Gwyther for preparing the two illustrations in this guide. Sections of this book appeared previously in 'Time Out of Joint: Hamlet and the Pure Form of Time,' *Deleuze Studies*, 5.4 (2011), 56–76, and I am grateful to Edinburgh University Press for kindly granting permission to include that material in this guide.

Abbreviations

Works by Gilles Deleuze cited

B   *Bergsonism*, trans. Hugh Tomlinson and Barbara Habberjam, New York: Zone Books, 1988.

DR   *Difference and Repetition*, trans. Paul Patton, New York: Columbia University Press, 1994/London: Continuum, 2004.

ECC   *Essays Critical and Clinical*, trans. Daniel W. Smith and Michael A. Greco, Minneapolis: University of Minnesota Press, 1997.

EPS   *Expressionism in Philosophy: Spinoza*, trans. Martin Joughin, New York: Zone Books, 1990.

ES   *Empiricism and Subjectivity: An Essay on Hume's Theory of Human Nature*, trans. Constantin V. Boundas, New York: Columbia University Press, 1991.

FLB   *The Fold: Leibniz and the Baroque*, trans. Tom Conley, Minneapolis: University of Minnesota Press, 1993/London: Continuum, 2006.

KCP   *Kant's Critical Philosophy: The Doctrine of the Faculties*, trans. Hugh Tomlinson and Barbara Habberjam, Minneapolis: University of Minnesota Press, 1984/London: Continuum, 2008.

L   Lectures, available at www.webdeleuze.com, cited by date of lecture.

LS   *The Logic of Sense*, trans. Mark Lester, with Charles Stivale, ed. Constantin V. Boundas, New York: Columbia University Press, 1990/London: Continuum, 2004.

NP   *Nietzsche and Philosophy*, trans. Hugh Tomlinson, London: Athlone Press, 1983/London: Continuum, 2006.

SPP   *Spinoza: Practical Philosophy*, trans. Robert Hurley, San Francisco: City Lights Books, 1988.

TRM   *Two Regimes of Madness: Texts and Interviews 1975–1995*, ed.

David Lapoujade, trans. Ames Hodges and Mike Taormina, New York: Semiotext(e), 2007.

Works by Gilles Deleuze and Félix Guattari

AO   *Anti-Oedipus: Capitalism and Schizophrenia I*, trans. Robert Hurley, Mark Seem and Helen R. Lane, Minneapolis: University of Minnesota Press, 1977/London: Continuum, 2004.

ATP   *A Thousand Plateaus: Capitalism and Schizophrenia II*, trans. Brian Massumi, Minneapolis: University of Minnesota Press, 1987/ London: Continuum, 2004.

WP   *What is Philosophy?*, trans. by Hugh Tomlinson and Graham Burchell, London: Verso, 1994.

Works by Gilles Deleuze and Claire Parnet

D   *Dialogues II*, trans. Hugh Tomlinson and Barbara Habberjam, New York: Columbia University Press, 2007/London: Continuum, 2006.

Introduction

Gilles Deleuze is one of the most influential post-war French philosophers. While his influence in the Anglo-American world began with the translation of his collaborations with Félix Guattari, *Difference and Repetition* has a good claim to be his philosophical masterpiece. It's difficult to situate *Difference and Repetition* within the philosophical tradition. Deleuze characterises his project as a 'transcendental empiricism', which suggests affinities with eighteenth and nineteenth-century German idealist thought. Nonetheless, Deleuze presents an account critical of both the transcendental idealist characterisation of experience and its account of knowledge. Similarly, we find strands of the early twentieth-century phenomenological project both affirmed and critiqued throughout *Difference and Repetition*. We can also see an ambivalent relationship to the structuralist tradition charted throughout the text, and a substantial engagement with the philosophies of science and mathematics. In this book, I have tried to present as many of these engagements as possible, but the emphasis is on Deleuze's own characterisation of himself as a 'pure metaphysician'. That is, I take Deleuze to be giving us an account of the nature of the world, broadly construed. What makes his project appear almost unrecognisable when compared with traditional metaphysical approaches is that he is attempting to provide a metaphysics of difference. As we shall see, his claim is that when we take identity as prior to difference, exemplified in the belief in judgement as the basis for philosophical enquiry, we are constrained to make a number of claims about the nature of the world and the nature of knowledge. These claims together form the traditional image of metaphysics. In *Difference and Repetition*, Deleuze renounces the priority of identity, which leads to a very different kind of metaphysical inquiry.

Challenges in Reading Deleuze

There are several challenges in engaging with Deleuze's text. The first of these is Deleuze's writing itself. Somewhat surprisingly, the prose of *Difference and Repetition* is more straightforward than that of many of Deleuze's texts. Nonetheless, it is still run through with neologisms, allusions to other texts, poetic phrasings, and technical vocabulary from a variety of discourses. One reason for this is Deleuze's love of taxonomy, which leads to a proliferation of distinctions, each of which plays a subtle role in the development of the argument as a whole. More fundamentally, however, as we shall see, Deleuze has a philosophically grounded mistrust of those forms of writing that communicate their ideas to us too easily, since they present the possibility of simply reinforcing our common sense beliefs rather than allowing us to engage in proper philosophical enquiry. If philosophy is going to challenge common sense, it has to be written in such a manner as to make us struggle, pause and think.

The second challenge is the variety of references to other thinkers found throughout *Difference and Repetition*. On the one hand, Deleuze develops an extended critique of much of the philosophical tradition, arguing that seeing difference as only comprehensible on the basis of identity has led us wrongly to construe the nature of the world and the philosophical endeavour. This critique takes in a number of thinkers from Plato, Aristotle, Descartes, Leibniz and Kant, through to Heidegger and the twentieth-century phenomenological tradition. On the other, Deleuze develops his alternative conception of philosophy both in contrast to these philosophers, and in relation to an alternative tradition of thinkers who have managed to free themselves at least partially from the structures of what he calls representation. Whether Deleuze is criticising his predecessors or developing moments of escape, his accounts of these other philosophers are often allusive. As such, without a broad acquaintance with the history of philosophy, *Difference and Repetition* becomes a text governed by jumps, breaks and non-sequiturs, built on a series of arguments from authority. Often, even a broad acquaintance will not suffice, as Deleuze's interest in a philosopher may focus on one or two sometimes marginal concepts.

Finally, it is not always clear what the structure of the text itself is. Deleuze does not make clear what his aim is in each of the chapters of *Difference and Repetition*, and a number of different readings of his project as a whole have emerged. It is often difficult to see exactly why Deleuze is introducing concepts (or even whole chapters) in the order in which they appear.

The approach of this text is to mitigate these difficulties as far as possible. Writing a guide to a text such as *Difference and Repetition* is a faintly paradoxical enterprise, as a certain perplexity of the understanding is a part of the project of the work itself. Nonetheless, I have tried as far as possible to present Deleuze's argument so as to make it accessible to an audience new to his work. Even without the stylistic challenges Deleuze's work presents, his philosophical thought is inherently complex and challenging, and as with any great philosophical writer, understanding his project will still require diligence on the part of the reader. In order to address the second challenge, I have included just as many references to other philosophers as to Deleuze. My hope is that by doing so, the reader will be able to understand the importance of the various allusions included in Deleuze's text. These references and explanations are not by any means exhaustive, but will hopefully allow the reader to develop enough of an understanding of the text to be able to integrate those encounters not covered. Finally, most books on *Difference and Repetition* have taken a thematic approach to the text. While this is certainly a productive approach, this guide closely follows the text of *Difference and Repetition* itself, and most of the major passages in the book are covered by a section of the guide. By dividing *Difference and Repetition* into manageable chunks, I have provided what I take to be the principal engagements going on in each section of the book, and allowed the reader to move between this guide and *Difference and Repetition* itself. The hope is to allow the reader not simply to understand the themes of the text, but to be able to read the text itself and understand the various transitions Deleuze makes within it.

The Structure of the Text

As you read different commentaries on *Difference and Repetition*, you will discover that there is not yet a consensus as to the structure of the text, or even the argument presented. While Deleuze makes the claim that neither difference nor repetition have been adequately understood, the significance he attributes to this claim is still contested. In this guide, I read *Difference and Repetition* as having the following structure:

The introduction relates the concepts of difference and repetition, noting that repetition cannot be understood within the concept of law. As we shall see, Deleuze's aim in this section is to show that repetition rests on a non-conceptual understanding of difference. While this fact is recognised by some philosophers, notably Kant, Deleuze's claim will be that we require a proper enquiry into the origin of these differences. Chapter 1 describes the limitations of our traditional conceptions of difference. Deleuze shows that understanding difference as the difference between x and y is inadequate. At the root of this account is Deleuze's claim that judgement (the attribution of predicates to objects), or representation, gives us at best a partial description of the world. Deleuze attempts to show that our understanding of the world in terms of judgement can only be made consistent on the basis of a belief that the world of judgement arises from a world of intensity.

Chapter 2 extends this result. While the first chapter focuses on a logical and metaphysical analysis of our relationship to the world, the second instead explores the world from a transcendental viewpoint, looking at the nature of experience. Deleuze is particularly keen to tackle Kant's understanding of the world. Kant's claim is that the world we perceive is the result of a synthesis on the part of the subject. That is, it is constituted. For Kant, this synthesis operates on the model of judgement, and this is the reason why the logical concepts of judgement traditionally used to explain the world accord with it. Deleuze's claim, however, is that Kant's account of the three syntheses of the transcendental deduction in fact presupposes three syntheses of time that themselves cannot be understood in terms of judgement. It is these that make the Kantian project possible. Furthermore, rather than presupposing the structures of the self and the categories of judgement, they explain their constitution in the first place. Thus, by the end of the second chapter, Deleuze makes the claim that the basic explanatory principles we use to understand the world are inadequate. While the world we perceive, and the concepts we use to describe it, operate in terms of selves and judgements, these are only effects of a deeper play of intensity.

Given the claim that the world is not simply one of subjects and objects, but one whose 'unground' is a field of intensity, we are led to the question, how are we to talk about this world? In the third chapter, Deleuze's aims are twofold. First, he attempts to show exactly *how* the traditional structures of thought occlude intensity. Thus, he describes eight postulates of what he calls the 'dogmatic image of thought' whereby the foundation of the world is understood in terms commensurate with judgement. In the process, he draws out the constraints on a more adequate account of a thinking that is able to describe the nature of the world in terms of intensity.

Chapter 4 explores this problem in more detail. Deleuze believes himself to have shown in the first two chapters that the fundamental nature of the world is intensive, but how are we to think this world? He draws out an answer based on certain advances in mathematics. In particular, the differential calculus provides a model for thinking in terms of intensity. What draws Deleuze to the calculus is the fact that it can be understood to operate according to entities that simply cannot be represented – that is, that simply cannot be incorporated into judgements. Thus, while the calculus is a definite conceptual structure, it is a conceptual structure with a determinate reference beyond the conceptual realm. It is this reference which allows us to prevent our thought from collapsing into the belief that everything can be understood in terms of extensity and judgement. As Deleuze notes, it is not simply in mathematics that we find a model of thinking that goes beyond judgement, and he provides several examples of other conceptual schemes, in the domains of physics, biology and sociology, that allow us to understand the nature of the world without reducing it to judgement.

Finally, Chapter 5 brings these themes together. We have a new understanding of the world in terms of intensity, and a new model of thinking in terms of Ideas. The question is, how do Ideas relate to intensity? In order to explain this relationship, Deleuze draws out a second set of syntheses that mirror those that he has given in terms of time, and presents a critique of the scientific theory of thermodynamics. The central aim of this chapter is to prevent Ideas simply being seen as replacing judgement. If Ideas were the only element that determined the nature of entities we found in the world, then we would be no better off than we were with judgement. Ideas would simply be a different way of encoding the properties we find in the world of judgement. Thus, Deleuze needs to show that the fields of intensity in which Ideas actualise themselves play a determinant role in constituting the world we find around us, and furthermore, that each field of intensity differs from every other.

While I take these to be the central themes of *Difference and Repetition*, in working through these issues, Deleuze draws out a number of implications. He notes that a rejection of extensity as foundation pushes towards a perspectival model of the world. The move away from judgement pushes us from an understanding of philosophy in terms of knowledge to one in terms of learning. The move away from representation gives a new urgency to projects in literature and the arts that attempt to explore the genesis of what in a different philosophical register has been called the 'thingliness' of things. Furthermore, *Difference and Repetition* contains a re-reading of the history of philosophy, developing an alternative tradition of thinkers of intensity, drawing in Lucretius, Duns Scotus, Spinoza, Feuerbach and Nietzsche, among others. Alongside this tradition runs a series of critiques of canonical thinkers from Plato to Heidegger. While we will not be able to explore all of these aspects of Deleuze's philosophy, we will touch on as many of these themes as possible.

How to Use this Guide
While this guide can be read on its own as an account of *Difference and Repetition*, it is most productively read alongside *Difference and Repetition* itself. My aim has been to provide a framework according to which Deleuze's account in his own words can be understood. This guide provides accounts of the main themes in each section of the text, providing accounts of the various interlocutors Deleuze introduces. The (same) English translation of *Difference and Repetition* has been published in two versions: the 1994 Columbia University Press/Athlone Press edition, and the 2004 Continuum edition. In this guide, I cite both editions as follows: (DR Columbia/Continuum).

I have used abbreviations for other works by Deleuze (and Guattari), and where Continuum editions exist, have also cited page numbers for both editions. Where English language texts are available, I have used these, but some texts, notably those on the calculus, are not available in English, and in these cases, the translations are my own. The final section of the book provides some aids to studying *Difference and Repetition*. The 'further reading' section gives details of where to find Deleuze's sources for various discussions. The glossary covers some of the main terminology of *Difference and Repetition*. I have also included a section on how to write about Deleuze.

1. A Guide to the Text

Introduction: Repetition and Difference

0.1 Introduction

Deleuze opens *Difference and Repetition* with the claim that 'Repetition is not generality' (DR 1/1). The incommensurability of generality, and the related concept of law, is the central theme of the introduction, and of much of the book itself. We normally see laws as applying to all particular entities that resemble one another in a pertinent way, that is, all particulars that fall under a generality. So, for instance, the laws of gravitation apply to particular bodies in so far as they have mass, Bernoulli's principle applies to all uncompressible fluids moving at low speeds. Likewise, for Kant, universal moral laws govern the behaviour of all beings who share the property of rationality. In all of these cases, it seems to be the case that repetition plays a central role in the formulation of laws. Scientific laws are formulated by repeated experimentation, and Kant's moral law appears, in the form of the categorical imperative, to provide a test of what actions can be repeated. Deleuze discusses three different ways of relating to the world in which we might think that we encounter repetition: scientific experiment, moral law and the psychology of habit. Deleuze's general strategy in these opening sections is to show that there is a problem with our notion of the law in natural sciences, and then to show how other conceptions of the law are ultimately founded on this one case. His argument is that in the case of scientific experiment, we do not really encounter repetition. In the case of moral law and the psychology of habit, while these do appear to offer us a true understanding of repetition, they do so only on the basis of drawing analogies with scientific repetition, so ultimately do not get beyond the limitations of this model.

0.2 Science and Repetition (1–3/1–4)

The first question, therefore, is why is it impossible for science to repeat? Henri Bergson, one of the central influences on Deleuze, presents the following key assumption of mechanism in his *Creative Evolution*: 'A group of elements which has gone through a state can always find its way back to that state, if not by itself, at least by means of an external cause able to restore everything to its place' (Bergson 1998: 8). This notion of repetition appears to be a precondition of the scientific method. It is by recreating the same situation that we are able to develop laws, by showing that bodies always behave the same way, thereby showing that the law is universal. Our common sense conception of repetition (which Deleuze will aim to overturn) seems to require both that we are presented with at least two objects (we need at least a second object to have a repetition of the first), and that they are absolutely identical with one another (otherwise we do not have repetition of an object, but two different objects). The fact that mechanism allows us to constitute the same situation several times appears to allow us to fulfil both of these criteria. Why does Deleuze believe that this model of repetition fails? While the physical world may be full of innumerable resemblances, experiment is not simply a case of observation, but of the active constitution of an experimental context. We choose the factors that we want to analyse by excluding other factors. More importantly, the entire notion of a factor presupposes a certain mode of understanding. In order to separate elements of a system, we have to presuppose that they are in some way already determinable discretely. These factors, moreover, are understood in terms that are essentially quantitative. That is, in order to conduct an experiment, we presuppose that the pertinent features of a system can be understood in numerical terms. Once this has been done, 'phenomena necessarily appear as *equal* to a certain quantitative relation between chosen factors' (DR 3/3). Deleuze therefore argues that physics comes to natural phenomena with a mathematical understanding of them, which opens the possibility of different situations being equal. In fact, physics is only able to recognise properties of states of affairs as *properties* to the extent that they are already constituted in terms of quantity: 'Resemblances are unpacked in order to discover an equality *which allows the identification of a phenomenon* under the particular conditions of an experiment' (DR 3/3, my italics). We can say, therefore, that science presupposes a principle of repetition that allows it to relate different orders of generality to one another, but it doesn't explain this principle.

Further, Deleuze argues that the notion of repetition emerges only hypothetically. The experiment generates a law of the form, 'given the same circumstances', i.e. a hypothetical law. In this case, repetition is given as an extrapolation from experiments which provide at best similar circumstances. As Deleuze writes, 'repetition can always be "represented" as extreme resemblance or perfect equivalence, but the fact that one can pass by degrees from one thing to another does not prevent their being different in kind' (DR 2/2).

0.3 Kant's Moral Law (3–5/4–5)

If repetition isn't found in the universality of the laws of nature, perhaps it can be found in the moral realm: 'the wise must be converted into the virtuous; the dream of finding a law which would make repetition possible passes over into the moral sphere' (DR 3/4). The figure that Deleuze draws on in order to work through this alternative hypothesis is Kant, due to his sharp distinction between natural law and rational law. One of Kant's key concerns in his moral writings is to account for the autonomy of the moral agent. Moral action is only possible if we can act freely. If we are motivated by something within the world – for example, by happiness – then, Kant argues, we are also *determined* by the world. Rather than being autonomous, we are determined by the particular structures of the empirical world which surround us in these cases. The question, therefore, is how are we able to provide a properly autonomous foundation for moral action? Kant's essential claim is that if we are to be autonomous, that is, self-legislating, then, given that we are rational creatures, self-legislation must involve giving ourselves rational laws to govern our conduct. Furthermore, in order that these laws be purely rational, they should not contain any empirical content whatsoever. That is, the principles of morals must be purely formal principles. So Kant appears to create a sharp distinction between two realms, and two kinds of laws. On the one hand, empirical laws, which deal with determinate content, and on the other hand, moral laws, which are purely rational and formal. In this latter realm, therefore, is the possibility that Deleuze considers 'of successful repetition and of the spirituality of repetition' (DR 4/4) actualised?

Kant proposes that if there is to be a formal criterion, it has to be based on the notion of rational consistency. The only way that we can provide a determination as to what we should do in a given circumstance is negatively. If the act can be performed without contradiction, then it is a moral act. He formulates the key criterion, the categorical imperative, as follows:

Act only in accordance with a maxim through which you can at the same time will that it be a universal law. (Kant 1998: 31)

The central idea behind Kant's account is therefore that if we can understand an action as hypothetically governed by a maxim that everyone held to without it producing a contradiction, then that action is a moral action. To use one of Kant's examples (Kant 1998: 32), suppose that I decide to borrow some money, knowing full well that I will not be able to pay it back. That is, I make a promise that I know I will not keep. There is nothing inherently self-contradictory in this maxim of action, but if we imagine that it became a maxim which was universally followed, then a contradiction would arise. If everyone made promises that they did not intend to keep, then the very idea of a promise itself would have no meaning: 'no one would believe what was promised him, but would laugh at all such expressions as vain pretenses' (Kant 1998: 32).

We can see on this basis that the notion of universality seems to function as a test for repetition. If an action could become a universal law, that is, if it could be repeated, then it is a moral act. In this sense, repetition is not just something that is present within the moral realm, but is even the test or criterion by which we determine if something belongs to the moral realm. Does Kant therefore manage to provide an account of repetition as strict universality?

Deleuze presents the following antinomy in *Difference and Repetition*:

Conscience, however, suffers from the following ambiguity: it can be conceived only by supposing the moral law to be external, superior and indifferent to the natural law; but the application of the moral law can be conceived only by restoring to conscience itself the image and the model of the law of nature. (DR 4/5)

As it stands, this criticism is quite obscure, but the first point is straightforward enough. The moral must be conceived of as separate from the natural. The natural realm is governed by causality, making free action impossible, therefore the moral must be seen as separate from it. Why must it then be seen according to the model of natural law? Deleuze explains in *Kant's Critical Philosophy* that this is an implication of the difference between the two realms:

It is thus in two very different senses that the sensible and the suprasensible each form a nature. Between the two Natures there is merely an 'analogy' (existence under laws). By virtue of its paradoxical character suprasensible nature is never completely realized, since nothing guarantees to a rational being that similar beings will bring their existence together with his, and will form this 'nature' which is possible only through the moral law. This is why it is not sufficient to say that the relation between the two Natures is one of analogy; one must add that the suprasensible can itself be thought of as a nature only *by analogy with* sensible nature. (KCP 33/28)

While we may posit the existence of the free moral realm, we lack any way of conceiving of it, since it differs in kind from the world we find around us. Thus, if we are to represent it to ourselves, we have to rely on an analogy with the world we find around us. We therefore project the model of empirical law onto the rational realm in order to understand the concept of moral law:

Moreover, the idea of a pure world of understanding as a whole of all intelligences, to which we ourselves belong as rational beings (though on the other side we are also members of the world of sense), remains always a useful and permitted idea for the sake of a rational belief, even if all knowledge stops at its boundary – useful and permitted for producing in us a lively interest in the moral law by means of the noble ideal of a universal kingdom of ends in themselves (rational beings) to which we can belong as members only when we carefully conduct ourselves in accordance with maxims of freedom as if they were laws of nature. (Kant 1998: 66)

In this case, Deleuze argues that Kant's central concept of duty is modelled on habit (or rather, the habit of contracting habits). He argues that our understanding of habit repeats the errors of natural laws. Thus, while habit relies on repetition of the similar, it doesn't provide a criterion by which we can select the relevant similarities ('everything resembles everything else'). It is only once we have done this that habits are explained, but only on the basis of ignoring the differences between events (equalisation).

0.4 Kierkegaard (5–9/5–10)

Deleuze claims that there are three thinkers who 'oppose repetition to all forms of generality': Kierkegaard, Nietzsche and Peguy (DR 5/6). I want to focus here on Kierkegaard's alternative to generality, and postpone an analysis of Nietzsche's eternal return for now. The key text for Deleuze, *Fear and Trembling*, presents an analysis of the binding of Isaac, the story of God's testing of Abraham's faith by asking him to sacrifice his only son (Genesis 22:1–19). Abraham proves willing to sacrifice Isaac, although God ultimately allows Abraham to sacrifice a ram in his place. For Kant, the fact that the commandment to commit murder contravenes the categorical imperative means that it could not have been a commandment given by God, and hence Abraham acted immorally in being willing to fulfil it. The position that Kierkegaard puts forward in *Fear and Trembling* is rather that the incommensurability of Abraham's actions with the moral law shows that Abraham's faith is higher than any ethical considerations:

> The paradox of faith, then, is this: that the single individual is higher than the universal, that the single individual – to recall a distinction in dogmatics rather rare these days – determines his relation to the universal by his relation to the absolute, not his relation to the absolute by his relation to the universal. (Kierkegaard 1983: 70)

What ultimately justifies Abraham's actions is a direct relationship with God that is incomprehensible from the point of view of universal law. This is a relationship that necessarily falls outside of the sphere of generality and law. Kierkegaard makes clear the relation of this moment of faith to repetition in *Repetition*, this time with a discussion of Job. Job is also tested by God, who allows him to suffer misfortunes to prove to the devil that Job's faith is not a consequence of God's protection of him from misfortune. In this case, Job's restoration is equated with repetition in a way that mirrors the return of Isaac to Abraham:

> So there is a repetition, after all. When does it occur? Well, that is hard to say in any human language. When did it occur for Job? When every *thinkable* human certainty and probability were impossible. Bit by bit he loses everything, and hope thereby gradually vanishes, inasmuch as actuality, far from being placated, rather lodges stronger and stronger allegations against him. From the point of view of immediacy, everything is lost. His friends, especially Bildad, know but one way out, that by submitting to the punishment he may dare to hope for a repetition to the point of overflowing. Job will not have it. With that the knot and the entanglement are tightened and can be untied only by a thunderstorm. (Kierkegaard 1983: 212–13)

Repetition, therefore, is this moment that falls outside of the categories of reason (the thunderstorm introduced by Kierkegaard). It is not a physical repetition (the Bible tells us Job gets back twice what he lost, putting the repetition outside of the sphere of quantitative identity). Rather than being based on universality, as it is for Kant, for Kierkegaard (and for Deleuze) it is based on singularity.

Summarising the philosophies of Kierkegaard, Nietzsche and Peguy, Deleuze provides four criteria for a philosophy of repetition. The final three of these parallel, but are incommensurate with, the three modes of natural law, moral law and habit:

1. Make something new of repetition itself: connect it with a test, with a selection or selective test; make it the supreme object of the will and of freedom. (DR 6/6)

The test in this case is God's commandment to Abraham to sacrifice his son. Abraham believes in repetition on the strength of the absurd to the extent that he believes he will get Isaac back in spite of the impossibility of the fact.

2. In consequence, oppose repetition to the laws of nature. (DR 6/7)

In the case of Kierkegaard, this is once again clear. Repetition for him falls outside of comprehensibility, and hence outside of the field of any possible scientific enquiry. In this sense, it at least offers the possibility of explaining the kind of repetition that is presupposed by, but falls outside of, the scientific endeavour.

3. Oppose repetition to moral law, to the point where it becomes the suspension of ethics, a thought beyond good and evil. (DR 6/7)

Once again, to the extent that Abraham's actions are incomprehensible from the point of view of ethics, his willingness to sacrifice Isaac represents a suspension of ethical principles in favour of God's commandment. God's 'temptation' therefore presents a direct alternative to Kant's test, the categorical imperative.

4. Oppose repetition not only to the generalities of habit but also to the particularities of memory. (DR 7/8)

Once repetition is understood in the context of a radical break, it becomes clear that our everyday conception of habit, which looks like a paradigm case of repetition, can no longer be considered so. Kierkegaard makes this point somewhat cryptically in a draft of his *Concept of Anxiety*:

Earnestness is acquired originality.
Different from habit – which is the disappearance of self-awareness.
Therefore genuine repetition is – earnestness. (Kierkegaard 1983: 327)

As we shall see, it is this deeper repetition that Deleuze will see as responsible for the kinds of surface repetition that are dealt with by law. Deleuze ultimately rejects Kierkegaard's actual account of repetition since the presupposed relationship between a subject (Abraham) and an object (God) borrows too heavily from the physical or moral worlds. Nonetheless, Kierkegaard prefigures Deleuze in seeing the need for a radical rethinking of the nature of repetition.

0.5 Extension and Comprehension (11–16/13–18)

Extension and comprehension are introduced by Deleuze in order to give an account of the third difference between repetition and generality. They are opposed in terms of (natural) law and in terms of conduct (moral law), but also in terms of representation. Representing an object is key to two processes, both of which Deleuze is critical of: representational memory and recognition. In the case of memory, representation is needed because the object to be remembered isn't present. In the case of recognition, it is because we need in some sense to compare our internal representation of the object with the object itself. How do we structure such a representation? We normally see objects as composed of substances and properties, and we describe these objects using the parallel conceptual terms of subjects and predicates. Depending on how many predicates we ascribe to a subject, we can determine which objects fall under that concept. For example, we can restrict the application of a concept by stipulating that it only applies to objects which have a certain property. So the concept of an animal applies to only those entities with the property of animality. By adding further predicates, we can narrow down the group of entities which fall under the concept. Thus the concept of a rational animal covers a subset of both of the groups to which those predicates are attributed. It therefore circumscribes a smaller collection of entities (traditionally taken to be mankind). This brings us to the comprehension and extension of a concept. These two features of a concept are defined in the *Port Royal Logic*, widely considered to be the definitive logic textbook until the mid-nineteenth century, as follows:

I call the COMPREHENSION of an idea, those attributes which it involves in itself, and which cannot be taken away from it without destroying it; as the

comprehension of the idea triangle includes extension, figure, three lines, three angles, and the equality of these three angles to two rigid Angles, &c.
I call the EXTENSION of an idea those subjects to which that idea applies, which are also called the inferiors of a general term, which, in relation to them, is called superior, as the idea of triangle in general extends to all the different sorts of triangles. (Arnauld 1850: 49)

So the class of objects that a concept ranges over is governed by its comprehension and extension. An object only falls under a concept if that concept comprehends the object, i.e. if it has all of the properties of the concept. The extension determines how many objects fall under the concept. Now, it should be obvious that the extension and the comprehension of a concept are inversely proportional. That is, the more we specify a concept, the fewer objects will be subsumed by it. If we are to remember a particular event, or recognise a particular object, then the extension of that concept must be 1, i.e. it must only refer to the particular experience or object under consideration. But this implies, as extension and comprehension are inversely proportional, that the comprehension of the concept must be infinite. Deleuze refers to the idea that every object can be uniquely specified by a concept as a 'vulgarized Leibnizianism' (DR 11/13). By this, he means that it implies something like a principle of identity of indiscernibles (that if two things share the same properties, they are in fact identical). If it were impossible for two different objects to have the same properties, then repetition itself would be impossible. So the question is, is it possible to distinguish each object from every other conceptually?

Deleuze's claim is that we cannot do this because in several cases concepts are 'blocked' from completely specifying objects. To get a sense of what Deleuze means by this, we can note that we often deliberately 'block' conceptual determinations. When we define a species, for instance, we attribute a set of properties to a thing. For instance, we might define a horse by the properties of being a mammal, having hoofs, being a herbivore, etc. In this case, we don't want to develop a concept that defines an individual, since we want a concept that allows us to talk about a group of individuals at the same time (horses). Rather than carrying on until we have specified a particular horse, we introduce what Deleuze calls an 'artificial blockage' (DR 12/14) by stopping this process of determination. Depending on where we introduce the artificial blockage, we will get more or less general concepts. Thus, by adding more determinations to the concept of mammal (and thereby increasing its comprehension), it will apply to a more and more specific class of mammals (its extension will decrease). Here we can relate repetition to difference, since purely in terms of these concepts of 'horse' or 'mammal', repetition is grounded in a difference which falls outside of the concept in question (DR 13/15). That is, in so far as we are only talking about the concept, 'horse', repetition is possible, as all particular horses are horses in exactly the same way. The difference between them is not in the concept, 'horse', but in another concept (perhaps they are different colours or sizes, or are used in different roles). Repetition is therefore difference without, or outside of, the concept. In this case, we could have carried on specifying the concept further and by doing so brought the difference within the concept, hence it being an artificial blockage; but the question is, are there natural blockages, that is, cases where it is impossible for us to capture the difference between two objects conceptually?

Deleuze presents three examples of cases where there are natural blockages, or differences that escape any possible conceptualisation. The first is atomism, whether physical or linguistic. The second is repression, where we repeat a trauma precisely because we cannot represent it to ourselves. The final case is that of incongruent counterparts, developed by Kant. As the second case is dealt with at length in Chapter 2 (2.9–2.12), I just want to deal with the first (briefly) and third cases here.

Deleuze's account of the first case is rather obscure, but the point he is making is simple. He suggests:

> Let us suppose that a concept, taken at a particular moment when its comprehension is finite, is forcibly assigned a place in space and time – that is, an existence corresponding normally to the extension = 1. We would say, then, that a genus or species passes into existence *hic et nunc* [*here and now*] without any augmentation of comprehension. (DR 12/14)

Rather than a species just being a convenient grouping, it would now be something that had a definitive existence, with each of the objects falling under the concept being absolutely identical. Deleuze is thinking of something like an atom here. Atoms are identical to one another (conceptually indistinguishable) in spite of the fact that they are separate individuals. While in the case of a species, we could add further determinations if we wished to distinguish particular members of a species, there simply are no further conceptual distinctions that can be made between different atoms. In this case, each atom is a repetition of the one before precisely because they differ, but still fall under the same concept. While we might question whether atoms really are identical with one another, Deleuze claims that the case is much more decisive in the case of words, where we can repeat *the same* word. This is because each particular instance of the word is conceptually indistinguishable from each other. In this situation, we cannot specify each instance conceptually, and so the 'vulgarized Leibnizianism' of complete conceptual determination breaks down. Leaving aside the second case, Freud's account of repetition, I want to focus on the final case, as the distinction between concepts and intuitions that it implies will be central to Deleuze's argument throughout the rest of *Difference and Repetition*.

0.6 Incongruent Counterparts (13–14/15, 23–7/26–31)

Kant's argument from incongruent counterparts is first introduced into a debate between Newton (and Clarke) and Leibniz on the nature of space. One of the central points of contention between Newton and Leibniz was the question of whether space was absolute, or relative to the objects which were contained within it. For Newton, we can make a distinction between absolute and relative space:

Absolute space, in its own nature, without relation to anything external, remains always similar and immovable. Relative space is some moveable dimension or measure of the absolute spaces; which our senses determine by its position to bodies; and which is commonly taken for an immovable space; such is the dimension of a subterranean, an aerial, or celestial space, determined by its position in respect of the Earth. (Newton 1934: Defs., Scholium II)

So for Newton, in practice, we determine the positions of objects in space by their relations to one another, since, for him, a frame of reference is defined by inertia, that is, by the fact that all objects within a frame of reference are moving at constant velocity. On this basis, it is very difficult to even differentiate between a relative and an absolute frame of reference. In spite of this, Newton claims that in order for these relations between objects to be possible, there must be an absolute frame of reference which is logically prior to the existence of objects themselves. Absolute space is therefore essentially a metaphysical posit within Newton's physics, which grounds the possibility of relations between objects.

    In contrast to Newton's analysis of space as absolute, Leibniz claims (at least on a first reading) that space is a secondary, derivative concept that emerges from the relations which exist between objects. He presents several arguments which seem to show the problematic nature of absolute space. First, it can be neither a substance nor a property, as *contra* substances, it is causally inert, and *contra* properties, it precedes objects rather than depending on them. Second, the notion of absolute space is problematic when we take into account Leibniz's view that every event must have a reason or cause. If space is independent of the things within it, it becomes inexplicable why the universe is where it is and not, for instance, three feet to the left of its current position. Third, if there is no way to distinguish one point of space from any other, then we can say that each point in space is identical to every other one, and so, as they are identical, space is just one point.

Leibniz presents the following alternative view:

> I have more than once stated that I held *space* to be something purely relative, like *time*; space being an order of co-existences as time is an order of successions. For space denotes in terms of possibility an order of things which exist at the same time, insofar as they exist together, and is not concerned with their particular way of existing: and when we see several things together we perceive this order of things among themselves. (Leibniz and Clarke 2000: 15)

We will return to Leibniz in the next chapter, but for now we just need to note that for him space is a distorted view of what are really conceptual determinations of objects. Space in this sense is therefore secondary to the 'order of things', and exists only in so far as it allows us to see the relations which obtain between these entities. Space emerges because the intellectual nature of the universe is only perceived confusedly by the finite subject. On this view, therefore, conceptual determinations precede space, which is in no way a real feature of the world, rendering Newton's absolute theory of space false. A corollary of this is that monads, the basic elements of reality for Leibniz, do not have any spatial properties. This does not mean that spatial properties are entirely arbitrary, however. They are what Leibniz calls, 'well-founded phenomena'. That is, they are analogous with what are in reality conceptual properties. The main point to take from Leibniz, in relation to Deleuze, is that for Leibniz, all of the properties which we encounter in space can be understood purely in conceptual terms. If that is the case, then because each object will be conceptually distinct for every other, repetition is impossible.

Kant first introduces the incongruent counterparts argument in his pre-critical work, *Concerning the Ultimate Foundation for the Differentiation of Regions in Space* (1768). Here, his aim is to show that the Newtonian view of space is correct:

> Let it be imagined that the first created thing were a human hand, then it must necessarily be either a right hand or a left hand. In order to produce one a different action of the creative cause is necessary from that, by means of which its counterpart could be produced.
>
> If one accepts the concept of modern, in particular, German philosophers, that space only consists of the external relations of the parts of matter, which exist alongside one another, then all real space would be, in the example used, *that which this hand takes up*. However, since there is no difference in the relations of the parts to each other, whether right hand or left, the hand would be completely indeterminate with respect to such a quality, that is, it would fit on either side of the human body. But this is impossible. (Kant 1968: 42–3)

Kant's point is that the conceptual determination of the hand, in this case, a set of relations between parts, is not sufficient to determine whether the hand is a left hand or a right hand. In both cases, the relations are identical, and so, conceptually, the hands are also identical. The fact that hands are left or right handed therefore means that there must be an 'internal difference' that is not a conceptual determination.

We can make this point clearer by noting that the property of handedness is intimately related to the nature of the space in which the object is placed. If, instead of a hand, we took the example of a triangle on a two-dimensional plane, it should be clear that it cannot be rotated so as to cover its mirror image. If we consider the same triangle in a three-dimensional space, however, we could 'flip the triangle over', thus making it congruous with its mirror image. The dimensionality of space therefore determines whether the counterparts are congruous or incongruent, meaning that handedness is a property of space, and not purely of conceptual relations. For this reason, Kant rejected his earlier Leibnizian interpretation of space in favour of a Newtonian conception.

In Kant's later critical philosophy, space is seen as transcendentally ideal, but empirically real. That is, while statements we may make about space may be true, their truth stems from the fact that we condition experience, rather than because space itself is absolute. Kant's system, and its claims to be able to give us *a priori* knowledge of the world, relies on distinguishing two faculties which together give us knowledge of the world: the understanding, which is active and representational, and intuition, which is passive and presentational. The incongruent counterparts argument lays the groundwork for this distinction by showing that space cannot be understood in conceptual terms. Space is an intuition, or a mode of sensibility, by which we apprehend the world. In the transcendental aesthetic of the *Critique of Pure Reason*, Kant makes two claims about intuition: that it is *a priori*, and that it is non-conceptual. For Deleuze, this difference in kind between the structures of space and time, and that of our conceptual understanding of the world, represents perhaps the most innovative moment of Kant's entire philosophy. As we shall see when we look at chapter two of *Difference and Repetition*, the central problem of Kant's theoretical philosophy, how concepts can be related to intuitions given their difference in kind, will find its analogue in Deleuze's own work.

0.7 Conclusion: Three Forms of Difference

There are (at least) three different conceptions of difference at work in the introduction, and it might be worth recapping them briefly.

First, there is conceptual difference. This is the kind of difference that can be represented. In this class are not only species produced by artificial blockages, but also the kinds of conceptual differences we can find by simply adding more and more precise determinations to our concepts: 'no two grains of dust are absolutely identical, no two hands have the same distinctive points, no two revolvers score their bullets in the same manner' (DR 26/29).

The second kind of difference is the difference of the incongruent counterparts themselves. This is a difference which has its principle outside of the conceptual realm: we tell the difference between the left hand and the right by a direct experience.

Kant hints at a third kind of difference, however, which is not relational: the difference which gives rise to the incongruent counterpart. Kant presents this difference in the *Regions in Space* essay:

It is already clear from the everyday example of the two hands that the figure of a body can be completely similar to that of another, and that the size of the extension can be, in both, exactly the same; and that yet, an internal difference remains: namely, that the surface that includes the one could not possibly include the other . . . this difference must, therefore, be such as rests on an inner principle. (Kant 1968: 42)

The inner principle which allows internal difference to emerge in the case of Kant's thought is the nature of space itself, and this remains the same whether space is taken to be absolute, as in Kant's early writings, or transcendental, as we find in his critical writings. Rather than remaining at the level of spatial difference itself, Deleuze will want to provide a transcendental account of the operation of this principle of difference which explains why cases such as left and right handedness appear in the first place. As well as the surface repetition of the incongruent counterparts themselves, therefore, there is a deeper repetition, 'the singular subject, the interiority and heart of the other, the depths of the other' (DR 24/27) that gives rise to this repetition. In other words, Deleuze wants to provide an account of the genesis of the kind of spatiality which Kant takes as his starting point.

The relationship between Leibniz and Kant sets out the project of *Difference and Repetition* clearly. Normally when we look at difference, we have two choices. Either we see it as conceptual difference, as in the case of Leibniz, in which case we have not really understood what difference is, or we take Kant's path, and recognise difference as non-conceptual. This then leads to the end of our enquiry since we lack the (conceptual) tools to do justice to it. In the two cases we have looked at here, what is responsible for repetition, whether atoms or space, is simply taken as given, rather than explained (and this holds true of Freud's account as well, which ultimately will presuppose the kind of physical repetition we find in law). Deleuze's project is therefore going to be to perform an enquiry into the principle of difference which neither sees it as conceptual nor sees its non-conceptuality as the end of our enquiry. In doing so, he will develop an account of difference which allows us to explain the kinds of differences presupposed but not explained by Kant and the atomists. Developing this new concept of difference is the primary aim of chapter one of *Difference and Repetition*.

Chapter 1. Difference in Itself

1.1 Introduction (28–30/36–8)
Chapter 1 begins with a discussion of indifference, or the absence of difference. Deleuze's aim in the opening few paragraphs is to provide an account of why representation emerges as an attempt to make difference 'leave its cave and cease to be a monster' (DR 29/38). What would a state of indifference involve? Deleuze gives two examples:

1. 'The undifferenciated abyss. The indeterminate animal in which everything is dissolved' (DR 28/36).
2. 'The white nothingness, the once more calm surface upon which float unconnected determinations like scattered members' (DR 28/36).

The first of these represents a space that has not been differenciated. Without difference, we cannot have anything other than pure abstract identity. Difference as a concept is what allows us to draw distinctions within this identity ('this differs from that'). The second quotation brings out the second role of difference: difference is a relation, and therefore allows things to be related to one another. Clearly, therefore, we need a concept of difference. Deleuze here outlines two ways in which we might understand difference. The first is that difference is imposed on the world, the second is that difference emerges of its own accord, or immanently from the world. Traditionally, difference has been conceived as operating in the first of these ways. The first of these is tied to representation and judgement, the second to immanence and univocity.

Deleuze associates representation with the question, 'what is it?', and this question implies an answer of the form, 'it is x'. This structure is the basic structure of judgement: the attribution of a predicate to a subject. The proper functioning of representation therefore requires two parts to it. First there is the subject (the 'it'), which defines the 'what' that is being asked about. Second there is the predicate, or property (the 'is x'), which is attributed to the subject. So in order to make a judgement about something, we need both a subject and a predicate. The undifferenciated abyss presents a situation whereby one of these conditions has not been met. There are no properties present in the subject, and so there is no possibility of making a judgement. In fact, we could take this further and say that as there are no limits to the abyss, there is no such thing as a subject present, either. The properties lacking a subject represent the second type of indifference. There are properties but no subjects to attribute them to. The process of representation therefore collapses again, and thinking is suspended.

The first of these possibilities, the abyss, brings us to the central problem of representation. While representation is able to qualify forms and subjects ('this square is red'), it is unable to account for the genesis of form itself. Form simply has to be imposed on something fundamentally non-representational; something that simply cannot be captured within the formal structures of judgement. Such an abyss is in a literal sense unthinkable. This is the dialectic of representation which operates in the opening of Chapter 1. If form, and with it the structure of the world of subjects and properties, emerge from an abyss, and if this emergence cannot be explained in terms of representation, how can it be explained? The difference between the formless abyss and form must be something that falls outside of representation. Difference is therefore Deleuze's name for this process of the emergence of form, which cannot be captured within the structure of the already formed. The fact that representation cannot think its own ground presents a serious problem, and in order to escape from this dilemma, it attempts to think difference from within the structure of representation itself. It attempts to mediate this concept of difference through the structures of identity, analogy, opposition and resemblance ('to "save" difference by representing it' [DR 29/38]). Deleuze's aim in this chapter is to show the failure of this project. In the process, he will make the claim that underlying representation is a structure that is different in kind from it. Underneath the represented world of subjects and properties is a differential field of intensity.

The structure of Deleuze's argument is therefore as follows. First, he is going to give an account of Aristotle's theory of species and genera, a paradigm case of representation. Second, he will make explicit the problem with this conception. Third, he will provide an alternative to Aristotle's equivocal conception of being by tracing an alternative lineage moving from Duns Scotus through Spinoza to Nietzsche. Fourth, he will try to show how Leibniz and Hegel's attempts to save representation fail. Finally, Deleuze will conclude with a discussion of Plato as the thinker who founds representation, but in the process shows the possibility of an alternative ontology. With a few minor deviations, we will be following this trajectory in this chapter.

1.2 Aristotle's Conception of Difference (30–3/38–42)

So who is the main target of Deleuze's criticisms? Deleuze begins by giving a short exposition of Aristotle's philosophy as the first formulation of representation. Deleuze's analysis of Aristotle essentially focuses on his concept of difference. His aim is to show how Aristotle's formulation of difference as relational and oppositional (x differs from y if x is not y) forces on him a certain conception of being. Deleuze's characterisation of Aristotle is central to Deleuze's own positive account, since it is the attempt to overcome its limitations that leads him to formulate what he terms a univocal conception of being, and with it a conception of intensive difference. His aim is going to be to show that how we understand being and difference are fundamentally interrelated. Following on from the introduction, Deleuze's claim will be that if we see difference as spatial, then we have to see being as fragmented (analogical). Alternatively, if we see difference in terms of intensity, then our understanding of being will instead be univocal. In this section, I want to go through some of the key terms of Aristotle's ontology, namely genus, species, difference and accident, relying on the account that the early commentator, Porphyry, gives of them, before moving on to why Deleuze thinks Aristotle's approach leads him into difficulties.

Porphyry defines the genus as 'what is predicated in answer to "What is it?", of several items which differ in species, for example, animal' (Porphyry 2003: 4). This follows from Aristotle's own definition: 'what is predicated in the category of essence of a number of things exhibiting differences in kind' (Aristotle 1984d: 102a). What does it mean to be predicated of items that differ in kind? If we take the case of Socrates, it should be clear that 'animal' can be predicated of him, to the extent that Socrates is a man (a rational animal). For Porphyry and Aristotle, however, there is no difference in kind between different men, but rather a difference in number. While it is the case that a given genus, such as animal, is predicated of an individual, such as Socrates, the genus cannot simply be directly used to define the individual. If it were used in this way, the genus would be the only function which was *essential* to each individual. This would mean that in essence each individual would be different only in number, whereas the definition of genus requires that it is predicated of what also differs in kind. We therefore need the intermediary category, which Aristotle and Porphyry call the species.

Porphyry first defines the species as 'that which is predicated, in answer to "What is it?", of many things which differ in number' (Porphyry 2003: 5). This case would be the one reached so far, where we have one genus, one group of individuals, and one level of species (a genus cannot simply have one species since in this case we could not meet the definition of a genus as applying to a number of things differing in kind). We can see that a given genus can be predicated of a species, and both the species and the genus can be predicated of an individual. We can therefore say that Socrates is both animal (according to his genus) and man (according to his species). In fact, we might want to make a more fine-grained definition by adding in more terms. Porphyry writes that 'the intermediate items will be species of the items before them and genera of the items after them. Hence these stand in two relations, one to the items before them (in virtue of which they are said to be their species), and one to the items after them (in virtue of which they are said to be their genera)' (Porphyry 2003: 6). A consequence of this is that we now need to define the species in terms of something other than the individual, since only the lowest species relates directly to things which differ only in number. Instead, we now define the species in terms of its genus. Thus we have a hierarchy, reaching from the highest genera to the individual, through which the individual is specified by a process of division from the genus through the various species, gaining determinations as it goes, since each genus will determine the essence of that below it. The last category we need to consider are accidents, which do not define a species. These can either be separable (as in the case of Socrates, who can be sitting or not sitting), or not separable (for instance, 'being black is an inseparable accident for ravens and Ethiopians' [Porphyry 2003: 12]), in that an Ethiopian could lose his skin colour without ceasing to be an Ethiopian, whereas a man without reason (at least potentially) is no longer a man.

What is the role of difference in this hierarchy? In order for two things to differ, Aristotle argues that they must also have something in common. We cannot have a difference between, for instance, a horse and an apple, as these two forms are too far apart from each other; they are what Aristotle calls 'other' to each other. Thus, a man and a horse differ in that a man is a rational animal and a horse is a non-rational animal. The difference of rational or non-rational makes sense because of the shared predicate of animal. If differences between things of different genera are too broad, how can we formulate a narrower conception of difference? Porphyry introduces three forms of difference: 'common difference', 'proper difference', and 'the most proper difference', but only the third of these is considered by him to be real difference. Common difference is the difference between two accidents, or non-essential predicates, and is not effective in determining a real difference between two entities. Proper differences deal with inseparable properties of things, and so do really serve to determine the difference between two things. The most proper difference, however, is specific difference. Specific difference is what allows species to be defined in Porphyry's tree by dividing the genus. So, if we take the genus, animal, we are able to determine the species, man, by dividing animals into two kinds: rational and non-rational animals. Difference is the criterion by which we divide the genus into two species. Conceptually significant difference therefore occupies a middle point between the extremes of otherness and accidental difference: 'Specific difference refers only to an entirely relative maximum, a point of accommodation for the Greek eye – in particular for the Greek eye which sees the mean, and has lost the sense of Dionysian transports and metamorphoses' (DR 32/40).

Porphyry therefore provides an account of the determination of objects that allows us to characterise all of their essential determinations through a process of division. We begin with a property which belongs to everything, for instance, substance, and by a repeated process of division of things into contrary classes, we eventually arrive at a complete determination of the subject. He puts this point as follows:

> For in the case of objects which are constituted of matter and form or which have a constitution at least analogous to matter and form, just as a statue is constituted of bronze as matter and figure as form, so too the common and special man is constituted of the genus analogously to matter and of the difference as shape, and these – rational mortal animal – taken as a whole are the man, just as they are the statue. (Porphyry 2003: 11)

Of course, Porphyry is not implying that what we have here is a temporal constitution (we don't find in the world beings that are only determined as animals, for instance). Rather, his point is that the series of genera and species provide an account of the logical order of determinations of a particular object.

1.3 Aristotle's Conception of Being (32–5/41–4)

I now want to look at some problems with the account of determination offered by Aristotle and Porphyry that Deleuze sets out. He divides the difficulties with Aristotle's model into problems of 'the Large', which arise from a difficulty related to characterising the top of the hierarchy of terms, the highest genus, and problems of 'the Small', which relate to the unity of empirical objects (DR 29–30/38). His claim is that such a model cannot deal with the extreme cases of determination. Thus, Aristotle's model relies on the 'extraction or cutting out of generic identities from the flux of a continuous perceptible series' (DR 34/43). This involves a problematic notion of resemblance between changing perceptions and an unchanging essence.

We can relate these difficulties to the two forms of indifference which are to be avoided. As we have seen, these are 'the black nothingness, the indeterminate animal in which everything is dissolved – but also the white nothingness, the once more calm surface upon which float unconnected determinations like scattered members' (DR 28/36). While Deleuze's characterisation of these problems may seem obscure, they relate to two key issues with Aristotle's theory. First, how do we determine the nature of the highest genus in the Aristotelian hierarchy (black nothingness), and second, how do we explain the constitution as well as the determination of the subject (the problem of white nothingness)? The problem of the highest genus is recognised by Aristotle. He sets it out in the *Metaphysics* as follows:

> It is not possible that either unity or being should be a genus of things; for the differentiae of any genus must each of them both have being and be one, but it is not possible for the genus to be predicated of the differentiae taken apart from its species (any more than for the species of the genus to be predicated of the proper differentiae of the genus); so that if either unity or being is a genus, no differentiae will either be one or have being. (Aristotle 1984b: 998b)

Now, a genus is 'what is predicated in the category of essence of a number of things exhibiting differences in kind' (Aristotle 1984d: 102a). Therefore, a genus, along with the differentiae, determines what it is to be an *X*. It should be clear that a difference cannot be the same type of thing as that which it differentiates. We can show this by taking as an example the case of living bodies. If the difference between living bodies was itself a living body, then we would be caught in an infinite regress, as in order for *this* living body to function as a difference, we would need to differentiate it from other living bodies. Thus, we would require a further difference, which would in turn need to be differentiated and so on to infinity. What thus differentiates living bodies, the difference sensible/non-sensible, must itself not be a living body. This, however, presents a serious problem when we apply this criterion to the case of being, as it now means that what differentiates beings into different species cannot itself be a type of being. Therefore, if being is a genus, then difference itself cannot be a being. As Deleuze puts it, 'Being itself is not a genus . . . because differences *are*' (DR 32/41). It is not simply the difference in being that would lack being, but as differences are inherited (man is a rational animal, but also a material substance), all differences would lack being. For this reason, the ultimate categories through which being is understood must be multiple, as they themselves are species in relation to the undefined genus.

This solution itself is problematic from the point of view of the science of metaphysics, however, as for Aristotle, science must relate to a unified class of things. But as we have just seen, Aristotle argues that there are several different classes of being. It therefore appears that there cannot be a coherent formulation of the concept of metaphysics. In order to resolve this problem, Aristotle argues that while these different senses of being are not identical, neither is it a case of simple equivocation to relate these various concepts together. Instead, these different senses are related to one another paronymously.

If we are to be able to talk meaningfully about the world, it cannot be the case that species and genera merely define general 'heaps' of things. Instead, they must group things together according to criteria which capture something common to their essence. For this reason, Aristotle opens his *Categories* with a discussion of three terms, homonymy, synonymy and paronymy:

When things have only a name in common and the definition of being which corresponds to that name is different, they are called *homonymous*. Thus, for example, both a man and a picture [of an animal] are animals.

When things have a name in common and the definition of being which corresponds to the name is called the same, they are called *synonymous*. Thus, for example, both a man and an ox are animals.

When things get their name from something, with a difference in ending, they are called *paronymous*. Thus, for example, the grammarian gets his name from grammar, the brave get theirs from bravery. (Aristotle 1984a: 1a)

What these definitions make clear is that some attempts to define species may not capture what is essential to the species itself. Since words apply to different objects, it might be the case that if we rely on the fact that the same term is used to designate different entities, we may be forced into a definition of a species which does not accurately capture what it is to be that particular thing. Thus, in the case above, the species, animal, may refer both to the man and the picture of a man, despite the fact that in these cases the term animal is being used in substantially different ways. Rather, we need to look for synonymous expressions, since it is these that capture something essential about the thing in question. How do these terms relate to the question of being? Being clearly cannot be synonymous, as the problem of the highest genus shows that it is impossible to give it a straightforward definition. Being could be homonymous, but in this case, each of the different categories of being would be arbitrarily related to one another. Being would therefore just be a conjunction of different terms – in effect, a 'heap', rather than a unified concept. Instead, Aristotle proposes that we consider being to be a paronymous concept. What would such a concept look like? Aristotle gives the following example:

Just as that which is healthy all has reference to health – either because it preserves health, or because it produces it, or because it is a sign of health, or because it is capable of receiving health – . . ., so too that which *is* is said in several ways, but all with reference to a single principle. (Aristotle 1984b: 1003a)

If we take the case of health, we can see that a paronymous definition has several consequences:

First, different things can all be said to be healthy. Second, the definition of health will apply to each of these objects in different ways. Clearly health is different from, for instance, a healthy diet, or a medical instrument which is capable of promoting health. Third, each of these different meanings is related to a central meaning, known as a *focal meaning*. For instance, if we see health as the proper functioning of the organism, we can see that there is an asymmetry between our uses of the term. While a healthy diet will have reference to this proper functioning, perhaps the intake of foods which allow the proper functioning of the organism, the definition of health itself does not need to incorporate anything from these secondary definitions.

It is quite straightforward to relate this idea of paronymy to the concept of being. Rather than simply being a heap, the different categories of being are all related to a single concept. Things can therefore be said to be. For instance, properties, substance and differentia can all be said to exist, despite being different from one another. Second, the ways in which these things exist may well be different, and yet still be related to one another. Third, these different notions of being will all relate to a central concept of being. If we look at the notions of substance and properties, for instance, it is clear that a property can only exist as a property *of* something. Therefore it is going to be logically secondary to a focal meaning, in this case the notion of substance to which properties are attributed.

As we shall see, this notion of paronymy is also central to the Scholastic tradition, where it takes the form of analogy. We can now return to the difficulty which Deleuze finds with this response to the problem of the highest genus. To deal first with the question of black nothingness, we can see that even if we can now solve the logical problem of how the terms at the top of the hierarchy are related, we are still left with a question as to how we are able to define the concept of being. Being still cannot be defined without presupposing a yet higher concept. Being is therefore put outside of the world of species and genera. As Deleuze writes, 'it is as though there were two "Logoi", differing in nature, but intermingled with one another: the logos of species . . . which rests upon the condition of the identity or univocity of concepts in general taken as genera; and the logos of Genera . . . which is free of that condition and operates both in the equivocity of Being and in the diversity of the most general concepts' (DR 32–3/41).

Second, Deleuze argues that while Aristotle provides an account of the *determination* of objects, he cannot provide an account of the *constitution* of objects. As we saw, properties are understood as properties *of* something, and the same could be said of differences. When we ask the question, 'what is it?', we have already presupposed the existence of a logical subject to which predicates will be attributed by means of an answer. This rules out in advance any possible account of the genesis of the subject. It is for this reason that Deleuze introduces the indifference of white nothingness. He is going to argue that we need to think the faintly paradoxical notion 'unconnected determinations' if we are to think of the emergence of the subject itself.

1.4 Duns Scotus (35–6/44–5, 39–40/48–9)

Aristotle's account is concerned with questions of what there is, that is, with questions of ontology. We have just seen that Deleuze finds substantial problems with this account. He therefore claims that 'there has only ever been one ontological proposition: Being is univocal' (DR 35/44). This claim is that the problems with the analogical conception of being cannot be solved, and hence we need to take an entirely new approach. In the next few sections, I want to trace Deleuze's development of this concept of univocity through the alternative tradition that he constructs. This tradition moves from Duns Scotus, through Spinoza, to Nietzsche. In the process, I hope it will become clear what exactly a 'univocal conception of being' entails.

Before discussing Scotus, we need to look at the conception of God presented by traditional theology. The central point to note is that medieval theologians saw a fundamental difference between the concept of finite things, and the concept of an infinite being such as God. It was taken for granted by the scholastics that God's nature is essentially simple (it is not composed of parts), whilst at the same time, it possesses every perfection (God is infinitely good, infinitely wise, etc.). This highlights a fundamental limitation to our understanding of God because when we look at objects that we have access to, objects in the finite world, we see that an object having several properties is a complex object. Now the very fact that a term like 'good' operates in these different ways when we use it to describe an object or person in the world or to describe God implies that when we use this term, we are equivocating. That is, that the same term names two different concepts, good-for-God, and good-in-the-finite-world. Such a position has certain advantages – in that it makes clear that God is a transcendent entity that cannot be adequately understood according to our categories of thought – but is ultimately untenable as it renders any relation to or understanding of God impossible.

It is here that Aquinas brings in the notion of analogy. As we saw with Aristotle, analogy allows us to relate terms that have something in common (a focal meaning), but yet differ. Aquinas' use of analogy relies on the likeness of cause and effect (our goodness is caused by God, so there must be some analogy between infinite and finite goodness, since effects resemble their causes). In this instance, therefore, God's goodness is the focal meaning by which finite goodness gets its own meaning. It is against this view that Scotus develops his own position: a univocal theory of religious language. He defines univocity as follows: 'I designate that concept univocal which possesses sufficient unity in itself, so that to affirm or deny it of one and the same thing would be a contradiction' (Duns Scotus 1978b: 20). Effectively, univocity therefore means that a word is used in the same sense in all contexts, unlike 'health', for instance, whose meaning changes depending on what we are relating it to. Scotus has two main reasons for supposing that being fits this category of univocity. First, he claims that we can believe that God *exists* without knowing anything further about him, even whether he is finite or infinite. Second, the alternative theory of analogy suffers from a key problem: in order for the analogy to work, we seem to require some knowledge of the relationship between God's nature and his attributes. Such an analogical argument presupposes some form of understanding of God's nature. Scotus instead takes being to be univocal and 'indifferen[t] to what is infinite and finite' (Duns Scotus 1987a: 2). Now this raises a problem, since we want to see God as separate from man. Deleuze raises this point as follows in one of his lectures:

Because I say: being is univocal, this means: there is no categorical difference between the assumed senses of the word 'being' and being is said in one and the same sense of everything which is. In a certain manner this means that the tick is God; there is no difference of category, there is no difference of substance, there is no difference of form. It becomes a mad thought. (L 14/01/74)

This view is clearly heretical, since it appears to be the case that as being is somehow prior to finite and infinite beings, being appears to operate as a genus, with finite and infinite beings as its species. Thus being would seem to occupy a place higher in the Porphyrian hierarchy than God. We might also want to ask how Scotus is able to explain the simplicity of the nature of God, given that God's nature seems to now be a compound of two different attributes: being and infinitude.

Scotus' resolution of these difficulties rests on his understanding of finitude and infinity. To return to Aquinas for a moment, in the *Summa Theologica*, Aquinas defines infinity as follows:

Something is said to be infinite from the fact that it is not limited. Now matter is in a certain way limited through form, and form in a certain way through matter. Matter is in fact limited through form inasmuch as before it receives a form, matter is in potency to many forms, but when it receives one, it is limited by it. Form however is limited through matter inasmuch as a form considered in itself is common to many things, but by being received in matter it becomes the form determinately of this thing. (Aquinas, cited by Tomarchio 2002: 176)

The concepts of finite and infinite are here *relational* concepts. The infinite is defined by not being limited, whereas the finite is defined through limitation (by matter). If the finite and infinite are understood in these terms, it is clear that we are going to end up with being as the highest genus, or at best an analogical conception of being, as these two terms are opposed to one another. Rather than finitude being defined by relation to a limit, Scotus instead therefore introduces the notion of an 'intrinsic degree' of being.

To see how such a concept can be formed, we can follow the account Richard Cross gives in his discussion of Scotus (Cross 1999: 40). Scotus firsts asks us to imagine an infinitely large magnitude. He then asks us to apply this model of extensive infinity to a qualitative perfection, such as goodness. The central claim is that much as we can determine spatial magnitudes, we are also capable of ranking perfections in such a way that we can conceive of an infinite perfection. In the case of a perfection, however, it cannot be constituted of parts in the way that the extensive magnitude is. An infinite extensive magnitude is constituted from an infinite number of finite extensive parts, but a perfection would not be infinitely perfect if it were composed of finite (and hence imperfect) qualities. The notion of infinity that Scotus is developing is therefore of an intensive, indivisible form of infinity, rather than the extensive, divisible form that Aquinas favours.

God is not, therefore, superior to man in the quantitative extension of his being, but rather in the qualitative nature of his being's intensity. This ultimately allows Scotus to solve the two difficulties of the highest genus and the simplicity of God. Instead of understanding infinity and finitude as species of being, they are rather modes or ways in which being subsists. Scotus gives the following example in terms of colour:

> When some reality is understood along with its intrinsic mode, that concept is not so absolutely simple that it is impossible that this reality be conceived apart from this mode, although it is then an imperfect concept of a thing. For example, if there were whiteness in the tenth degree of intensity, however simple it may be in reality, it is nonetheless possible that it be conceived under the concept of so much whiteness, and then it would be conceived perfectly by means of a concept adequate to the thing itself. Or, it is able to be conceived precisely under the concept of whiteness, and then it is conceived according to a concept that is imperfect and lacking in perfection in the thing. But the imperfect concept is common to this and that white, and the perfect concept is more proper. (Scotus, *Ord.* I, d. 8, pars 1, q. 3 n. 138–9, taken from Hall 2007: 107)

Infinite being is like infinite whiteness in this example. Finite being in turn is like a finite degree of whiteness. In neither case are the notions relational. Infinite whiteness is not defined by a lack of limitation, but positively, in terms of its own intensity. Likewise, a finite degree of whiteness is not defined in relation to some other quality, but is intrinsic to the colour itself. Finitude and infinity are therefore modes, rather than properties of being.

When we looked at Porphyry's theory of species and genera, we saw that Porphyry defines these as what are given in response to the question, 'what is it?' Man, for instance, is defined by the genus, animal, and the difference, rationality. Differences are, and so we can make a real, existential distinction between rationality and animality. The fact that there is a real distinction between these two terms means that man shares something with another animal, such as a horse, whilst differing in another respect (rationality). If this kind of distinction was applied to finite and infinite being, then being would be the genus of God and man, as the identity under which they are distinguished. In this case, being would be higher than God. Scotus' notion of the distinction allows us to avoid this difficulty. Clearly there is a difference between whitenesses of different degrees of intensity.

When we look at the concept of the intensity itself, however, it should be apparent that this notion of intensity cannot be grasped as really distinct from the whiteness itself. If we take away the concept of whiteness, we simply have the concept of 'degree', which is meaningless on its own – 'degree of what?' Nevertheless, the degree clearly does distinguish different 'whitenesses'. We can note however, that it is possible to formulate a concept of whiteness that does not make reference to its degree of intensity. Such a concept would, however, be 'an imperfect concept of a thing' as whiteness always shows itself with a given intensity. It should be clear that we can apply this conception to the notion of being. Scotus' claim would then be that being always presents itself with a given degree of intensity which is inseparable from it. While we can therefore formulate a concept of being without reference to its intensity, such a conception is only formal, as actual being is always finite or infinite.

Intensity as it stands is purely a difference in the degree of something's being, and is also pre-categorial. As such, it does not constitute the kind of distinction that would allow a proper separation between God and man. Such a position in fact is the one that Deleuze wants to develop in his own philosophy. For Scotus on the contrary, the difference in degree between God and his creation becomes a difference in kind once we recognise that infinite intensity is simply incommensurate with any form of finite intensity. The gap between finite and infinite is therefore still a chasm which allows the separation of God and his creation to be maintained. While being can conceptually be said univocally, in practice, we always encounter being with a given intensity, and so in reality being is always encountered in different forms:

As said of the ten categories, neither metaphysically nor naturally does the term 'being' signify one concept; and being is not a genus of these, neither naturally nor metaphysically. However, logically speaking, being is univocal. (Duns Scotus, *In De an.*, q. 22, n. 33 taken from Hall 2007: 20)

By making this difference a difference in kind, Scotus separates man from God, but at the cost of making the thesis of univocity a purely formal thesis. This is why Deleuze claims that Scotus 'only *thought* univocal being' (DR 39/49).

1.5 Spinoza (40/49–50)

Spinoza represents for Deleuze the second major thinker of univocity. Spinoza goes beyond Scotus by moving from a conception of univocal being as purely abstract to one whereby we in practice encounter one being. He makes it 'an object of pure affirmation' (DR 40/49). At this point it would be useful to go through three of the key terms in Spinoza's philosophy (substance, attributes and modes) in order to highlight how the structures of univocity are taken up on Deleuze's reading. Spinoza defines substance as follows: 'By substance I understand that which is in itself and is conceived through itself, that is, that the conception of which does not require the conception of another thing, from which it has to be formed' (Spinoza 1992: Part I D3). Spinoza is here very close to Descartes' definition of substance as 'a thing which exists in such a way as to depend on no other thing for its existence'. At this point, however, an important difference arises in regard to how we distinguish substances. For Descartes, the fact that a substance exists implies that it is numerically distinct from other substances. Thus, for Descartes, the mind and the body are two actually distinct substances. In fact, we have more than just two substances. Each person has a separate mind, or soul, and so there are a number of real, numerically distinct, substances which share the same attribute. How does this relate to the question of how to distinguish or determine entities? For Descartes, 'there are numerical distinctions which are at the same time real or substantial' (EPS 30). Spinoza disputes this claim, arguing that substances with the same attribute could only be distinguished by their particular mode (i.e. whether the substance of thought is your or my thought). As substance is logically prior to its modes, it is impossible to distinguish substances with the same attributes numerically (Spinoza 1992: Part I P5). This does not just mean that there is only one substance, but as it falls outside of numerical distinctions, substance is better described as singular (without number). I want to turn to this theme now by introducing Spinoza's notion of the attributes.

Spinoza defines an attribute as 'that which the intellect perceives of substance as constituting its essence' (Spinoza 1992: Part 1 D4).

In Descartes' terms, an attribute is the essence of a substance, so, for instance, the essence of material substance is extension. So in answer to the question, 'what is it to be a material substance?', we would reply, 'it is to be extended'. For Descartes, substances are individuated numerically, which means that we can distinguish them simply by indicating which one we are talking about ('this is my body, and that is yours'). Extension plays a purely definitional role in this case. For Spinoza, however, there is only one substance, and so he cannot simply rely on thought and extension being conceptual distinctions of two different substances. Given that the world contains (at least) both things and ideas, Spinoza has to explain how it is possible for the same substance to be expressed by two different essences, thought and extension.

As Deleuze recognises, this problem mirrors one which Scotus dealt with. The question for Scotus was how an infinite being could both be understood as simple, which was a standard part of the definition of God, yet at the same time be composed of a number of proper attributes: how could God be simple, yet still be one, true and good? Scotus' solution was to rely on the notion of a formal distinction between the different attributes so that while they were not actually distinct as things separate from one another, they were nevertheless formally distinct in that they picked out genuine differences for reason within the infinite being. Truth, goodness and unity were therefore formally, but not really, distinct features of the infinite being (Scotus uses a similar logic for the Trinity).

Attributes operate in a similar way for Spinoza. They are formally distinct from each other, but they cannot be really distinct, as they express the essence of the same substance. There are some key differences between Scotus' account of the attributes of God and Spinoza's account of the attributes of God or substance. First, Scotus' attributes are really just what Deleuze calls 'signs' for the intellect. They express a way in which the nature of God is to be taken up by the finite subject. It is to an extent ambiguous how they are to be read in Spinoza. His definition of 'what the intellect perceives of a substance, as constituting its essence' can be read both as subjective (by focusing on the intellect's perception) or as objective. Second, for Scotus, God is a separate entity to the world, whereas for Spinoza, as there is only one substance, the expression of the essence of God in the attribute cannot merely be a formal feature. Rather, the expression *is* the world. For Spinoza, therefore, the intellectual and physical realms are just the expression, or explication, of the essence of God. In this sense, 'instead of understanding univocal being as neutral or indifferent, he makes it an object of pure affirmation' (DR 40/49). Whereas the essence of God is known formally for Scotus (as a 'sign'), it is now known expressively and concretely. We therefore have a progression between the nature of God being known analogically for Aquinas; univocally, but only in a formal manner for Scotus; and now univocally and affirmatively for Spinoza.

So Spinoza's metaphysics presents the world as the expression of the essence of God. This brings us to the final part of his system I want to discuss: the mode. If the world is the essence of God, and God is infinite, how do we account for the existence of finite things within the world, which Spinoza calls modes? Spinoza argues that finite things are modifications of infinite substance. He defines them as follows: 'By mode I mean the affections of substance; that is, that which is in something else and is conceived through something else' (Spinoza 1992: Part 1 D5). Here we rely on the second of Scotus' distinctions, the modal distinction. Earlier on, I mentioned how Spinoza disagrees with Descartes' equation of real and numerical distinction. Spinoza instead argues that substance is really distinct, but not numerically distinct. Modes operate in the opposite manner. Modes are modifications of a singular substance, and so are not really distinct. They are, however, numerically distinct from one another. If modes are to be distinct, but not seen as existentially distinct from one another (as they are all moments of a singular substance), we need some other way of distinguishing them. This is in essence the same problem that we found in Scotus' attempt to develop a univocal conception of being which was at the same time applicable to finite and infinite beings. Scotus' solution was to replace Aquinas' notion of the finite/infinite distinction (which was founded on limit) with a distinction founded on intensity. Thus being is like the concept of whiteness. While we can formulate a concept of whiteness separately from the intensity by which it manifests itself, such a concept would be inadequate. Intensity is the mode by which whiteness manifests itself. According to Deleuze, Spinoza develops a similar account of the nature of finite modes. Just as intensity is only modally distinct from whiteness, finite modes are only modally distinct from substance itself.

What is the role, therefore, that univocity is playing in Spinoza's philosophy? First, we can see that the nature of substance itself is not given according to a categorial form of definition. In order to define something for Aristotle, we need a genus and a difference. This led to the problem of the highest genus, as the highest genus would seem to require a higher identity in order to be defined, but the presence of such a higher identity would imply that the highest genus was not, in fact, the highest genus. In such a case, determination relies on a numerical distinction between terms. We must be able to separate the rational animals from the non-rational animals (as separately existing entities) in order to define man as a rational animal. We define something by saying that it is 'this and not that'. Spinoza's substance, however, has an essence which is expressed through the attributes. This essence is not one that can be given in terms of the categories, however, as Spinoza's substance is not subject to any form of numerical distinction – it is singular. On this basis, it cannot be determined through the 'this and not that' structure of representation, even in relation to a possible but non-existent object. Substance does have a structure and an essence, however, as is shown by the finite modes which as a whole express substance, and which are distinguished from one another in terms of their intensity. Substance is determined by a difference, but it is not a difference between concepts (everything is substance), but rather a difference that is internal to substance. This is therefore one of the most difficult ideas in Deleuze's metaphysics: substance expresses its essence by differing from itself. This is made possible on the basis of the univocal conception of being, whereby all modes express *the same* being. Spinoza's system therefore makes no distinction between different ways in which things exist. Although the world appears to be made up of different substances, in actual fact, everything is simply an expression of the same substance.

1.6 Nietzsche (36–7/45–7, 40–2/50–2, 52–5/63–7)

Despite the fact that Spinoza represents an advance over the work of Scotus, Deleuze claims that for Spinoza, 'substance must be said itself *of* the modes and only *of* the modes. Such a condition can be satisfied only at the price of a more general categorical reversal according to which being is said of becoming, identity of that which is different, the one of the multiple, etc.' (DR 40/50). Deleuze's point is that the relation of modes to being is still structured like the terms of a judgement. The modes are said *of* being, in the same way that we might say *of* a man that he is rational, and so we still understand being as if it were a subject, even if we know that in reality it is singular rather than one, and thus different in kind from the object of a judgement. In order to overcome this limitation, we need somehow to replace our account of being as the highest term in our hierarchy with difference, whilst retaining the insights given by the intensive understanding of difference; it is Nietzsche, Deleuze claims, who provides the means to do this. I want to come back to his work in the next chapter, but there are two points in Nietzsche's writings that Deleuze is basing his argument on at this point. The first is section 13 of Essay I of the *Genealogy of Morality*, where Deleuze sees Nietzsche as opposing the subject–property view of reality, and the second is aphorism 341 of the *Gay Science*, where Nietzsche presents the eternal return. Deleuze sees the eternal return as Nietzsche's formulation of the univocity principle.

Let us begin by looking at the section from the *Genealogy of Morality*. Here, Nietzsche presents a contrast between two basic attitudes towards the world, that of the lamb and the bird of prey:

There is nothing strange about the fact that lambs bear a grudge towards large birds of prey: but that is no reason to blame the large birds of prey for carrying off the little lambs. And if the lambs say to each other, 'These birds of prey are evil; and whoever is least like a bird of prey and most like its opposite, a lamb, – is good, isn't he?', then there is no reason to raise objections to this setting-up of an ideal beyond the fact that the birds of prey will view it somewhat derisively, and will perhaps say: 'We don't bear any grudge at all towards these good lambs, in fact we love them, nothing is tastier than a tender lamb' . . . A quantum of force is just such a quantum of drive, will, action, in fact it is nothing but this driving, willing and acting, and only the seduction of language (and the fundamental errors of reason petrified within it), which construes and misconstrues all actions as conditional upon an agency, a 'subject', can make it appear otherwise . . . no wonder, then, if the entrenched, secretly smouldering emotions of revenge and hatred put this belief to their own use and, in fact, do not defend any belief more passionately than that *the strong are free* to be weak, and the birds of prey are free to be lambs: – in this way, they gain the right to make the birds of prey *responsible* for being birds of prey. (Nietzsche 2006a: §13)

Nietzsche is here presenting an argument which combines moral and ontological aspects. The natural state of affairs is that of the bird of prey, who exercises his strength, and sees itself as good. The lamb, however, sees the bird of prey as evil, and therefore sees itself as good. The symmetry between these two positions is misleading, however, and each rests on fundamentally different ways of seeing the world. For the bird of prey, its action is simply an expression of its strength, or, in more Nietzschean terms, we might say that the bird of prey itself is an expression of strength: 'It is just as absurd to ask strength not to express itself as strength . . . as it is to ask weakness to express itself as strength' (Nietzsche 2006a: §13).

The lamb's reaction is a moral reaction, and one that is made possible by an illusion fostered by grammar: it posits a subject who is responsible for exercising its strength. Nietzsche gives the further example of lightning. When we say that 'lightning strikes', we are forced by the structure of language to posit a distinction between a subject ('lightning') and an act ('striking'). Now we might recognise in this case that in fact there is nothing other to the lightning than its striking itself – there is no hidden subject behind the act – but language opens up a way of thinking of the world in terms of agents and actions. Once the lamb understands the bird of prey as an agent acting, he can posit the (illusory) possibility of the agent withholding this action. Thus, the bird of prey, once it is seen as a subject, becomes culpable for what it does.

We can use this distinction between two different ways of understanding the world to clarify Deleuze's key distinction between sedentary and nomadic distributions. Distributions in this sense are for Deleuze ways of thinking about what something is essentially, or more generally, what kinds of things the world is composed of. Let us begin with a sedentary distribution: 'A distribution of this type proceeds by fixed and proportional determinations which may be assimilated to "properties" or limited territories within representation' (DR 36/45). Deleuze's conception here is that the world is cut up by applying pairs of predicates to the world, thus distinguishing, for instance, the rational from the non-rational, the animate from the non-animate. It is something like the Aristotelian division of the world into species and genera by dividing identities with differences. We can also see the scheme from the *Genealogy of Morality* at play. The sedentary distribution is agrarian, and encompasses the domesticated point of view of the lamb. Just as Aristotle sees the world in terms of subjects possessing properties, the lamb sees the world in terms of agents responsible for actions. Deleuze writes further that 'even among the gods, each has his domain, his category, his attributes, and all distribute limits and lots to mortals in accordance with destiny' (DR 36/45).

The notion of limit is important here, if we recall its centrality in Aquinas' division of the finite from the infinite. The limit is also what allows us to determine something as possessing one property and not another. Something cannot be both rational and non-rational at the same time, and in this sense Aristotle uses these categories to define the logical space which something occupies. Each term limits the other, but also, to the same extent, defines it, so that the properties form reciprocal pairs. In other words, to determine something, we in effect characterise it as 'this and not that'. This characterisation can also be related once again to the lamb. The lamb determines itself as good in opposition to the bird of prey, which it first determines to be evil. Difference in this sense is therefore fundamentally tied to the related notions of spatial metaphor (two objects differ in that we characterise them as occupying different delimited logical territories) and negation. Finally, it provides 'a hierarchy which measures beings according to their limits, and according to their proximity or distance from a principle' (DR 36/46); in other words, according to how closely a being conforms with its essence or is a degenerate instance of it. A sedentary distribution therefore is a way of ordering the world that is hierarchical, and proceeds by the delimitation of the world according to oppositional determinations. The notion of difference is grounded in negation and operates according to a spatial metaphor.

The second form of distribution is the nomadic distribution. Deleuze makes clear that this conception of a distribution relies on 'a space which is unlimited, or at least without precise limits' (DR 36/46). Rather than being defined by the 'this and not that' conception of difference that Deleuze finds in Aristotle, it is defined by the notion of intensive difference which, as Scotus showed, does not require definition in oppositional terms. It is therefore not a spatial conception of organisation. Deleuze introduces the univocal conception of being in order to explain those features of the world which escaped something like an Aristotelian conception of the world. The nomadic distribution is intimately connected to this univocal conception: 'Oedipus' chorus cries: "which demon has leapt further than the highest leap?" The leap here bears witness to the unsettling difficulties that nomadic distributions introduce into the sedentary structures of representation' (DR 37/46). If a sedentary distribution is fundamentally tied to an understanding of the world in terms of subjects and properties, how are we to understand this notion of a nomadic distribution? The key point is Deleuze's claim that everything goes to the limit of what it can do. He elaborates on this as follows:

Here limit [*peras*] no longer refers to what maintains a thing under a law, nor what delimits or separates it from other things. On the contrary, it refers to that on the basis of which it is deployed and deploys all of its power; hubris ceases to be simply condemnable and *the smallest becomes equivalent to the largest* once it is not separated from what it can do. (DR 37/46)

When we separate the bird of prey from its action, or lightning from its striking, we institute the two moments of an ontology of judgement: the subject and the property. This moment of separation of something from what it can do is what gives us the Aristotelian idea of a world of fixed things. If something is not separated from what it can do, then instead of an ontology of being, we have an ontology of forces, or becoming. There are not static points from which movement originates, but rather just movement itself. We can tie together a number of results at this stage. Just as Scotus shows that analogy can only operate within a prior uni-vocal framework, Nietzsche shows that the point of view of the lamb is derivative of that of the bird of prey. Deleuze similarly argues that 'nega-tion results from affirmation: this means that negation arises in the wake of affirmation or beside it, *but only as the shadow of the more profound genetic element* – of that power or "will" which engenders the affirmation and the difference in affirmation' (DR 55/67). Difference is therefore primary in this scheme. This leads us to the last aspect of Deleuze's discussion of univocity: how are we to conceive of a univocal conception of becoming?

1.7 The Eternal Return (40–2/50–2)

Nietzsche formulates the eternal return as follows:

What if some day or night a demon were to steal after you into your loneliest loneliness and say to you: 'This life as you now live it and have lived it, you will have to live once more and innumerable times more' . . . Would you not throw yourself down and gnash your teeth and curse the demon who spoke thus? Or have you once experienced a tremendous moment when you would have answered him: 'You are a god and never have I heard anything more divine.' (Nietzsche 2001: §341)

This principle has two important aspects for Deleuze at this point in *Difference and Repetition*. First, the question we need to ask is, what is it that eternally returns? Second, the eternal return seems to operate as a test; what is it a test for? Let us begin with the first question. Deleuze has laid down two different ways of understanding the world. A sedentary dis-tribution essentially understands the world as a collection of things with properties. If Deleuze's aim is to give us a conception of difference that is not subordinated to identity, then understanding the return in terms of subjects is clearly not going to be adequate in any case, since these are centres of identity. Instead, what returns is the nomadic distribution. Deleuze's analysis of Spinoza saw being as the ground for the modes. For Deleuze, taking up the eternal return, the ground (or, as we shall see, unground) for modes is going to be a pre-judicative field of becoming: it is the intensive, nomadic distribution which returns. 'Only the extreme, the excessive, returns; that which passes into something else and becomes identical . . . Eternal return or returning expresses the common being of all these metamorphoses . . . of all the realised degrees of power' (DR 41/51). The priority of difference does not, therefore preclude the existence of identities, but asserts that what returns is not these identities themselves, but something prior to identity, which Deleuze characterises as difference.

The eternal return appears as a test – whether we can bear the heaviest burden of the demon's truth. What is this a test for? The lamb and the bird of prey both see the world in terms of different distributions; the former according to the sedentary distribution, the latter according to the nomadic distribution. In this case, deciding between them is straightforward, but it may be difficult to see whether something is governed by a sedentary or nomadic distribution. The eternal return allows us to differentiate those two classes. Only that which is pure affirmation, or which is not separated from what it can do, can truly will the repetition of everything that makes it what it is. Those who cannot affirm this do not have their ground in the affirmative field of differences, but are instead, like the lamb, grounded in the sedentary distribution. The fact that they make a distinction between what can be done and what is done (they posit agency), means that they as agents are not the same as their actions. For the lamb, therefore, positing its own return is not identical with positing the return of everything which is. The eternal return therefore allows us to differentiate 'the superior form of everything that "is"' (DR 41/51) from those beings that are really not (as the sedentary distribution is not a well-founded way of understanding the world). In doing so, it allows us to characterise that set of entities which genuinely are, and are not merely secondary effects, just as the lamb's attitude is a secondary effect of the bird of prey's.

1.8 Infinite Representation (42–4/52–4, 48–54/59–65)

Towards the conclusion of the chapter, Deleuze notes that the move to a univocal conception of being isn't the only response we can make to Aristotle. At this point, he makes a distinction between two different ways in which we can characterise philosophies that are based on the notion of judgement. The first form, which we have been dealing with, is finite representation. This is based on the idea that judgements describe the essential structure of things. In other words, they set out the essential determinations which make up something. What makes it finite is the notion of limit. Aquinas' definition of limit, for instance, showed that finite things failed to properly express their form because they were limited by matter. This led to a distinction between the essence of something and its appearance, in that something expresses its essence to the degree that its actual finite form embodies its essence ('their degree of proximity or distance from a principle' [DR 37/46]). Deleuze's claim is that infinite representation replaces the notion of matter with a broader notion of representation. Rather than finite forms occurring in matter, everything that is exists as a moment of an infinite concept which encompasses everything. In effect, this is the claim that the world is therefore conceptual 'all the way down': 'Instead of animating judgements about things, orgiastic representation makes things themselves so many expressions, or so many propositions: infinite analytic or synthetic propositions' (DR 43/53). I want to spend a bit of time outlining how these approaches might function. In relation to the discussion of representation so far, the following comment by Deleuze sums up the difference between finite and infinite representation:

> The signification of the very notion of limit changes completely; it no longer refers to the limits of finite representation, but on the contrary to the womb in which finite determination never ceases to be born and to disappear, to be enveloped and deployed within orgiastic representation. (DR 42–3/53)

1.9 Hegel (44–6/54–6, 51–3/62–4)

There are two ways of putting this approach into practice. We can either take a synthetic approach, which is what Hegel does, or we can see objects as fully defined by an infinite number of properties, thus making truths about them analytic, which is Leibniz's proposal. In the case of Hegel, therefore, this means that the kind of thinking which has characterised representation so far is only a moment in a wider movement of thought. Thus, finite thinking, or 'the understanding' in Hegel's terms, the mode of thought of Aristotle, is really just a single moment in a broader process called speculative reason. It is only by reifying speculative thought that we end up with the problems we have encountered so far; that is, by denying that there is a greater moment to representation than finite representation, we find ourselves unable to explain the concept of totality.

Central to Hegel's explanation of infinite representation is the notion of dialectic. Essentially, Hegel wants to argue that rather than the meanings of terms simply being given by definition, we find when we analyse the movement of thought thinking these terms that their meaning arises from the content itself. Hegel's *Science of Logic* therefore traces the development of concepts from the simplest concept, that of pure, undifferentiated being, through to what he calls the Absolute Idea, or the Notion. By tracing the development of ideas themselves, we are able to see the inherent connections between them. Philosophy is therefore this movement of concepts themselves. For Hegel, therefore, the problems of finite representation emerge when we ignore this movement, and assume that concepts are just given. In this way, Hegel criticises his predecessors as follows:

Such presuppositions that infinity is different from finitude, that content is other than form, that the inner is other than the outer, also that mediation is not immediacy (as if anyone did not know such things), are brought forward by way of information and narrated and asserted rather than proved. (Hegel 1999: 41)

Finite representation therefore emerges for Hegel from the fact that we take for granted the nature of the distinction between the finite and the infinite. We presume that: '*There are* two worlds, one infinite and one finite, and in their relationship the infinite is only the *limit* of the finite and is thus only a determinate infinite, an *infinite which is itself finite*' (Hegel 1999: 139–40). If we just view the infinite as a 'beyond' of the finite, and remain with finite thinking, however, we end up with an infinite which is itself limited, and hence is finite: 'Owing to the inseparability of the infinite and the finite – or because this infinite remaining aloof on its own side is itself limited – there arises a limit; the infinite has vanished, and its other, the finite, has entered' (Hegel 1999: 141). The heart of the difficulty is that the infinite is supposed to be that which is beyond limitation, but the basic structure of determining the infinite is by opposition, in other words by saying what the infinite is not. But by doing so, we introduce a limit into the notion of the infinite. Possessing a limit, however, is what defines finite things. For this reason, Hegel defines this understanding of the infinite as a 'spurious infinite' (Hegel 1999: 142).

We attempt to determine the infinite as a beyond, but in determining it, we limit it and make it finite. We thus have an infinite progression and alternation between finite and infinite terms. If we are truly to understand the infinite, and hence the finite, we need to see both as moments of one process:

> The image of the progress to infinity is the *straight line*, at the two limits of which alone the infinite is, and always only is where the line – which is determinate being – is not, and which goes *out beyond* to this negation of its determinate being, that is, to the indeterminate; the image of true infinity, bent back into itself, becomes the *circle*, the line which has reached itself, which is closed and wholly present, without *beginning* and *end*. (Hegel 1999: 149)

The true infinite emerges when we step back from attempting to formulate the infinite through the progression, and recognise that the process of the circular movement of the finite into the infinite and back again is itself the infinite. Such a process involves seeing the infinite as essentially a contradictory structure – the identity of identity and difference. The finite is in a perpetual process of vanishing or negation, and this movement itself is seen as the infinite. Everything therefore falls under conceptual determination. Hegel's claim is thus that it is only by moving to a different way of understanding concepts, namely speculative reason, that we are able to truly understand either of the categories of finitude or infinitude.

What, therefore, is the relationship between the infinite and finite that Hegel develops? Deleuze's claim is that infinite representation is no better than finite representation. In distinguishing the two, he writes that 'it treats identity as a pure infinite principle instead of treating it as a genus, and extends the rights of the concept to the whole instead of fixing their limits' (DR 50/61). The finite and the infinite are still understood oppositionally, as each is not the other, but at the same time, they are united together, in that they are part of one process. Now, if two terms are opposed to each other, but are both asserted simultaneously, then we have a contradiction. This is why Deleuze claims (and Hegel would agree) that speculative reason operates by pushing difference past opposition to contradiction. In that everything is one element (the infinite), it appears as if we have a univocal theory much like Spinoza's. In actual fact, however, Hegel's theory preserves the central features of representation: 'Goethe, and even Hegel in certain respects, have been considered Spinozists, but they are not really Spinozists, because they never ceased to link the plan[e of infinite representation] to the organization of a Form and to the formation of a Subject' (SPP 128–9). Deleuze makes three main criticisms of this approach. First, '[Hegel] creates movement, even the movement of the infinite, but because he creates it with words and representations, nothing follows' (DR 52/63). Deleuze's claim is that Hegel has misunderstood the cause of the movement of thought by continuing to represent it, rather than seeing it as escaping representation. The aspect of representation which Deleuze takes to be critical here is the universal. '"Everyone" recognises the universal because it is itself the universal, but the profound sensitive conscience which is nevertheless presumed to bear the cost, the singular, does not recognise it' (DR 52/63). The singular, or singularity, which is neither particular nor universal, is excluded by beginning with a term which is essentially universal. We can return to the figure of Abraham. Abraham cannot be understood within the framework of the universal, which is the precise reason for Kierkegaard's introduction of him in *Fear and Trembling*.

The second criticism is that this movement is always around a particular point. Deleuze is claiming that Hegel relies on a 'monocentring of circles' (DR 49/60) which Deleuze claims comes about through Hegel's adherence to the species–genus model. In the case of the finite and the infinite, movement 'revolves' around the central moment of the true infinite. Hegel has not got rid of the idea of a central identity, therefore.

The third point, which relates the previous two, is that the idea of opposition, which Hegel uses to unite the particular and universal, is too rough to provide an adequate description of the world. 'Oppositions are roughly cut from a delicate milieu of overlapping perspectives, of communicating distances, divergences and disparities, of heterogeneous potentials and intensities' (DR 50/61). That is, Deleuze asserts that simply relying on a reinvigorated understanding of the distinction between finite and infinite will not provide the kinds of fine-grained distinctions needed to describe the world adequately. It's worth noting that whilst there are a number of structural parallels between Hegel's work and that of Aristotle, there are also a number of conceptual innovations. The fact that these parallels exist is not enough, therefore, to refute Hegel's philosophical position. Exploring possible Hegelian responses to these criticisms would take us far beyond the scope of this guide, however.

1.10 Leibniz (43–4/54, 46–52/56–63)

If Hegel is seen by Deleuze as dealing with the Large by introducing infinity into it (the notion of contradiction as the largest difference), Leibniz is characterised as introducing the infinite into the finite by concentrating on the very small. I have already spent some time talking about Leibniz in the last chapter when we looked at Deleuze's use of the incongruent counterparts argument (0.5–0.6), and we will discuss Leibniz further in relation to the calculus when we look at Chapter 4 (4.2). For now, I just want to give an outline of the reasons why Deleuze classifies Leibniz as a thinker of infinite representation. At the beginning of this chapter, we saw how Deleuze's central claim is that we need to find an alternative way of conceptualising the world to that provided by judgement. Now Leibniz holds to the view that all truths take the form of subject-predicate judgements: 'In every categorical proposition (for from them I can show elsewhere that other kinds of propositions can be dealt with by changing a few things in the calculus) there are two terms, the subject and the predicate' (Leibniz 1989b: 11). It is certainly the case that some truths take this form, such as the claim that 'man is a rational animal', or that 'seven is a prime number'. If we hold that our judgements are able to accord with the world, then it is going to be the case that the basic elements of existence are also going to be substances of some form possessing properties (what Leibniz calls monads). If we see the basic substances in existence as purely defined in terms of substances and properties, however, we encounter a problem when we deal with relations between substances, since these don't seem to fit this structure. If we say, for instance, that 'Paul is taller than John', then it doesn't seem clear what is the subject and what is the predicate (we might want to say that 'Paul' is the subject, and 'is taller than John' is the property, but what about if we rephrase the proposition as 'John is shorter than Paul'?). Similarly, relations of cause and effect seem to involve two subjects and a relation between them. If all propositions can be reduced to judgements, therefore, we seem to be left with a world of non-causally interacting entities – 'the monads have no windows through which something can enter or leave' (Leibniz 1989a: §7). We now have to deal with two problems. First, how do we explain interactions without relations, given that we appear to live in a world of causally interacting substances; and second, how do we differentiate different monads? The solution to the first problem is to see each of these monads as somehow containing the relations between different substances as properties. This means that 'taller than John' will be a property of Paul, and 'shorter than Paul' will be a property of John. If causal interactions are going to be understood purely as properties of each subject, then each monad will have to contain all of its causal interactions with the rest of the world. Leibniz therefore writes that:

This interconnection or accommodation of all created things to each other, and each to all others, brings it about that each simple substance has relations that express all the others, and consequently, that each simple substance is a perpetual, living mirror of the universe. (Leibniz 1989a: §56)

Each monad is therefore made up of an infinite number of properties which together describe the totality of what would be its relations with the universe, and hence, in a sense, the universe itself. To this extent, the infinite, in the sense of even the smallest elements of the universe, is contained within each monad. The whole variety of difference is therefore brought into the notion of the essence of each particular monad. Deleuze writes that: 'The inessential here refers not to that which lacks importance but, on the contrary, to the most profound, to the universal matter or continuum from which essences are finally made' (DR 47/58). The second question was, how do we differentiate monads given that each expresses the whole of the universe? While each monad expresses the entire universe, each does so from a particular perspective, and so only that which is proximal to the monad is expressed distinctly. Events which are at some remove from the monad are only perceived confusedly:

Monads are limited, not as to their objects, but with respect to the modifications of their knowledge of them. Monads all go confusedly to infinity, to the whole; but they are limited and differentiated by the degrees of their distinct perceptions. (Leibniz 1989a: §60)

The difference between monads is therefore the difference between different perspectives on the world. Different perspectives are not opposed to each other, and so Leibniz appears to have succeeded in coming up with a form of non-oppositional difference which explains all of the accidents of entities. If he had done so, then he would have developed a conception of non-oppositional difference founded on judgement, thus providing an alternative to Deleuze's philosophy. In the end, however, this project fails, because the concept of difference is still founded on an identity. If we ask what these different perspectives are perspectives of, then we are given the answer that they are perspectives of the universe. The notion of the universe itself has to pre-exist the different perspectives of it, since it is through this notion that God determines which of the monads can exist and which cannot. Only those which are compossible, that is, can simultaneously co-exist within the same world, can exist. We cannot have a world in which Adam both sinned and did not sin, as this would be a contradiction, nor a world in which different monads see the world in such radically different ways, as then the impression of causality would break down. 'There are, as it were, just as many different universes [as there are monads], which are, nevertheless, only perspectives on a single one' (Leibniz 1989a: §57). Leibniz's notion of difference therefore still relies on the convergence of these different perspectives on a single identity, the universe itself:

> Leibniz's only error was to have linked difference to the negative of limitation, because he maintained the dominance of the old principle, because he linked the series to a principle of convergence, without seeing that divergence itself was an object of affirmation. (DR 51/62)

1.11 Phenomenology (55–7/67–9)

Now Deleuze does have a place for the notion of difference as opposition, although he says that 'negation is difference seen from its underside, seen from below' (DR 55/67). He also argues that it is only 'the shadow of the more profound genetic element' (DR 55/67). As we shall see, the notion of law dealt with in the introduction (0.2) relies on a spatial way of thinking (5.1–5.3). We can see that the same is true of the concept of negation. If we think about something not being something else, then we normally think of them as being spatially separated from one another. This pencil is not this piece of paper to the extent that they occupy different positions within the same space. Deleuze argues that extensive space is an illusion, but one that emerges quite naturally from the way in which we relate to the world. Intensive difference is generative of our notion of objective space, and it is this space which forms the basis of oppositional difference. If we forget the fact that this conception of space is generated from something more primitive, then we end up in a situation where it is possible to introduce the notions of opposition and negation. The world thus has a tendency towards oppositional difference, but we make a mistake when we take this tendency to be a completed state of things.

In order to explain how we generate the illusion of identity, Deleuze now presents a revision of one of the central claims of the phenomenologist, Maurice Merleau-Ponty's *Phenomenology of Perception*. In order to explain how this genetic account functions, we need to look at three statements from *Difference and Repetition*:

1. Infinite representation includes precisely an infinity of representations – either by ensuring the convergence of all points of view on the same object or the same world, or by making all moments properties of the same Self. (DR 56/67)

2. The immediate, defined as 'sub-representative', is not therefore attained by multiplying representations and points of view. On the contrary, each composing representation must be distorted, diverted and torn from its centre. Each point of view must itself be the object, or the object must belong to the point of view. (DR 56/68)

3. Difference must become the element, the ultimate unity. (DR 56/68)

The section of Merleau-Ponty's text to which Deleuze is referring here is his account of the movement from our own perspective on the world to a positing of objective being. Merleau-Ponty writes as follows:

But, once more, my human gaze never *posits* more than one facet of the object, even though by means of horizons it is directed towards all of the others . . . If I conceive in the image of my own gaze those others which, converging from all directions, explore every corner of the house and define it, I have still only a harmonious and indefinite set of views of the object, but not the object in its plenitude . . . If it is to reach perfect density, in other words, if there is to be an absolute object, it will have to consist in an infinite number of different perspectives compressed into a single coexistence, and to be presented, as it were, to a host of eyes all engaged in one concerted act of seeing . . . The positing of the object therefore makes us go beyond the limits of our actual experience which is brought up against and halted by an alien being, with the result that finally experience believes that it extracts all its own teaching from the object. It is the *ek-stase* of experience which causes all perception to be perception of something.

Obsessed with being, and forgetful of the perspectivism of my experience, I henceforth treat it as an object, and deduce it from a relationship between objects. (Merleau-Ponty 1962: 69–70)

Merleau-Ponty's point is that perception is always originally from and of a certain perspective. I can never see such a thing as a totalised object. As I move around the object, I begin to notice that although my perspective on the object changes, when I return to my original position, something similar to the original perspective returns. On this basis of the fact that my own memory appears to preserve some perspectives, I posit what Merleau-Ponty calls 'the memory of the world' (Merleau-Ponty 1962: 70), which includes all possible perspectives on the object. Now, with an understanding of the object based on an infinite number of possible perspectives, my own view ceases to be relevant (I become 'forgetful of the perspectivism of my experience'). I now suppose that rather than the object emerging from the accumulation of perspectives on it, the perspectives are in fact inessential, and logically posterior to the object itself.

The final stage is to recognise that now the object is not considered to be constituted by perception, we need another explanation of how it is constituted. We thus alight on the idea that it can be deduced 'from a relationship between objects'. This relationship is, of course, the relationship of opposition and limit. At this point, therefore, negation enters our world, as a precondition for limit. This account is therefore the account of the generation of an illusion, which, as Deleuze puts it, is nonetheless well founded. It shows how negation and limit enter the world through representation ignoring its genetic conditions (perspectivism). How does this then fit in with Deleuze's account?

Such an account fits with Deleuze's characterisation of infinite representation as the convergence of all points of view (quotation 1). Opposition comes into play through the gradual elimination of perspectives. It also fits with Deleuze's desire that each point of view instead be the object, or the object must belong to the point of view (quotation 2). Such a view is a return to a form of perspectivism such as that found in Merleau-Ponty. What about Deleuze's final claim that 'difference must become the element, the ultimate unity'? In the next paragraph, Deleuze claims that 'the intense world of differences, in which we find the reason behind the qualities and the being of the sensible, is precisely the object of a superior empiricism' (DR 57/68–9). This suggests that Deleuze's analysis is going to go beyond the kind of perspectivism Merleau-Ponty proposes.

For Merleau-Ponty, what makes possible the field of perspectives is the body, but the notion of a body operates as an identity. Instead, Deleuze is going to try to explore what makes possible the kind of account Merleau-Ponty gives. Such an account will be what Deleuze calls elsewhere a 'transcendental empiricism', since it will deal with the conditions of real experience. Intensive difference will therefore take the place of identity as being generative of our experience of the world. This means that while Deleuze can accept the phenomenological criticism of the objective understanding of the world, he can also reject phenomenology's own account as not truly explaining the genesis of its own account. Phenomenology rejects the notion that the self-identical object gives coherence to perception, but fails to recognise that perspective itself still needs an explanation, this time in terms of difference. Phenomenology provides a description of phenomena, but what is needed is a genealogy of phenomena. Thus, Deleuze claims that 'the whole of Phenomenology is an epiphenomenology' (DR 52/63).

1.12 Plato (59–69/71–83)

The close of Chapter 1 introduces the figure of Plato into Deleuze's discussion, taking up Nietzsche's slogan, 'to overturn Platonism' (DR 59/71). Plato represents an important but ambivalent figure in Deleuze's history of philosophy. On the one hand, Plato holds that everything partakes in being. On the other, Aristotle's central concern, the question, 'what is it?', is already present in Plato's dialogues, for instance, when Socrates attempts to answer the question, 'what is justice?' in the *Republic*. At first glance, it appears as if Plato's approach to this question mirrors that of Aristotle. For instance, in the *Sophist*, the visitor defines the nature of an angler by a progressive method of dividing classes into smaller and smaller groupings, distinguishing between acquisitive and productive arts, and within acquisitive arts between willing exchange and taking possession, and so on down to distinguishing between fishing with nets and spear fishing (Plato 1997c: 218a-221d). Deleuze notes, however, that we cannot see this procedure as operating in the same way as species and genera were determined for Aristotle. Aristotle criticises Plato's method of division, for instance, by noting that 'someone who states the definition as a result of the division does not state a deduction' (Aristotle 1984c: 91b35). Aristotle's point is that the determination of entities according to genera and species is a purely taxonomical procedure that allows us to classify entities of a similar kind. It seems that when we read a Platonic dialogue such as the *Sophist*, or the *Statesman*, a much more significant project is going on, however. If we look at the *Statesman*, for instance, the definition of statesmanship as 'knowledge of the collective rearing of human beings' (Plato 1997d: 267d) occurs quite early in the dialogue. Once we have this definition, however, we are still faced with the real difficulty, since it appears that there are a large number of people who fulfil this description: 'merchants, farmers, millers and bakers' for instance (Plato 1997d: 267e). As Deleuze puts it, for Plato, 'difference is not between species, between two determinations of a genus, but entirely on one side, within the chosen line of descent' (DR 60/72).

Plato's question is rather, which candidate is truly the statesman? Whereas Plato is normally understood as using myth to allow non-philosophical readers to understand the point of the dialogue, Deleuze gives it a more philosophical role. The *Statesman* introduces the fable of two cosmic eras, that of Cronos, and the present age of Zeus. Each of these gods allows ordered existence to carry on in the world by ensuring that the universe continues to revolve around its circle. These gods' governance of the universe provides us with a model by which to assess which of the claimants is the true statesman. We can see in the god a metaphor for Plato's theory of Ideas, the theory that what determines the nature of something temporal is its relation to an eternal super-sensible entity. So actions are just in so far as they participate in, or resemble, the Idea of justice. The true statesman is therefore the one who participates in (or best represents in the temporal world) the eternal Idea of statesmanship, whereas the false claimant does not. Now, obviously a statesman cannot be a god, but there are two ways in which he can resemble one, which Plato outlines in the *Sophist*:

Visitor: One type of imitation I see is the art of likeness-making. That's the one we have whenever someone produces an imitation by keeping to the proportions of length, breadth, and depth of his model, and also by keeping to the appropriate colours of its parts.

Theaetetus: But don't all imitators try to do that?

Visitor: Not the ones who sculpt or draw very large works. If they reproduced the true proportions of their beautiful subjects, you see, the upper parts would appear smaller than they should, and the lower parts would appear larger, because we see the upper parts from further away and the lower parts from closer. (Plato 1997c: 235d–236a)

The true statesman resembles the Idea of the statesman in the first of these senses, as the form itself cannot be given in appearance, since it is not spatio-temporal. The pretender only resembles the appearance of the Idea, not the Idea itself. They are instead tied to the world of appearance. The problem, therefore, is to distinguish the candidates who bear a true likeness from those which merely appear to do so.

For Aristotle, the essential nature of something was determined by a process of division much like that of Plato. For Plato himself, however, we have just seen that the definition alone does not determine whether something partakes in the relevant form. 'The Idea is not yet the concept of an object which submits the world to the requirements of representation, but rather a brute presence which can be invoked in the world only in function of that which is not "representable" in things' (DR 59/71). Deleuze therefore sees Plato as situated at a decisive moment in the history of philosophy, as he instigates the kind of genealogical project which will later make Aristotle's notion of representation possible.

Deleuze presents Plato's procedure as follows: 'The four figures of the Platonic dialectic are therefore: the selection of a difference, the installation of a mythic circle, the establishment of a foundation, and the position of a question-problem complex' (DR 66/79). We therefore begin by determining the definition through the method of division. The mythic circle to which Deleuze refers is either the myth of the *Statesman*, or more generally the Platonic doctrine of anamnesis, that we have knowledge of Ideas because we remember them from our existence prior to our birth. The foundation is then given by the relation of appearance to the realm of Ideas, allowing us to ask the question of descent. Plato therefore ultimately grounds the world of becoming on the world of being. We should note that there are a number of parallels between Plato and Nietzsche. For both, the question is one of genealogy (in Nietzsche's case, whether something is based on a sedentary or nomadic distribution), and they both involve tests of selection. Plato selects genuine copies, and real knowledge which is based on being or the Ideas. Nietzsche selects those entities whose existence is founded on a principle of becoming. Both rely on myth (the demon) and a relation between questions and problems. Deleuze's project therefore parallels Plato's, with his account of superior empiricism, as determining the differential origin of perspective, mirroring Plato's own project of tracing appearances to their Ideal origins. Rather than an investigation in search of a primal identity (the Ideas), Deleuze is attempting to trace phenomena to their origin in a field of difference.

Chapter 2. Repetition for Itself

2.1 Introduction

Chapter 2 draws together two themes that we have already encountered. In the introduction, we saw how the argument from incongruent counterparts points to the possibility of differences that escape from any conceptual identification. Chapter 2 explores the phenomenon of repetition, where we have elements that are absolutely identical (if they are not identical, then there is no repetition), but yet must also be different (if they are not distinguishable, then we once again have no repetition, as we only have one event). As Deleuze notes, representation might try to provide a concept of repetition by noting that while the elements that make up the repetition are identical with one another, 'a change is produced in the mind which contemplates: a difference, something new *in* the mind' (DR 70/90). Repetition is in this case made possible by the way in which the subject takes up the elements. In this sense, repetition is tied to the notion of synthesis. Once again, we will find that there are two forms of repetition: bare, material repetition, which operates at the surface, and a clothed, spiritual repetition which makes bare repetition possible. Furthermore, beneath the representation of repetition, the second mode of repetition will be an intensive repetition, reiterating the result of Chapter 1.

The second theme is somewhat broader than repetition itself, but is related to it. In the introduction, we briefly discussed Kant's claim that some aspects of our knowledge of the world are known *a priori* because we ourselves condition our relation to the world. So, for instance, in the first part of the *Critique of Pure Reason*, the Transcendental Aesthetic, Kant attempts to justify our faith in geometry by showing that space must be something that we ourselves impose upon the world. As we organise external objects spatially, we know that geometry, which is the science of this mode of organisation, must necessarily correspond to the structure of the external world. The coherent world of objects we find around us is, then, for Kant, the result of a synthesis. Further, Kant's claim will be that wherever we find synthesis, we need to presuppose a subject that is responsible for that synthesis, as well as an object to be synthesised. As we shall see in the next section, Kant's transcendental philosophy, while it takes the objects of experience to be constituted, is liable to repeat the mistakes Deleuze finds in traditional metaphysics. One of the key questions for Chapter 2, therefore, is whether it is possible to give an account of the organisation of experience which does not rely on the activity of a subject. This question is important for Deleuze because he needs to show that he can provide an alternative to the Kantian notion of synthesis. Put in other terms, if Kant's account of synthesis is correct, then organisation will always imply a central identity. A proper concept of difference will therefore be impossible to develop.

Deleuze begins Chapter 2 with an analysis of Hume, and it is in Deleuze's early 1953 book on Hume, *Empiricism and Subjectivity*, that we can find an account of the difference between Hume's project and Kant's:

We embark upon a transcendental critique when, having situated ourselves on a methodologically reduced plane that provides an essential certainty – a certainty of essence – we ask: how can there be a given, how can something be given to a subject, and how can the subject give something to itself? . . . The critique is empirical when, having situated ourselves in a purely immanent point of view, which makes possible a description whose rule is found in determinable hypotheses and whose model is found in physics, we ask: how is the subject constituted in the given? The construction of the given makes room for the constitution of the subject. (ES 87)

So here we have two very different projects. For Kant, we begin with the notion of the subject and object, and attempt to explain how the two can enter into a relationship with one another. In this case, therefore, the 'methodologically reduced plane' is the field of representation, with its concomitant positing of judgement. Taking judgement as our model is, according to Deleuze, destined to lead us to the same kinds of difficulties we encountered with Aristotle in the last chapter. Hume's approach instead begins with the 'given' that precedes the subject, and attempts to show how it is constituted, which in turn allows us to explain how the subject systematises the given into its own categories. Deleuze's aim in this chapter will be to provide a 'Humean' deduction of how the world is constituted that does not rely on a subject. In order to do so, he distinguishes between Kant's notion of synthesis, which he calls active synthesis, and another form of synthesis that is actually responsible for bringing subjects into existence, called passive synthesis. By explaining how subjects come into being, Deleuze also aims to show why it is that philosophers have been misled into believing in something like a Kantian account of the constitution of the world that presupposes rather than explains the existence of subjects. In order to do so, he will show how each of the three active syntheses Kant takes to explain the possibility of experiencing a world of objects presupposes a prior synthesis whereby the subject is constituted. In the next section, therefore, I want to make a short digression into one of the most important sections of Kant's critical philosophy, the transcendental deduction of the *Critique of Pure Reason*, in order to outline the three syntheses that Deleuze is dealing with.

2.2 Background: Kant's Three Syntheses of Time

We saw in relation to the argument from incongruent counterparts (0.6) that for Kant there was a fundamental difference between sensibility (intuition in Kant's terms) and the understanding. That argument showed that there was a difference in kind between the way the understanding organises the world, and the way objects are presented in space. This led to determinations, such as handedness, that could not be specified purely conceptually. This brings in a new question, however. If the empirical world is the product of our cognitive faculties, how are two faculties which are different in kind able to relate to each other? Kant himself raises this difficulty by noting that 'appearances might very well be so constituted that the understanding should not find them to be in accordance with the conditions of its unity' (Kant 1929: A90/B123). That is, there could be nothing in intuition to which the understanding can apply itself. He begins by claiming that knowledge involves some kind of synthesis. In other words, to make a statement involves bringing together different concepts into a unity. Kant defines synthesis as 'the act of putting different representations together, and of grasping what is manifold in them in one act of knowledge' (Kant 1929: A77/B109). As we can see, this model of synthesis is very closely related to judgement, and an act of judging *is* this conjunction of what is manifold in one single act (A is B). Kant's essential claim is that the judgements we make about the world seem to accord with it because the world of experience is itself constituted by a series of syntheses by the same faculties, but operating in a transcendental manner, that is, prior to our conscious experience of the world. Because of this parallel between our judgements about the world and its constitution, the model Kant uses for synthesis is judgement.

Kant's solution to the difficulty of the relation of the faculties involves arguing that conceptual thought plays a necessary role in experience. Whereas perception simply requires intuition, experience also involves the notion that we experience a world of objects. Now, when we look at our experience of the world, Kant argues, the notion of an object is not directly given in sensible intuition. Rather, our experience of a world made up of things – instead of, for instance, sense-data – *presupposes* a conception of an object, or object-hood. The question of the deduction can therefore be reformulated as: what is it that allows us to experience a world of objects rather than simply appearances? The claim that the transcendental deduction makes is that it is the understanding – which is the faculty of concepts (or, as we shall see, rules) – which gives us the concept of an object. As such, the understanding plays a necessary role in experience, and the gap between the different faculties has been bridged. To prove this result, Kant argues that experience rests on a threefold synthesis, which in turn requires us to posit a subject and an object, leading us to introduce the categories as rules which relate to the constitution of objects.

The first synthesis is what Kant calls a 'synthesis of apprehension'. He begins with the claim that if we experienced everything at once, our experience would just be of an undifferentiated unity. For this reason, Kant makes the claim that we have to experience different moments at different times. Just having a collection of moments is not enough, however. We also have to experience these moments as a part of *the same* temporal sequence. Without some kind of unifying synthesis of time on our part, all we would encounter is a series of moments without relation to one another. Now, Kant claims that our ability to relate particular empirical experiences to one another relies on a deeper, transcendental synthesis. In order to be able to relate different moments in time to one another, we also need to be able to synthesise time itself into a unified structure. This first synthesis therefore '[runs] through and [holds] together' (Kant 1929: A99) the various moments of time in order to allow us to be presented with a unified temporal framework.

The synthesis of apprehension allows us to recognise different moments as belonging to the same temporal sequence. Kant notes that we often make use of these kinds of relations in our imagination's use of associative principles, particularly in the contraction of habits. So, if we see a pattern, or hear a melody often enough, we come to expect the next sign, or musical note. Now, this is an empirical synthesis on the part of our imagination, to the extent that our particular habits themselves are not conditions for the possibility of experience. The possibility of contracting a habit in general *does* imply a second transcendental synthesis on the part of the subject, however:

If cinnabar were sometimes red, sometimes black, sometimes light, sometimes heavy, if a man changed sometimes into this, sometimes into that animal form, if the country on the longest day were sometimes covered with fruit, sometimes with ice and snow, my empirical imagination would never find opportunity when representing red colour to bring to mind heavy cinnabar. (Kant 1929: A100–1)

In order to be able to reproduce empirically past moments that have an affinity with present moments, we need a transcendental synthesis of production in the imagination to generate those affinities that the empirical imagination discovers. If we turn to Kant's example of drawing a line, we can see what this deeper synthesis is. In order for there to be the possibility of associating representations, they have to be in themselves associable. That is, in order to relate different moments together, I must be able to compare moments that have passed with my present experience. If I draw a line in thought, it must be the case that I can reproduce the previous moments as being contiguous with the present one in order for the thought to be complete.

This synthesis in turn implies a third synthesis. In order to have experience, we don't just need to have an affinity between different moments of experience, but these different moments of experience need to be related to one another as a unity for consciousness. 'Without consciousness that that which we think is the very same as what we thought a moment before, all reproduction in the series of representations would be in vain' (Kant 1929: A103). Kant puts this point as follows:

It must be possible for the 'I think' to accompany all our representations; for otherwise something would be represented in me that couldn't be thought at all, and that is equivalent to saying that the representation would be impossible, or at least would be nothing to me. (Kant 1929: B131–2)

When we walk around a building, we are given a series of perspectives on it. Now, a condition of seeing these different perspectives as being perspectives on the same building is that I am able to relate them together as being *my* perceptions of the building. Otherwise, we would simply have a series of fragmentary appearances. We can go further than this, and say that without the unity of consciousness we would not just see appearances of different buildings. We would simply see a series of appearances without any kind of unity – they wouldn't relate *to* anything. Now, this is a key point. Kant has claimed that in order for experience (that is, a relation to the world that gives us knowledge, rather than just sensation or appearances) to be possible, we need to be able to see appearances as belonging to the same subject. In order for this to be the case, they need to exhibit some kind of unity. It is the concept of the object that gives all of these moments of appearance a unity, as it is by seeing all the moments of appearance as referring to the same underlying object that we are able to unify them. The concept of the object thus makes the unity of consciousness possible. We can note that, while for Kant we need the concepts of a subject and an object to make experience possible, precisely because they make experience possible, we don't have direct experience of subjects and objects. Rather, they are necessarily prior to experience (and to synthesis). As such, while we need to presuppose them, we cannot say anything about them. This point will be important when we look at Kant's criticisms of Descartes in relation to Deleuze's third synthesis of time (2.6).

We can now return to our initial question. How does Kant show that the faculties can be related to one another? Well, for experience to be possible, the subject needs to synthesise appearances into objective unities. How is it able to do this? The categories give us the essential characteristics of what it is for something to be an object (to be a substance, to have properties, etc.), and so it makes sense for the categories of the understanding to provide the rules by which the synthesis takes place. Thus we have a situation whereby appearances are synthesised into experience by relating them to the notion of an object, and in order to relate appearances to the notion of an object, we need rules governing objects in general, and these are the categories of our conceptual thought (the understanding in Kant's terms).

Kant's account is important because it shows the interrelations between several concepts which we saw Deleuze opposing in the previous chapter. Kant essentially shows that the notions of objecthood, judgement and synthesis are all interconnected. Because we see experience as being about a subject relating to an object, we are forced to invoke the concept of judgement. Now, given that all of these concepts reciprocally imply one another, how can we develop the kind of subrepresentational account that Deleuze is seeking? Deleuze's response, as we shall see, will centre on the concept of synthesis driving this account. His claim is that Kant has essentially taken a psychological account of what it is for the temporal world of objects to emerge for us and reiterated it at a transcendental level. Conscious synthesis for Kant takes the form of judgement. When I count, or bring together the moments of a judgement ('the table is red'), it is I who actively relates these representations (the table, redness) to one another. By using this model, Kant ties synthesis to the subject, and hence any form of synthesis that is not ultimately governed by judgement is going to be ruled out. Deleuze's approach is therefore going to be to try to provide an alternative account of the synthesis of time which does not rely on this sharp divide between the activity of consciousness and the passivity of the given:

> It is impossible to maintain the Kantian distribution, which amounts to a supreme effort to save the world of representation: here, synthesis is understood as active and as giving rise to a new form of identity in the I, while passivity is understood as simple receptivity without synthesis. (DR 87/109)

In doing so, he will try to show how our experience is also the result of syntheses which occur prior to consciousness, and hence prior to our imposition of the structure of judgement. Providing an account of this kind is going to be the primary focus of Chapter 2.

2.3 Deleuze's First Synthesis of Time: Hume (70–9/90–100)

Deleuze begins with Hume's 'famous thesis' that 'repetition changes nothing in the object repeated, but does change something in the mind which contemplates it' (DR 70/90). If, to take Deleuze's example, we have a sequence, AB AB AB, then it is obviously the case that repeating cannot be a function of the objects, AB, in the sequence themselves. If they were somehow altered by the process of repetition, then it would no longer be the same thing that was repeated (it would differ by the simple fact that it was a 'repeat'). So what is it that allows us to expect B when we perceive A? In other words, what is it that allows us to contract habits? Kant has an explanation of how different moments that are independent can be related to one another by the synthesis of reproduction of the imagination, but for Hume, such an account would not be adequate:

> When any hypothesis, therefore, is advanc'd to explain a mental operation, which is common to men and beasts, we must apply the same hypothesis to both . . . The common defect of those systems, which philosophers have employ'd to account for the actions of the mind, is, that they suppose such a subtility and refinement of thought, as not only exceeds the capacity of mere animals, but even of children and the common people in our own species; who are notwithstanding susceptible of the same emotions and affections as persons of the most accomplish'd genius and understanding. Such a subtility is a dear proof of the falshood, as the contrary simplicity of the truth, of any system. (Hume 2000: 1.3.16)

Hume's point is that the ability to contract habits is not restricted to creatures with cognitive faculties as subtle as those Kant describes, and so any explanation in terms of those faculties cannot be accurate. Rather than an inference from a number of supporting cases, Deleuze argues that Hume sees habit formation as a process whereby past instances of the AB sequence are contracted together to form generalities by the imagination. The imagination operates like a 'sensitive plate' in order to develop a qualitative impression of the AB relation, rather than the quantitative relation of the understanding, which relies on storing a sequence of prior moments.

Now, on this level we have a conception of time, in that habit anticipates the future on the basis of the past. After having observed AB enough times, we anticipate a future, B, when we perceive A. So habit gives us a relation between the past and the future. In what sense is this a *synthesis* of time? Hume says the following about our perception of time: 'For we may observe, that there is a continual succession of perceptions in our mind; so that the idea of time being for ever present with us' (Hume 2000: 1.2.5). Habit turns this succession into a synthesis of time by systematising it, thus generating a field of past instances and a horizon of anticipation of the future. Rather than simply having a succession, certain impressions are retained (qualitatively), and others are anticipated on the basis of our retained impressions. We therefore have a model of time whereby aspects of the past are retained, and aspects of the future are anticipated from within the present.

Deleuze's account of method aims to show how active syntheses are possible on the basis of passive syntheses, and so we also need an account of how these higher syntheses are possible. The first point to note is that the systematisation of the flux of experience is, for Deleuze, the constitution of the subject: 'Habit is the constitutive root of the subject, and the subject, at its root, is the synthesis of time – the synthesis of the present and the past in the light of the future' (ES 92–3). I want to come back to this point in a moment, but if syntheses are constitutive of subjects, we can now see how the active syntheses are possible. Deleuze claims that once the subject emerges, then 'on the basis of the qualitative impression in the imagination, memory reconstitutes the particular cases as distinct, conserving them in its own "temporal space". The past is then no longer the immediate past of retention, but the reflexive past of representation, of reflexive and reproduced particularity' (DR 71/92). So Deleuze's claim is that when we represent this process to ourselves, we do so through the types of structures Kant has outlined. Doing so gives us a false impression that the work of synthesising time is being carried out by those faculties themselves, whereas in fact by simply representing the process they have falsified it. The synthesis of a temporal manifold therefore, according to Deleuze, relies on a prior synthesis whereby the notions of past and future are generated, and the indifferent moments of sensation are related to one another through habit. Thus, Kant's active synthesis in terms of the higher faculties relies on a prior synthesis that cannot be accurately represented by these faculties.

What is the nature of the subject that is constituted through this process of the contraction of habit? Well, the subject is simply the organisation of impressions themselves. It is thus constituted by a synthesis, rather than being the agent of synthesis. Habit is thus not being understood here as a form of activity on the part of the subject, but rather as a mode of expectation, or in Deleuze's terms, contemplation. Now, it is this contemplation of time as involving anticipations and retentions that Deleuze claims is the subject. Such an understanding of habit as passive is not possible for an account such as Kant's, because synthesis has to be seen as an activity of a subject. There are a number of implications that Deleuze draws out of this model of contemplation.

First, this synthesis of time is organised according to rhythms of anticipation, rather than simply as a succession of moments. Rather than mathematical time, which is modelled on space, the time of habit is qualitative, and, like Henri Bergson's duration, forces us to wait.

Second, if the subject is simply the synthesis of time into an organised structure, then it is going to be the case that wherever we encounter such a synthesis or organisation of time, we will encounter a self: 'there is a self wherever a furtive contemplation has been established' (DR 78/100). This means that habit is not itself a psychological phenomenon, but instead operates throughout the world. In fact, as this synthesis is constitutive of the psychological realm, it will operate in the material world prior to it. We can see, for instance, that the heart contracts, not in the sense of the actual movement it makes, but to the extent that it organises an essentially indifferent succession into a series of moments of a particular duration (the heartbeat). Now, if the heart can be seen as operating according to a habit, then so can almost everything in the world. Deleuze puts this point as follows:

Perhaps it is irony to say that everything is contemplation, even rocks and woods, animals and men, even Actaeon and the stag, Narcissus and the flower, even our actions and our needs. But irony in turn is still a contemplation, nothing but a contemplation. (DR 75/96)

A consequence of this is that if everything is a contemplation, then although the organisation of time is subjective, all time is organised. Essentially, the world is constituted as a field of co-existing rhythms operating with different tones, rather than as pure succession.

Third, when we look at how habit functions, even when a habit is driven by a need on the part of an organism, it is not the case that the habit itself is constituted in terms of the objects themselves. If I am thirsty, for instance, I do not anticipate or expect the molecular structure, H_2O, but rather water. Habit does not operate in terms of that which generates impressions, but rather in terms of signs. Habit does not, therefore, operate with representations of things, but rather with what Deleuze and Guattari will later call affects.

This leads us on to the fourth point. Deleuze has said that the heart contemplates, and obviously, the heart is a part of us. What is the relation between us and our heart, and all of the other organs and constituents of organs that make us up? We ourselves, according to Deleuze, are systems of syntheses:

The self, therefore, is by no means simple: it is not enough to relativise or pluralise the self, all the while retaining for it a simple attenuated form. Selves are larval subjects; the world of passive syntheses constitutes the system of the self, under conditions yet to be determined, but it is the system of a dissolved self. (DR 78/100)

The notion of sign is important here, because the relations between levels of the self cannot be understood as if the self were a series of distinct elements brought into relation with one another. We don't have interactions between different substances, but interactions between levels of the same substance. Rather than a causal interaction between entities, we therefore have signals between levels. Our heartbeat appears as a 'sign' in our world, but this sign does not resemble the movement of the heart itself. The signs transmitted between levels are different in kind from the selves that generate them.

2.4 Deleuze's Second Synthesis: Bergson (79–85/100–7)
Deleuze's first synthesis parallels Kant's first synthesis, and aims to show how we are constituted along with a coherent temporal framework.

Why is the first synthesis not sufficient to explain experience? Deleuze's claim is that the first synthesis constitutes a structure of time that has a past and a future, but these pasts and futures are only understood as moments of the present, that is, as habit and anticipation. This particular present, with its particular anticipations, can itself become past and be replaced by another present. In this sense, as Deleuze puts it, '*there must be another time in which the first synthesis of time can occur*' (DR 79/100).

Now, if we turn back to Kant's model of the three syntheses (2.2), we can see that the final two syntheses provide an account of how different presents can be related to one another. Kant's claim was that our imagination reproduced a past present, which is recognised as such by the understanding. As Deleuze notes, reproduction therefore involves the co-existence of these two presents: the present within which I remember, and the memory itself. To differentiate the past event from the event of recollection, 'it is of the essence of representation not only to represent something but also to represent its own representivity' (DR 80/102) – to represent the past as past. Deleuze's claim is that on this model, the past is simply understood as 'the mediation of presents' (DR 80/101), a claim which has two important consequences. First, such an account presumes that the nature of the past *simply is* a series of presents which have passed. Second, it presupposes that there is no difference between presents that are now in the past and the 'current' present. At this point, Deleuze turns to Bergson's critique of associationism in his 'great book' *Matter and Memory* to show the inadequacy of such an account (DR 81/103).

In order for a past experience to be associated with a present experience, Kant claims that we need a prior synthesis whereby impressions are brought into 'affinity' with one another. As Deleuze writes, 'the limits of this representation of reproduction [of former presents] are in fact determined by the variable relations of resemblance and contiguity known as forms of association. In order to be represented, the former present must resemble the present one' (DR 80/102). The difficulty with founding reproduction on resemblance is that 'we should seek in vain for two ideas which have not some point of resemblance or which do not touch each other somewhere' (Bergson 1991: 163). The point Bergson is making is that once we have separated memories into a series of passive givens, in a manner such as Kant's, the principle whereby they are related to one another appears to be arbitrary: 'why should an image which is, by hypothesis, self sufficient, seek to accrue itself to others either similar or given in contiguity with it?' (Bergson 1991: 165).

We can relate this point to Deleuze's criticisms of the notion of law (0.2). There we saw that in order for a law to function, we had to see it as ranging over a field of discretely determined entities. But this made it impossible for us to provide an account of how those entities themselves were determined. Similarly here, once we have reached the level of discretely determined appearances, it is impossible to determine the principles by which they are related to one another, primarily because their self-sufficiency means that they are not internally related to other memories. For this reason, we require an external force, such as the active synthesis of consciousness, to impose a set of relations on them. If this act of relation is external to the elements, and comes after them, then we cannot explain how it is able to operate according to an affinity we find within them. Bergson presents the following alternative: 'In fact, we perceive the resemblance before we perceive the individuals which resemble one another; and in an aggregate of contiguous parts, we perceive the whole before the parts' (Bergson 1991: 165). Bergson's point is that there is a self-relation of the moments prior to their constitution as individuals that can be given to an active synthesis. This in effect is the claim that active synthesis is transcendentally dependent on a prior passive (non-conscious) synthesis.

Bergson provides an alternative account of the way memory functions by rejecting the assumption that the past, or memory, resembles the present, or perception. We can begin to outline this account by noting that three domains are run together in Kant's account: recollection-memory, habit-memory, and perception. Habits are produced by the re-presentation of actual past experiences by the imagination, just as, presumably, the imagination reproduces particular events from the past that we recollect. These moments are represented as the equivalent of perceptions. As we know from experience, however, there is a clear difference between the notion of habit, which involves orienting ourselves towards a world of things, and the reminiscence of a particular event, which may involve a detachment from concerns and present experience.

If we want to understand how these two notions are related, we need to begin by recognising that consciousness, for Bergson, is fundamentally oriented towards action. That means that the present moment of time is to be understood in terms of the connection between perception and action (i.e., in sensory-motor terms). Our principle concern is with our orientation towards future possibilities, rather than towards the past. In this respect, however, the memory is obviously of use, as it allows us to act on the basis of prior experience. This was the basis of Kant's claim that forming habits required an affinity of perceptions, in order that relations of similarity and contiguity could be formed between the past and present. Now, as Bergson believes that memory is different in kind from perception, it cannot be the case that memories are simply representations like perception itself. Rather, memory 'begets sensation' (Bergson 1991: 141) when it is brought to bear on a present situation. So the present is the site of the integration of two movements which are different in kind. This leads to a number of questions. If the past is unlike the present, how is it structured? And, if the past is unlike the present, how is it able to be integrated into the present?

Beginning with the first question, we can note that there appears to be a process of selection involved in action. What is similar to the present is brought to bear on present experience. As Bergson notes, children often have far greater facility of recall than adults, which is inversely proportional to their ability to select the experiences appropriate to the present context (Bergson 1991: 154). If the detail of one's recollections is inversely proportional to action in this way, then 'a human being who should dream his life instead of living it would no doubt keep before his eyes at each moment the infinite multitude of the details of his past history' (Bergson 1991: 155). So memory that functions by recollection contains a greater and greater part of the past, until we reach a point at which it is completely detached from action and hence, in the state of pure memory, contains a complete record of the past. Now, for Bergson, memory is different in kind from the present, which relates itself by succession to the future. We can now give a clearer account of its structure.

If we recognise that Kant's model sees memory as disconnected and successive (Bergson's characterisation of 'self-sufficient atoms'), then the rejection of this model is going to mean that we no longer see memory as composed of separate parts. If that is the case, then we will not be able to separate one particular set of memories from others. This implies that memory stores the whole of the past, rather than just moments of particular interest to the subject. Now, given that the past cannot be divided up into elements, it must be the case that the whole of the past is also present in our practical relations to the world. Selection on the basis of similarity will not explain how only a small part of the past is related to the present, as selection implies detachable elements, and as we saw, similarity is presupposed rather than explained by the empiricist model. Instead of a process of selection, we have a process of expansion and contraction between different levels of our memory. At the level of pure memory, which is most remote from action, we have memories at their most expanded, whereby the particularity of different experiences is apparent. As we contract memory towards a point, we move from particularity to generality, until we arrive at the point of the present itself, where, while the whole is still present, it is manifested in the form of habit where all particularity of past experience has been lost. This gives us Bergson's diagram of the cone of time:

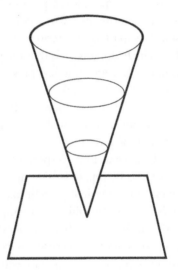

Figure 1: Bergson's cone of memory

In fact, this 'cone' is divided up into a whole series of co-existing planes of memory, which represent different degrees of the contraction of the past depending on the requirements of the circumstances which allows us some freedom in our response to stimuli. Thus:

> A foreign word from a foreign language, uttered in my hearing, may make me think of that language in general or of a voice which once pronounced it in a certain way . . . [these two associations] answer to two different mental *dispositions*, to two distinct degrees of tension in memory; in the latter case they are nearer to the pure image, in the former, they are more disposed toward immediate response, that is to say, to action. (Bergson 1991: 169)

Bergson's account of how this process of contraction operates is a little obscure, but he describes it as follows:

Memory, laden with the whole of the past, responds to the appeal of the present state by two simultaneous movements, one of translation, by which it moves in its entirety to meet experience, thus contracting more or less, though without dividing, with a view to action; and the other of rotation upon itself, by which it turns towards the situation of the moment, presenting to it the side which may prove to be the most useful. (Bergson 1991: 168–9)

Deleuze presents this account of the pure past in terms of three paradoxes. What makes these paradoxes paradoxical is the inability of representation to characterise its own account of representation. Provided we understand the past as non-representational, the problems they highlight dissolve. The first paradox is that the past cannot be constructed on the basis of the present: 'If a new present were required for the past to be constituted as past, then the former present would never pass, and the new one would never arrive' (DR 81/103). Deleuze's point here is that if we see time as a series of atomic moments and try to conceptualise the notion of the past, then we encounter a simple logical problem. In order for *this* present to be responsible for the constitution of the past, it would have to be replaced by a new present. But a new present can only emerge if the original present has *already* been constituted as passed (otherwise there would be no temporal 'space' for it). Thus, we cannot represent the past as being formed by a succession of moments. Now if the past cannot be successively constituted from our representation of the present, it must co-exist with the present. The second paradox is that of co-existence. If the past cannot be constituted from the present, it must be different in kind from it. Now, as what characterises the present is the self-sufficient, atomic nature of the presents which make it up, the past must be non-atomic. If that is the case, then it cannot be only a part of the past which co-exists with the present, but the whole of it. The final paradox is that of pre-existence. The past, as it is a condition of the passing of the present, must exist prior to the present.

Now, while reproduction relies on the pure past in order to relate different presents to one another, when we consciously recollect a past event, it always appears to us as a present which has passed. Ultimately, it is an underlying passive synthesis that provides the affinity between the past and the present that the active synthesis presupposes. So the active synthesis of reproduction rests on the passive synthesis of memory, which is itself not representable. The passive synthesis thus provides the account of the past that was obscured by the mediation of past presents in Kant's model.

We can now see how these two syntheses lead to two concepts of repetition. In fact, there are four repetitions at play in *Difference and Repetition* at this point, as we have two levels, habit and memory, and two modes of synthesis operating at these levels, active and passive synthesis. We now need to see how these two levels interact. To return once more to the question of association, the problem with the representational account was that it was unable to explain *how* different moments came to be selected as a basis for habit, as every moment possessed an affinity of some sort with every other moment. Now, Hume appears to solve this problem by introducing the notion of a contractive faculty of the imagination, rather than the Kantian account, which operated more like an inference from previous cases to the present case through shared properties. We still need to know how the imagination is able to select what it contracts, or what it fixes on as the basis for its anticipation. This is where the synthesis of the past comes into play. As we have just seen, Bergson represents the past as a cone, each level of which contains the entirety of the past, but at different levels of contraction and relaxation. At the widest level of the cone, we have the absolute relaxation of memory, the pure past. At the point of the cone, the past was contracted down to a point of practical generality. Between the two the past was layered in different degrees of contraction and relaxation. Each of these layers of contraction and relaxation can be seen as a field of different similarities and differences between events, just as in Bergson's example of hearing a word in a foreign language can evoke either the meaning of the word, or the first time that I heard it. These two syntheses are therefore related as follows: 'The sign of the present is a *passage* to the limit, a maximal contraction which comes to sanction the choice of a particular level as such, which is in itself contracted or relaxed among an infinity of possible levels' (DR 83/105). The imagination that Hume talks about is therefore the point of actualisation of a particular plane of memory in relation to action. We therefore have two different contractions: the contraction of the plane itself, and then the contraction that relates the plane of memory to the actual world. Bergson's account supplements Hume's by providing a model of time within which the first synthesis can take place, but also by explaining how different contractions of the same temporal field are possible: 'each chooses his pitch or his tone, perhaps even his lyrics, but the tune remains the same, and underneath all the lyrics the same tra-la-la, in all possible tones and all pitches' (DR 83–4/105–6).

We can therefore say there are two forms of passive repetition – the repetition of habit, which is 'empirical', and is the repetition of instants, and the repetition of memory, whereby the same past is repeated at a series of different levels, with different degrees of contraction and relaxation. Habit synthesises essentially indifferent elements into a field of temporality, or duration, and in doing so creates what Deleuze calls 'material' or 'bare repetition. It does repeat, as in the case of the heart-beat, but only on the basis of the 'clothed' repetition which underlies it. This repetition is based on memory, and is responsible for what Deleuze calls 'Destiny': the fact that everything is determined by the past, but a past that still allows for freedom through the selection of the level at which the past is played out.

2.5 The Third Synthesis 1: The Pure Form of Time (85–9/107–11)

While the first two syntheses give us a model of temporality, at present we are in a position where one of the two syntheses appears to be privileged. It appears to be the case that the second synthesis, memory, serves habit, allowing those elements of the past which are at the service of the present to be brought into play. In the final synthesis, Deleuze is therefore going to claim that both syntheses are dependent on a third synthesis that grounds, or rather, ungrounds, them (we will return to the difference between grounds and ungrounds in Chapter 4). If we return to our account of passive synthesis, we can note that the third synthesis is not directly constitutive of a subject, but is rather a synthesis of time prior to the subject as either constitutive or constituted. As such, it would be reasonable to say that the third synthesis is in fact neither active nor passive, and in fact, Deleuze does not refer to it as a passive synthesis. Nevertheless, as with the two prior syntheses, Deleuze needs to show why the third synthesis leads us to the illusion that a representational active synthesis is responsible for the constitution of our world. In order to do so, his strategy is slightly more complex than in the prior syntheses. Deleuze will take up a claim from Kant that positing a substantial subject is the result of a paralogism, that is, a logically fallacious argument. He will further argue that Kant's solution to the paralogism, the positing of a transcendental unity of apperception (the 'I' in the transcendental deduction) rests on Kant's false belief that all synthesis requires a subject. Instead, Deleuze will claim that the unground for his own transcendental deduction is time itself. In the following sections, I want to go through

Deleuze's claims in the following order. First, I want to look at what is special about Kant's philosophy of time, and why it opens the possibility of a pure form of time. Second, I want to look at how this model of time leads to a critique of the subject through Kant's *Paralogism*, and why Deleuze believes that Kant is wrong to posit a pre-categorial self as the ground for the transcendental deduction. Third, I want to look at what Deleuze calls the symbol of the pure and empty form of time, that is, its dramatic representation in the works of *Hamlet* and *Zarathustra*. Finally, I want to turn to what Deleuze calls the 'esoteric' doctrine of the third synthesis, and relate this to the notion of intensive difference we discovered in Chapter 1 of *Difference and Repetition*.

I want to begin with one of Deleuze's statements on the third synthesis relating three different concepts: the empty form of time, the third synthesis, and time out of joint. It is, I think, the last of these terms that opens up the third synthesis:

What does it mean: the empty form of time or third synthesis? The Northern Prince says 'time is out of joint' . . . The joint, *cardo*, is what ensures the subordination of time to those properly cardinal points through which pass the periodic movements which it measures (time, number of the movement, for the soul as much as for the world). By contrast, time out of joint means demented time or time outside the curve which gave it a god, liberated from its overly simple circular figure, freed from the events which made up its content, its relation to movement overturned; in short, time presenting itself as an empty and pure form. (DR 88/111)

To get clear on what time out of joint might mean, it's helpful to begin with the notion of what time in joint would mean. In a lecture from 1978, Deleuze makes the following claim:

Cardinal comes from cardo; cardo is precisely the hinge, the hinge around which the sphere of celestial bodies turns, and which makes them pass time and again through the so-called cardinal points, and we note their return: ah, there's the star again, it's time to move my sheep! (L 14/03/78)

Deleuze is referring here to the account given in Plato's *Timaeus* of the nature of time. The *Timaeus* tells the story of the creator (Demiurge), who seeks to create the universe by imposing form on chaotic matter. The Demiurge 'took over all that was visible – not at rest but in discordant and disorderly motion – and brought it from a state of disorder to a state of order, because he believed that order was in every way better than disorder' (Plato 1997e: 30a). As the creator himself is perfect, he desires to create the universe as far as possible as an image of himself. The creator himself is eternal, but given the nature of the world as already in motion, he can only create the world as a likeness to eternity:

> Now it was the Living Thing's nature to be eternal, but it isn't possible to bestow eternity fully upon anything that is begotten. And so he began to think of making a moving image of eternity: at the same time as he brought order to the universe, he would make an eternal image, moving according to number, of eternity remaining in unity. This number, of course, is what we now call 'time'. (Plato 1997e: 37d-e)

So how does time come about? Well, the first thing to note is that before the universe is organised according to time, it is still in motion, although this motion is 'disorderly'. Thus, motion is not dependant on time, which appears afterwards. In fact, Timaeus believes that time is grounded in the elements which are most perfect in the universe, the celestial bodies. In what way do the celestial bodies form the ground of time? The planets move in an orderly manner, which is what allows time to be related to measure (the star that represents the time to move the sheep in Deleuze's example).

> In this way and for these reasons night-and-day, the period of a single circling, the wisest one, came to be. A month has passed when the Moon has completed its own cycle and overtaken the Sun; a year when the Sun has completed its own cycle. (Plato 1997e: 39c)

Time here is simply the measure of motion. What is central to this Platonic model is that we cannot have an empty form of time, as time is a way in which something else (in this case, the number, or measure of motion) presents itself. Time is simply an imperfect way in which the eternal patterns of the world present themselves. Since time is just an expression of another form of order, once we remove this underlying order, time itself disappears. Time is ancillary to the intelligible. To put time out of joint will therefore be to move to an understanding of time that is not based on this kind of Platonic subordination of time to intelligible motion. If time is instead primary, then we open up the possibility of a pure form of time, prior to any particular content. Now, although we might feel that rejecting something like the Platonic conception is not a particularly radical move, we can see that the subordination of time to an eternal, intelligible and also representational model is central not just to Plato's conception, but also to pre-Kantian philosophy in general. Leibniz, for instance, argues that space and time are simply 'well founded phenomena' by which we inadequately perceive the true 'conceptual' order of things. As such, time is really a mode in which the essential structure of succession appears to us. In this case too, therefore, time is secondary to a rational, conceptual and representational way of ordering things. Time is predicated on a prior representational structure. To be 'in joint' is therefore to be hinged, tied to cardinal numbers, and tied to a prior representational order. In what sense, therefore, does Kant make time 'out of joint?'

We can give a schematic answer to the first question by noting the result of the Kantian theory of intuition that rather than time being a mode of succession, succession is a mode in which time appears to us. In fact, for Kant, succession is simply a way in which we organise time. Deleuze puts this point forward as follows:

Time cannot be defined by succession because succession is only a mode of time, coexistence is itself another mode of time. You can see that he arranged things to make the simple distribution: space-coexistence, and time-succession. Time, he tells us, has three modes: duration or permanence, coexistence and succession. But time cannot be defined by any of the three because you cannot define a thing through its modes. (L 14/03/78)

Thus, by making time a faculty that is different in kind from the understanding, Kant presents it as something more than simply derivative of succession. Rather, succession is a way of ordering time. This opens the way for a consideration of the empty form of time as time prior to succession. Deleuze will take up this notion to make the claim that the successive structure of habit and the co-existent structure of memory are both simply modes of one underlying pure form of time.

2.6 The Third Synthesis 2: Two Different Paralogisms (85–7/107–10)

Deleuze relates this notion of time out of joint to the subject by claiming that 'nothing is more instructive than the difference between the Kantian and the Cartesian Cogito' (DR 85/107). Descartes' cogito, the claim that 'this proposition, *I am, I exist*, is necessarily true whenever it is put forward by me or conceived in my mind' (Descartes 1984a: 17), is the lynchpin of Descartes' system, the point of certainty which grounds the positive claims of Cartesian philosophy. Descartes' claim is that in doubting, the I which doubts can at least be known with certainty. Kant's claim in the paralogisms is basically that Descartes has made the error of assuming that time is an inessential determination of thinking. That is, the I that doubts is able to reflect directly on its nature as a thinking thing ('Descartes could draw his conclusion only by expelling time' [DR 86/109]). In fact, as we saw in the transcendental deduction, all thinking has to take place in time. It is an *essential* determination of thinking.

Here we come to Descartes' essential problem. Objects conform to our cognition, and in this sense the category of substance is something we use to construct a world that is amenable to judgement. As the transcendental deduction shows, it is one of the categories that makes thinking about objects possible. Now, Descartes is attempting to apply a determination ('I think') to an object that is undetermined (the 'I am'), but according to our notion of substance, substance is a way of organising something which is given. According to Kant, the mistake is that Descartes hasn't considered how the object can become determinable (under what form it can be given). For Kant, the answer is that objects are given in intuition, and therefore that the 'I am' can only be determined provided it is given to us by the intuition of time. But clearly the 'I am' that Descartes introduces as a thinking thing is not an object which is given to us in intuition. As Kant notes, when we introspect, we don't find the self as a given object: 'No fixed and abiding self can present itself in this flux of inner appearances' (Kant 1929: A107). Descartes is therefore guilty of attempting to apply a determination outside of its proper sphere of application, by not using it as a form for synthesising intuitions, and it is this that leads him into error.

This brings us to the split in Kant's philosophy. We can see what is going on here by relating the situation back to the transcendental deduction. There, Kant made the claim that 'it must be possible for the "I think" to accompany all my representations' (Kant 1929: B131). What made this possible was a prior synthesis by the transcendental unity of apperception. This prior synthesis was something about which we couldn't say anything, as it was the ground for the categories (it was prior to notions such as substance). Now, Descartes' error therefore emerges because he conflates two different levels: 'the unity of apperception, which is subjective, is taken for the unity of the subject as a thing' (Kant 2005: 240). This means that since we can only be given to ourselves in time, when we reflect, what we observe isn't the activity itself (which is transcendental), but merely the empirical after-effect of it (the 'I think' is merely an analytic result of an underlying process of synthesis):

> The spontaneity of which I am conscious in the 'I think' cannot be understood as the attribute of a substantial and spontaneous being, but only as the affection of a passive self which experiences its own thought . . . being exercised in it and upon it but not by it. (DR 86/108)

When we introspect, therefore, what we encounter is not an active subject, but a subject intuited under the form of time, and subject to the same patterns of determination that any temporal object is subject to: a passive self.

Kant argues that in order for us to be able to accompany all of our representations by an 'I think', there must be a prior, active synthesis, as the unity of the manifold is experienced through the passive form of time. This inference to the conditions of possibility of the 'I think', however, rests directly on the notion that all synthesis involves an active subject. His definition of synthesis as 'the act of putting different representations together, and of grasping what is manifold in them in one act of knowledge' (Kant 1929: A77/B109) implies that the elements of time are simply passively given, and that all synthesis takes place by an active self. Given the passive nature of the 'I think', which is determinable under the form of time, Kant is therefore obliged to posit a transcendental ego which makes the 'I think' possible. Deleuze has an alternative explanation of how we are able to confront a unified world, which is that syntheses can also be passive. As we have seen, passive syntheses are constitutive of a subject, rather than the result of a subject's activity. In this regard, what makes the 'I think' possible for Deleuze is 'a synthesis which is itself passive (contemplation-contraction)' (DR 87/109). In this sense, Kant posits the transcendental unity of apperception simply because he has ruled out a constitutive role for time itself by assigning all organisation to the understanding. If the transcendental unity of apperception isn't responsible for unifying our world of appearances, what is? For Deleuze, time itself is going to be responsible for constituting both the passive self and the world that the passive self encounters. In order to explain how this occurs, he will introduce a new moment: the eternal return. There are two doctrines of the eternal return to consider: the exoteric doctrine which provides us with a symbol of the eternal return, and the esoteric doctrine which, as we shall see, we have already encountered in Chapter 1.

2.7 The Third Synthesis 3: Hamlet and the Symbol of the Third Synthesis (88–92/111–16)

Once concepts are understood as being different in kind from our intuition of time, time cannot be seen as the moving image of eternity, since it is no longer the expression of an underlying representational structure, whether the 'number of movement' or the true 'order of things'. Time is no longer simply a confused intellectual determination. Clearly, however, we do see space as involving co-existence, and time as involving successive states. How, then, does Kant's view that time is non-conceptual relate to conceptual determinations? Or, what is the pure and empty form of time? Kant reverses the order of determination that we found in the previous model. Rather than time being a mode of the appearing of an underlying succession, for Kant, succession is a way of synthesising a prior intuition of temporality. This opens the way to escaping from an understanding of the temporal as a derivative form of representation, and grounds representation instead on something fundamentally non-representational. Succession is now a determination of an intuition of time which is not inherently successive. In a similar way, Deleuze is going to argue that the two co-existing moments of the two passive syntheses are ultimately united in a pure form of time that pre-exists both of them. This pre-existing notion of time is, paradoxically, the future, which is determined simultaneously as the present, and as the past that co-exists with the present. Before we turn to the 'esoteric' doctrine of the third synthesis, Deleuze provides an image or symbol of the structure of time through the narratives of *Hamlet*, *Oedipus*, and *Zarathustra*. In this section, I just want to outline the first and last of these 'symbols'.

Deleuze here takes up Rosenberg's conception of drama. Traditionally, drama is seen in terms of the actions of the characters. A play such as *Antigone* is driven by the act of Antigone burying her brother, Polyneices, an act forbidden by King Creon. In the case of dramas such as this, Rosenberg notes that what is being offered is something like a legal conception of the individual. When we look at the law, Rosenberg notes,

The concepts of morality or social law, applying exclusively to human beings and ignoring possible analogies with other living creatures, tend to define the individual not as an entity enduring in time but by what he has done in particular instances. A given sequence of acts provokes a judgement, and this judgement is an inseparable part of the recognition of the individual. (Rosenberg 1994: 136)

Now when we look at the legal conception of the person, it isn't the case that the unity of the individual can be given in terms of their acts themselves. Rather, when someone comes before a judge, what the judge sees is not a unity governed by personality, but rather a series of acts which are unified by the last act's relationship to the law. So, as Rosenberg notes, the acts of a murderer are in large part no different from the acts of anyone else, and are only made criminal by the fact that they precede the murder itself: 'entering an automobile, stepping on the gas, obeying the traffic lights' (Rosenberg 1994: 138). In this sense, when we look at a criminal act, it is the law that provides a framework for the analysis of action, and which imposes a structure of artifice that unifies the conduct of the perpetrator. In the case of the law, Rosenberg notes that if it is suddenly discovered that the alleged perpetrator did not commit the crime, his entire identity before the law disintegrates. The actions of 'stepping on the gas' and 'obeying the traffic lights' now take on an entirely innocent aspect. In this sense, the law operates according to an active synthesis, as it provides the active principle uniting indifferent determinations. We can therefore see Rosenberg's conception of classical drama as being one of time in joint. Here, the phenomenal manifestations of characters in classical drama are merely manifestations of an underlying law, or an underlying judgement: the fate of the character. Hence, 'psychology can establish the plausibility of Macbeth's or Lear's behaviour, but for the sufficiency of his motivation, we must not refer to a possible Macbeth or Lear "in real life" but to the laws of the Shakespearean universe' (Rosenberg 1994: 140).

How does this differ with *Hamlet*? Deleuze notes that Hamlet's claim that 'time is out of joint' can be read as an essentially philosophical claim. Here we can see that *Hamlet* was not a purely arbitrary choice on the part of Deleuze. In fact, we can see in the structure of the play itself an intimation of the reversal of the roles of time and succession/action/movement.

The first half of *Hamlet* sees Hamlet himself not as an identity in the legal sense. As Rosenberg points out, the drama prior to Hamlet's return from England concerns his inability to act:

I do not know
Why yet I live to say 'This thing's to do;'
Sith I have cause and will and strength and means
To do't. (Shakespeare 2003: IV.iv.43–6)

Now, as this quote makes clear, Hamlet is very much aware of what he should do, but he is simply not able to do it. To this extent, we have an odd dramatic structure, since, if characters are understood in terms of the relations of acts to the judgement of the law, then Hamlet's various speeches, and use of speech in the first half of the play, are simply irrelevant to the structure of his role. As Deleuze writes, 'Hamlet is the first hero who truly needed time in order to act, whereas earlier heroes were subject to time as the consequence of an original movement (Aeschylus) or aberrant action (Sophocles)' (ECC 28). Rosenberg's interpretation is precisely this, that Hamlet exists as a person, rather than an identity, and hence exists outside of the role that the play assigns him. The task of taking on the role of avenging his father is simply too big for him. The sea voyage is therefore necessary to the structure of *Hamlet*, as it represents the break whereby Hamlet becomes equal to the task allotted to him. What does this involve? Deleuze talks about the first half of Hamlet in terms of the '*a priori* past'. In this sense, Hamlet exists in the past in relation to the event (he is yet to become equal to his action). Now, here the two notions of the past and of inaction should remind us of Bergson's theory of the pure past. Hamlet, in the first half of the play, exists in a state of relation to a past that is disconnected from the present. In this sense, there is a failure to relate the past to action, which is mirrored by Hamlet's failure to identify himself with the actual structure of the law. As Deleuze puts it in his discussion of Hamlet and Oedipus, 'they are in the past and live themselves as such so long as they experience the image of the act as too big for them' (DR 89/112). The second time, the action, is the moment of the present, where the self becomes capable of acting. This is where the emergence of our representation of the self emerges as a parallel to the self of habit ('the projection of an ideal self in the image of the act' [DR 89/112]); but it is only against the future that these two moments can be related. It is only the future that allows the self of the past and the present to be brought into a 'secret coherence'. This secret coherence is the coherence exhibited by the eternal return.

We can note parallels between *Hamlet* and *Zarathustra*. Both involve their central characters moving from a state where they are not equal to their action to the act itself. The bulk of *Zarathustra* is therefore governed by Zarathustra's inability to think the eternal return ('O Zarathustra, your fruits are ripe, but you are not ripe for your fruits' [Nietzsche 2006b: 117]). This first part of *Zarathustra* is bound up with the question of the past. 'Of Redemption' is central in this respect, in that it explores two different relationships to the past. As Zarathustra says, 'this alone is revenge itself: the will's unwillingness towards time and time's "it was"' (Nietzsche 2006b: 111). Now this conception of time, with its 'dreadful chance', is the past of representation. In this framework, temporality itself is seen as the ground for resentment, man is not the ground for his own actions (he cannot will backwards), and so he is in this sense alienated from what he is by the structure of temporality. In this, we can perhaps see the structure of the paralogisms – the inability of man to find the ground of his own activity through recourse to a determinable identity. The spirit of revenge is therefore engendered by the passing of time, and its incommensurability with the will. The eternal return is thus that which offers us the possibility of a more appropriate relation to temporality ('the redemption of time'). It functions on the one level as an ethical principle, which Deleuze formulates in a way which parallels that of Kant ('what ever you will, will it in such a way that you also will its eternal return' [NP 68/63]).

Deleuze claims that the second part of *Zarathustra* is concerned with Zarathustra's transformation, as he finally becomes adequate to the thought of the eternal return. In the last part of the book, Zarathustra finally throws off his 'pity for the higher man' (Nietzsche 2006b: 266) and truly embraces the form of temporality explicit in the eternal return. The final stage, Deleuze claims, is unwritten, and would have dealt with the death of Zarathustra. In essence, we can read the eternal return in this formulation purely in terms of the first two syntheses. We act by incorporating the pure past into the present (we repeat), but this generates something truly novel, the future as new. In other words, it is on the basis of the return of the past (through memory) that the future is constituted as being in excess of the present. It is thus the future that allows us to relate the past to the present.

2.8 The Third Synthesis 4: The Esoteric Doctrine of the Eternal Return (90/113, 93–6/117–19)

While we can give the eternal return a tripartite structure in terms of the act as incorporating the past into the present in order to relate to the future, 'such an exposition remains purely introductory' (DR 90/113). While the image of the third synthesis relates the past to the present via the future, the third synthesis in reality 'concerns – and can concern – only the third time in the series' (DR 90/113). Having reached the end of our account of the three syntheses we are now in a position to see what Deleuze means by this account of the future, or third synthesis. The important comment is his claim that 'the future, which subordinates the other two to itself and strips them of their autonomy, is the royal repetition' (DR 94/117). Given the first two syntheses, we need to explain the interaction of the two very different forms of time themselves. The question of how memory is able to relate to habit is much like Kant's question of how two different faculties can relate to one another. Deleuze's answer to this question in terms of time is ultimately Spinozist. Succession and co-existence are simply different 'attributes' of time. Habit and memory can relate to each other because they are simply different modalities or expressions of the form of time itself. We can think (somewhat figuratively) of memory and habit as simply being different ways of presenting the same underlying form of time. By taking this approach, the problem of the priority of succession over co-existence, or vice versa, is put out of play. They are both expressions of the same ontologically prior temporal form, which in itself is neither successive nor co-existent. As such, while they are different modalities, they are related by being different modalities of the same empty form. The pure and empty form of time is therefore that which bifurcates itself into the past of memory and the present of habit. If we understand time apart from its references to the subject it constitutes, we have a pure form of time that is neither successive nor co-existent. The third synthesis is responsible for constituting the space of the first synthesis, what Deleuze calls the 'field of individuation' (DR 246–7/307–9, 2.10, 5.5), within which the subject is constituted. It is also responsible for constituting the relations between these fields of individuation, which are expressed by memory. Deleuze characterises this function as the 'differenciator of difference' (DR 117/143), or the 'difference which relates different to different' (DR 119/145), or as the 'dark precursor'. As we saw (2.4), Deleuze followed Bergson in seeing resemblance as dependant on a sub-representational process. Here too, Deleuze's claim is that the dark precursor does not relate two fields of individuation according to a resemblance between them, but rather because it finds expression in both simultaneously, while resembling neither, much in the manner that memory resembles neither of the presents it relates.

We can see, therefore, how this account relates to Kant's own. By making time different in kind from the understanding, Kant opens up the possibility of a pure form of time that is not itself simply the expression of a prior intellectual order. Now, because Kant associates all synthesis with an active subject, time is simply a material which can be taken up by the understanding. This means that he cannot fully develop the implications of this move, and is instead forced to posit the transcendental unity of apperception as responsible for the synthesis of time. Once we recognise the possibility of syntheses that are not active, we can understand time as auto-synthetic. Time orders itself according to the modalities of habit and memory. We can get clearer on what the pure form of time is by noting that 'the eternal return is neither qualitative nor extensive, but intensive, purely intensive. In other words, it is said of difference' (DR 243/303). What returns cannot therefore be actual states of affairs. To read it as such would be to read it in terms of time in joint, a mistake that Deleuze accuses Vico of making (DR 92–3/116). That is, the future, the pure form of time, is the same field of intensive difference that we encountered in the previous chapter. We can now see that repetition occurs not because the same forms repeat, but because the same field of intensive difference engenders these different forms. What returns, therefore, is the pure form of time in the form of intensive difference, in different actual expressions.

This final form of the eternal return therefore unites the first two chapters of *Difference and Repetition*. While the first chapter begins from an analysis of our metaphysical concept of difference, and arrives at a field of intensive difference, Chapter 2 begins with our experience of habit, and shows that what makes habit possible is memory, and that in turn, the relation between habit and memory is made possible by the field of intensive difference that is the future. Thus, the metaphysical account of Chapter 1 is reinforced by the transcendental account of Chapter 2. We therefore have two eternal returns in *Difference and Repetition*, the genealogical doctrine of the second chapter and the ontological doctrine of the first.

2.9 Freud (16–19/18–22, 96/119–20)

The conclusion of the account of the eternal return marks a natural break in Chapter 2. Deleuze's introduction of the theme of 'biopsychic life' (DR 96/119) marks a new topic, or rather, a repetition of the previous topic, this time in terms of Freud rather than Kant. In this section Deleuze aims to show once again that at the root of the psyche is a field of intensive difference. In doing so, he plots out a similarly ambivalent relationship: while Freud recognises that repetition falls outside of representation (just as for Kant the incongruent counterpart could not be conceptualised by the understanding), he ultimately understands the source of our compulsion to repeat to be the brute repetition of matter rather than the intensive repetition of difference.

Freud's account of repression sets up a relation between repetition, repression and representation: 'the patient does not *remember* anything at all of what he has forgotten and repressed, but rather *acts it out*. He reproduces it not as a memory, but as an action; he *repeats* it, without of course being aware of the fact that he is repeating it' (Freud 2003b: 36). The analyst's treatment of a patient involves helping the patient to form a representation of an initially unrepresentable trauma, which the patient repeats without being able to represent this repetition. This notion of an unrepresentable repetition at work in the project of psychoanalysis therefore bears certain structural analogies with that which Deleuze is interested in. To explore why Freud makes this claim, we need to begin with the notion of pleasure. Now, it seems to be a truism that we act in order to maximise our own pleasure. So what is pleasure for Freud? Essentially, we can see the psyche as a system subjected to excitations from both inside and outside. In so far as these excitations threaten the stability of the psyche (traumas and shocks which the mind cannot adequately get to grips with), these excitations are interpreted by consciousness as 'unpleasure'. A relaxation of the psyche, which involves a reduction in energy which hasn't been incorporated into the psychic system, is seen, on the contrary, as involving pleasure. The psyche is therefore a system which seeks to minimise the amount of energy that could destabilise it. The principle that the psyche attempts to maximise pleasure is therefore tied to a principle of homeostasis, the constancy hypothesis: 'one aspiration of the psychic apparatus is to keep the quantity of excitation present within it at the lowest possible level, or at least to keep it constant' (Freud 2003a: 47).

Now, it's clearly the case that we do not simply experience pleasure in our lives. Most of our experiences of unpleasure, however, can be explained away by looking at the system as a whole. We defer immediate pleasure in order to experience greater pleasure later on (the reality principle), or we repress particular drives in order that other parts of the psychic system can experience pleasure. Repetition does not operate in this way. Reliving past traumas, for instance, or even the stability of our characters, are situations where it appears that our repetition of behaviours is either underdetermined by the pleasure principle, or worse, actually opposed to it: 'We are much more strongly affected by cases where people appear to be the *passive* victim of something which they are powerless to influence, and yet which they suffer again and again in an endless repetition of the same fate' (Freud 2003a: 60). Deleuze sees Freud's attempt to account for this fact as providing a transcendental account much like his own three syntheses of time.

2.10 Freud's First Synthesis (96–8/119–22, 111–14/136–40)

The first thing to note about Deleuze's characterisation of Freud's project is that he claims that the concern of *Beyond the Pleasure Principle* is not 'the exceptions to this principle, but rather to determine the conditions under which pleasure effectively becomes a principle' (DR 96/120). Now, prior to the organising principle of the ego, Deleuze argues that we can see 'biopsychical life' as 'a field of individuation in which differences in intensity are distributed here and there [*Ça et là*] in the form of excitations' (DR 96/119). Within such biopsychical life, we will, of course, have variations in the level of excitation of the system at various points and at various moments. In this sense, pleasure, as a process, will be operative within the system (the level of excitation will sometimes drop). In this context, Deleuze makes a rather swift (and problematic in English or German) linguistic argument to equate the 'here and there [*Ça et là*]' of biopsychical life with Freud's id [*Ça*]. Now, in spite of the problematic nature of the argument, it does seem like a reasonable equation, and it allows us to raise the key question of this section, which is, how does pleasure cease to be a process in order to become a principle that organises the life of the unconscious? An answer such as 'pleasure is pleasing' is tautologous, and misses the point. If we try, as Freud has, to give an account of pleasure that does not already presuppose the existence of a subject who values it, then we have to be able to account for how this value gets attached to this particular biological process in the first place. That is, how a (value neutral) process becomes a principle of organisation and action.

What happens when we receive some kind of excitation from the world? Well, obviously, this excitation needs to be recognised in some way (we need to be conscious that something has happened), and also to be stored (we need to incorporate it into memory). Now, Freud's contention is that 'it is not possible within a given system for something both to enter consciousness and also to leave a memory trace' (Freud 2003a: 64). The reason for this is that if traces of excitation remained in consciousness, then they would prevent the system from registering new excitations. We therefore need to see the processes of memory and consciousness as operating within two parallel systems, much as habit and memory were different in kind in the first account of the three syntheses. We can begin with the most primitive form of life, an 'undifferentiated vesicle of irritable matter' (Freud 2003a: 65). Since a part of this organism is turned towards the world, it naturally becomes affected by various external stimuli. As it is affected by these various shocks, its nature changes so that it is able to transmit them without its elements changing. This, for Freud, is the origin of consciousness. As the system evolves, it develops protection against excessive stimulation from the outside by partially reverting to the inorganic (the skull), and, in higher creatures, by separating off the perceptual aspects further (the development of particular senses). Such a model allows Freud to explain a number of key results of psychoanalysis. It is not simply the case that all stimulation comes from outside the organism. The organism will also suffer disturbances from processes within it. Now, since these processes operate within the organism, the trauma produced by them cannot be reduced by the presence of a barrier, as was the case with shocks from the outside. Traumas which affect the organism from the inside therefore have a far greater role within the economy of the organism than those which affect it from the outside. We can further note that the organism will tend to interpret internal trauma as originating from the outside in order to allow its defences to be brought into play, which leads to the notion of projection.

So, what is a trauma? A trauma is a situation where we have energy flowing through the psyche that has not been annexed or incorporated into the psychic system of the organism (unbound energy). In cases of trauma or pain, Freud claims, rather than seeking to maintain the lowest possible level of psychic energy, the organism may attempt to stabilise the psychic system by suspending the pleasure principle, and instead annex the free flowing energy into the system of the psyche. This means that the pleasure principle does not always govern the operations of the psyche. This process of annexing energy from the outside can explain some of the situations where it appears as if the pleasure principle has been contravened. In the case of severe trauma, the system experiences unpleasure in order to retain its overall integrity. War trauma, for instance, would be a retrospective attempt to master the phenomena in question, that is, to assert control over them. Now, in the case of war trauma, this attempt to master and bind energy within the system leads to the repetition of past experiences which lead to unpleasure on the part of the subject. Freud therefore claims that such compulsions to repeat simply cannot be understood according to the pleasure principle.

Prior to the application of the pleasure principle, there needs to be some process of binding or annexation of excitation so that excitations can have 'systematic resolution', rather than arbitrarily traversing the life of the organism. So some kind of integration or organisation is necessary for us to be able to relate pleasure to a principle. Freud himself makes this point as follows:

As the drive-impulses all act on our unconscious systems, it is scarcely a new departure to assert that they follow the primary process, and it is also no very great step to identify the primary psychic process with Breuer's 'free-flowing' cathexis, and the secondary one with his 'annexed' or 'tonic' cathexis. This would then mean that it was the task of the higher echelons of the psychic apparatus to annex excitations originating from the drives and reaching it via the primary process. Any failure of this annexion process would bring about a dysfunction analogous to traumatic neurosis. Only when the annexion has taken place would the pleasure principle (or, once the latter has been duly modified, the reality principle) be able to assert its dominion unhindered. In the meantime, however, the psychic apparatus's other task of controlling or annexing the excitation would be very much to the fore – not, it is true, in opposition to the pleasure principle, but independently of it, and to some extent quite heedless of it. (Freud 2003a: 74–5)

The pleasure principle therefore rests on the integration of excitations that are originally unbound. It's helpful here to note that there are parallels with the first synthesis of time. Just as there the contraction of impressions led to the constitution of a subject, here the binding of free flowing energy leads to the constitution of a system capable of supporting the pleasure principle. The binding of energy is, therefore, for Deleuze, a process actually constitutive of a subject with the pleasure principle operating as an active synthesis on top of this process: 'an animal forms an eye for itself by causing scattered and diffuse luminous excitations to be reproduced on a privileged surface of its body. The eye binds light, it is itself a bound light. (DR 96/120). Deleuze's point is also that as the self is constituted by the integration or contraction of excitations, it simply *is* these excitations. This gives us the reason why Deleuze calls these contracting egos 'narcissistic'. What they relate to is, in a sense, themselves, or an image of themselves, in the form of the excitations that they bind. The movement of binding therefore finds satisfaction in a narcissistic relation to its own image. In this sense, the fact that the egos constituted by the binding process are narcissistic parallels the way in which the selves that were contracted habits in the first synthesis of time related not to objects, but to signs. So just as a heartbeat appears as a sign in our world that doesn't resemble the movement of the heart itself, the binding of excitations constitutes egos that do not relate directly to objects, but to images of themselves.

It is not the case that pleasure gives rise to habit, therefore, in the sense that we might talk of repeating something enjoyable, but rather it is the existence of habits that leads to pleasure. In the discussion of habit, Deleuze claimed that habit was only conceived of as reproduction when it was incorporated into a mathematicised 'temporal space' by the imagination. Similarly here, it is only by relating pleasure to the past and the future and by instituting the pleasure principle that we are able to see pleasure as operating prior to habit. That is, by talking about 'pleasure in general', we introduce the 'idea of pleasure'. Once pleasure is no longer related to a passive synthesis, but is seen as organised in relation to a principle, we have an active synthesis that relates to an ego. The result of this is that the pleasure principle will now be seen as primary, since without some kind of external organising principle, it is impossible to explain how indifferent processes can form a coherent system, and how individual excitations can be related to one another (how habits are formed). One final thing to note is that binding and the pleasure principle relate to different objects. Binding operates on free excitations in order to enable the pleasure principle to relate them together into a system.

There are therefore two principles operative within the psyche. The first is to increase pleasure within the psychic apparatus by reducing the quantity of energy within it. This is the pleasure principle. The second is a principle that attempts to convert unbound energy into bound energy by mastering excitations. This is the compulsion to repeat, which will become the death drive. Freud's claim is that it is only once excitations have been annexed by the psyche that the pleasure principle can become operative.

At this stage, it is worth noting that by grounding the compulsion to repeat in the original structure of the organism, Freud has opened the possibility of analysing this compulsion as a basic function of life itself. While the compulsion to repeat can operate in accordance with the libido, it can also operate as a tendency of life to return to an earlier stage. Freud characterises this tendency to return in the following terms:

At this point we cannot help thinking that we have managed to identify a universal attribute of drives – and perhaps of *all* organic life – that has not hitherto been clearly recognized, or at any rate not explicitly emphasized. A drive might accordingly be seen as *a powerful tendency inherent in every living organism to restore a prior state*, which prior state the organism was compelled to relinquish due to the disruptive influence of external forces; we can see it as a kind of organic elasticity, or, if we prefer, as a manifestation of inertia in organic life. (Freud 2003a: 76)

What leads Freud to this conclusion? Central to this conception are, I think, two primary assumptions in the account we have been looking at so far. The first is that the organism is defined essentially as closed off from the world. Organic life's engagement with the world is seen as essentially traumatic and disruptive for Freud. Second, there is the belief that organisms, in their particular development, tend to repeat their development as a species. If we combine these two assumptions, then we have the claim that change (and hence development) is traumatic, and therefore generates a tendency for the organism to return to a prior, less traumatic state. Now, Freud claims that this movement can be seen in the fact that fish, when spawning, return not simply to their own birthplace, but also 'to the previous domain of their species, which, in the course of time, they have exchanged for others' (Freud 2003a: 77). Here the second claim, the recapitulation theory of embryo development, comes into play, as each animal carries with it the history of its development from the simplest forms of life. In fact, this movement is not simply to the earliest forms of life, but to the origin of life itself in the move from the inorganic to the organic. Thus, the drive to repeat is not simply a drive to return to an earlier form of life, but in fact, a death drive. In this sense, the compulsion to repeat/return and the death drive are equivalent: '*The goal of all life is death*, or to express it retroactively: *the inanimate existed before the animate*' (Freud 2003a: 78). Freud's account of the origin of repetition therefore ultimately traces it back to the constitution of consciousness itself. Life can be seen as playing out the relations between two different drives. First, there is the libido, which aims at conserving life by protecting the organism from external traumas that threaten to destabilise it. This conservation of life is ultimately to be understood as simply making more complex the more fundamental drive, the death drive, which seeks to return the organism to its primal state.

A key feature of this account is that the death of an organism is not (necessarily) something that is due to external factors, but rather something that is inherent to the organism itself. The organism seeks to return to the inanimate. The obvious question to ask about this claim is, why is it the case that life exists at all if it seeks its own dissolution? Well, death is at first 'still easy for living matter; the course of life that had to be gone through was probably short, its direction determined by the newly created organism's chemical structure' (Freud 2003a: 78–9). Over time, however, the complexity of life means that more and more detours are incorporated between life and death. These drives delay the movement towards death, and so appear to be conservative. They are the 'guardians of life' in that they allow the organism to perpetuate itself, but in the end, these drives, such as the sexual drives, are ultimately subordinated to the death drive. They are determined by the fact that the organism wants to choose its own death, rather than succumb to external influences.

In essence, this death drive plays the same role that the eternal return plays in Deleuze's account. The ground of Freud's account is here characterised as a mode of repetition. Once again, however, we can see that rather than repetition being conceived of as a field of intensive difference, it is here understood as an extensive, physical structure, much as time was equated with passive extension in Kant's philosophy. As we shall see, Deleuze will retain the structure of the death drive, but instead understand death in terms of a field of intensive difference. Before turning to Deleuze's account of the third synthesis as the death drive, we need to briefly look at the second synthesis.

2.11 Freud's Second Synthesis (98–111/122–35)

Is the model of the psyche as it stands adequate? At present, passive synthesis involves the binding of excitations that occur within the biopsychical system. Now, clearly pleasure does operate within this system, but it is also the case that 'biopsychical systems' have some kind of relation to an outside. As Deleuze puts it, 'A child who begins to walk does not only bind excitations in a passive synthesis, even supposing these were endogenous excitations born of its own movements. No one has ever walked endogenously' (DR 99/123). That is, our actions have an object. Now, as we might expect, given the account of the three syntheses of time, this second stage, the relation of the biopsychical system to a world of objects, is going to involve two different syntheses, an active and a passive synthesis. As the active synthesis is the most straightforward, I will begin with that.

We can start by recalling one of the central axioms of Kant's model of active synthesis, which was that the subject makes the object possible, and *vice versa*. If Kant is right about the interdependence of subjects and objects (and Deleuze takes him to be right, at least at the level of representation), then a relation to an object is going to require a subject that relates to it. In this sense, Deleuze writes the following:

Active synthesis is defined by a test of reality in an 'objectal' relation, and it is precisely according to the reality principle that the 'ego' tends to 'be activated', to be actively unified, to unite all its small composing and contemplative passive egos, to be topologically distinguished from the Id. (DR 98/122)

If we recall that pleasure relates to individual bindings, or drives within the unconscious, then it becomes apparent that the organism cannot simply function according to the pleasure principle alone. Sometimes one drive may seek satisfaction in a way which threatens the integrity of the organism. Freud therefore supplements the pleasure principle with the reality principle, which overrides the interests of the particular satisfaction of drives in favour of the pleasure (and survival) of the organism as a whole. This in turn leads to the constitution of the represented subject:

We know that the pleasure principle belongs to a primary operational level of the psychic apparatus, and that so far as self-preservation is concerned it is never anything but useless, indeed highly dangerous, given the challenges posed by the external world. Thanks to the influence of the ego's self-preservation drive it is displaced by the *reality principle*, which, without abandoning the aim of ultimately achieving pleasure, none the less demands and procures the postponement of gratification, the rejection of sundry opportunities for such gratification, and the temporary toleration of unpleasure on the long and circuitous road to pleasure. (Freud 2003a: 48)

As well as the extension of active synthesis, we also have an extension of a passive synthesis. This revolves around the somewhat obscure notion of a virtual object:

The child constructs for itself another object, a quite different kind of object which is a *virtual* object or centre and which governs and compensates for the progresses and failures of its real activity: it puts several fingers in its mouth, and appraises the whole situation from the point of view of this virtual mother. (DR 99/123)

Why might we need a separate conception of an object to deal with passive syntheses? Well, the first point to note is that if the child is going to continue to be able to bind excitations, then clearly it needs to relate in some way to a source for those excitations. This implies some kind of relationship to the outside (it needs to relate to some kind of object that generates excitations). Now, as we noted, binding does not relate to objects, but rather to signs – binding is an integration of excitations rather than a relation to a representation. This means that the kind of external object that allows for the generation of excitations will be different in kind from the actual objects of representation (just as the heartbeat doesn't resemble the motion of the heart). Bearing this in mind, we can understand Deleuze's claim that 'sucking occurs only in order to provide a virtual object to contemplate in the context of extending the passive synthesis' (DR 99/123). Here we find a similar situation, since in sucking its thumb, the child is not interested in the actual object it relates to (the thumb), but rather in providing virtual signs for a passive synthesis. Thus, the thumb takes the place of the mother's breast as providing excitations for the organism. Now, given that passive syntheses do not operate with representations, the child does not take the thumb to be the breast, but rather that aspect of the breast which satisfied the original binding process. This aspect is an action, or an image of an action. The thumb therefore provides a series of excitations that can be bound by a sub-representational passive synthesis.

Once we accept this account of the nature of the virtual object, we can start to piece together Deleuze's analysis of it. The fact that we have two types of objects, one of which is actual, and one of which is virtual, should put us in mind of the notion of the pure past that Deleuze introduced in his discussions of the syntheses of time, and in fact, he characterises virtual objects as 'shreds of pure past' (DR 101/126). So how are they constituted? Deleuze gives the following description of the constitution of the virtual object:

We see both that the virtuals are deducted from the series of reals and that they are incorporated in the series of reals. This derivation implies, first, an isolation or suspension which freezes the real in order to extract a pose, an aspect or a part. This isolation, however, is qualitative: it does not consist simply in subtracting a part of the real object, since the subtracted part acquires a new nature in functioning as a virtual object. (DR 100/125)

When we are dealing with an object of representation that we intend towards, we cannot help but think of the object as a totality. We cannot help but think that if we walked around the object then we would continue to be presented with different perspectives on it. Now, the binding process isn't concerned with the totality of the object, but only with those aspects of the object which are capable of generating excitations. It thus subtracts from the total object those aspects that are capable of creating excitations in it. It is only interested in a particular gesture, motion or aspect, and not, for instance, the object which actually moves to create the gesture. But as a representation has to be a coherent object separate from the particular perspective from which it is presented, the process of subtraction actually changes its nature (a gesture without a gesturer is incoherent as a representational object, for instance). Virtual objects are then incorporated in the series of reals. Virtual objects have to in some sense motivate behaviour – they have to be found in the world somewhere. So when the child sucks his thumb, it is relating to a virtual object, but only on the basis that this is incorporated into, or supervenient on, an actual object.

The virtual object performs a second function, which is that, once again, positing a non-actual series paralleling the actual world allows us to explain the notion of association. Deleuze poses the following question:

The difficulties in conceptualising repetition have often been emphasised. Consider the two presents, the two scenes or the two events (infantile and adult) in their reality, separated by time; how can the former present act at a distance upon the present one? How can it provide a model for it, when all its effectiveness is retrospectively received from the later present? (DR 129)

When we looked at the syntheses of time, the problem with understanding association as operating purely in terms of actual memory was that everything was like everything else in some way. That meant that it was impossible to explain why a particular experience conjured up *this* memory. For Deleuze, what ties together two series of events is that the same virtual object is at play (incorporated) in both series. This explains why a past event can still influence the present, not because of the actual events themselves, but because of the virtual object incorporated into them. This also explains why it is the case that we can see, for instance, in someone's character, a repetition of the same relationships, or the same actions, in different situations. The subject does not reason by analogy on the basis of their past responses, but is reacting to the same event incorporated into a different state of affairs.

In this sense, we can say that what is repeated is something that has never actually been present, but rather that the 'same' virtual object is present in disguise in the various states of affairs that make up the repetition. There is no first term to the series itself, however, as repetition takes place in response to the drives rather than the ego and its object.

2.12 Freud's Third Synthesis: The Death Drive (110–14/135–40)

The question which opens up the third synthesis is as follows: 'Do the disguises found in the work of dreams or symptoms – condensation, displacement, dramatisation – rediscover while attenuating a bare, brute repetition (repetition of the Same)?' (DR 16/18–19). That is, given that we need to find a foundation for repetition, is this foundation going to be a kind of repetition which is different in kind from empirical repetition? A foundation for repetition that simply rests on another bare repetition will be inadequate, since rather than explaining repetition, it will presuppose it. Deleuze's claim is going to be that underlying repetition for Freud is a material repetition, rather than a spiritual repetition:

> Even beyond the pleasure principle, the form of a bare repetition persists, since Freud interprets the death instinct as a tendency to return to the state of inanimate matter, one which upholds the model of a wholly physical or material repetition. (DR 17/19)

Now, what is interesting about this claim is that Deleuze is not here rejecting the death instinct, but rather claiming that the error is with Freud's interpretation of it. Deleuze makes the claim that the virtual and actual objects 'inevitably become confused, the pure past thereby assuming the status of a former present, albeit mythical, and reconstituting the illusion it was supposed to denounce, resuscitating the illusion of an original and a derived, of an identity in the origin, and a resemblance in the derived' (DR 109/135). This illusion, therefore, is that the origin of the compulsion to repeat is in an actual, albeit potentially mythical event. Once we succumb to this illusion, it is a short step to positing a Freudian death drive. For Deleuze, the retention of the death drive will be premised on a reinterpretation of what death amounts to. For Freud, death is understood in terms of a material repetition. Deleuze is instead going to understand death in terms of the other category of repetition, spiritual repetition.

In fact, Deleuze here introduces the same distinction that has been running through Chapter 2 between active synthesis and passive synthesis. Now, the parallel isn't perfect here, but death within the Freudian model is a principle that operates in relation to a synthesis of undifferentiated elements. It comes into play at the point at which these elements become organised as something separate from them and active in its own right (it is a principle over and above that which it is a principle of). The death drive in Freud's terms thus operates according to an active synthesis. As with Deleuze's discussions throughout this chapter, we will find that as well as the active synthesis, there is a passive synthesis that underlies it. Thus, Deleuze writes as follows:

> Blanchot rightly suggests that death has two aspects. One is personal, concerning the I or the ego, something which I can encounter in a struggle or meet at a limit, or in any case, encounter in a present which causes everything to pass. The other is strangely impersonal, with no relation to 'me', neither present nor past but always coming, the source of an incessant multiple adventure in a persistent question. (DR 112/138)

Freud's model is clearly closer to the first of these forms of death, although it is somewhat broader than Freud's own case. This first model of death is not simply 'the model of an indifferent inanimate matter to which the living would return' (DR 112/137), and there is an open question of whether Deleuze is here making a deeper point about 'this death [that] always comes from without, even at the moment when it constitutes the most personal possibility, from the past, even at the moment when it is most present' (DR 113/138).

So what is the true nature of death? Well, we saw that the third synthesis of time in the case of *Zarathustra* was represented by Zarathustra's death. Deleuze's discussion of Freud also sees death as 'a pure form – the empty form of time' (DR 112/137). Death therefore refers us to the field of intensities of Chapter 1, it is 'the state of free differences when they are no longer subject to the form imposed upon them by an *I* or an ego' (DR 113/138). So, the real notion of death is in fact the collapse of a given structure in the face of some kind of pure becoming. In this sense, death is a perpetual drive that destabilises identities, and makes transition possible: 'The experience of death is the most common of occurrences in the unconscious, precisely because it occurs in life and for life, in every passage or becoming, in every intensity as passage or becoming' (AO 330/363). Life is therefore pervaded with death, to the extent that it is run through with experiences which destabilise the structure of the organism, and the identity of the ego. For Deleuze, therefore, there is something equivalent to the death drive, but this does not operate according to an entropic principle as we find in Freud's model. Structures are not destabilised through a drive to return to a state where there is no energy in the system, but rather through the emergence of intensities into the field of representation. The death drive does not operate according to a principle, but simply is the manifestation of intensive difference into the realm of the unconscious ('this energy does not serve Thanatos, it constitutes him' [DR 113/139]). This leads to a reversal of our understanding of death. Since intensive death is a part of life (the destabilising of identities), our 'death' in this sense is coextensive with life: 'it finally ceases to die since it ends up dying, in the reality of a last instant that fixes it in this way as an *I*, all the while undoing the intensity, carrying it back to the zero that envelops it' (AO 330–1/363).

Deleuze's interpretation of the death drive is therefore one that replaces the fundamentally entropic model that we find in Freud's interpretation with one that opens up onto the univocal ontology that we looked at in the last chapter. So the final question is, why do we repeat that which we cannot represent? Earlier, Deleuze has stated that 'the present is the repeater, the past is repetition itself, and the future is that which is repeated' (DR 94/117). It is therefore the field of intensive difference which expresses itself in the present. Now, as this is different in kind from representation, it cannot occur within the field of representation as it is in itself. In this sense, the intensities which constitute us express themselves throughout our lives in a variety of contexts 'in disguise'. When we are dealing with intensive difference, therefore, 'the path it traces is invisible and becomes visible only in reverse, to the extent that it is travelled over and covered by the phenomena it induces in the system' (DR 119–20/146).

Chapter 3. The Image of Thought

3.1 Introduction

Chapter 3 of *Difference and Repetition* can be seen as generalising the results of Chapter 2. In the previous chapter, Deleuze argued that taking judgement as a model for thinking led Kant into a number of errors which ultimately prevented him from formulating a clear transcendental account of the conditions of experience. Most notably, since judging requires a subject, Kant was unable to explain the constitution of the subject itself (which occurs through a sub-representational passive synthesis), instead having to presuppose it. Chapter 3 extends this approach, looking at the 'image' of thought in philosophy more generally. Deleuze's central claim is that the traditional image of thought mistakes a representation of thinking for thinking itself, or, to put the matter differently, thinking in terms of judgement is unaware that its foundations cannot themselves be understood in terms of judgement. As we shall see, Deleuze's problem with the image of thought is not that it is just a representation of thought, but rather that it takes this representation, which is a moment of thinking, to be the entirety of thought. It is this feature that makes it a *dogmatic* image of thought. In setting out the structure of the image of thought, Deleuze invokes eight postulates (DR 167/207) that he takes together to define the traditional philosophical conception of thinking. All of them revolve around common sense. The first four deal with what we might call a technical notion of common sense, namely, the faculty of cognition that allows the other faculties (whether difference sense modalities, or different ways of relating to objects) to communicate with one another. Thus, the question is, how does philosophy traditionally explain how we encounter a world of objects amenable to the structure of judgement? The second set of four postulates deals with common sense in terms of language, focusing on the role of truth and falsity, and the genesis of meaning (or, once again, sense), and the grounds for communication. The key issue here is how representational philosophy believes language is able to make meaningful assertions about the world. While Deleuze's primary aim in this chapter is to develop a critique of the theories of thinking and of language that support judgement as the model of thought, within this critique we will also see Deleuze developing a sketch for his own theory of thinking, the relations of the faculties, and language. This will be extended into the next chapter into a theory of the Idea adequate to thinking intensity.

3.2 Feuerbach and the Postulate of the Principle (129–33/164–8)

In Chapter 1, Deleuze presented a critique of traditional Aristotelian philosophy. Chapter 3 opens by raising the question of beginnings, and considering another critic of Aristotle: Descartes. Deleuze alludes to an incomplete dialogue written by Descartes: *The Search for Truth by means of the Natural Light*. In this dialogue, Eudoxus, 'a man of moderate intellect but possessing a judgement which is not corrupted by any false beliefs and a reason which retains all the purity of its nature' (Descartes 1984b: 401), who represents Descartes, engages in a debate about how to conduct philosophy with two other characters: Epistemon (Knowledgeable), who represents the Aristotelian Scholastic tradition, and Polyander (Everyman), who is ignorant of philosophy. Descartes' aim in the dialogue is to show the insufficiency of the Aristotelian method of definition, and to replace it with a method that relies on reason alone. In order to demonstrate this method, Descartes has Eudoxus propose that Polyander attempt the method of doubt. By doubting everything given by the senses and the imagination, we realise that the only thing that cannot be doubted is one's own existence as a doubting thing, but how might we characterise this doubting thing – what kind of being is it? When we came across this question in Porphyry, we discovered that the answer to the question, what is x?, could be given by its species, which in turn was given by its genus and its difference. In this case, man is a rational animal. Eudoxus here explicitly criticises such an approach, however, on the grounds that it relies on terms that are not given by reason alone, and hence are not transparent to it:

First, what is an *animal*? Second, what is *rational*? If, in order to explain what an animal is, he were to reply that it is a 'living and sentient being', that a living being is an 'animate body', and that a body is a 'corporeal substance', you see immediately that these questions would be pure verbiage, which would elucidate nothing and leave us in our original state of ignorance. (Descartes 1984b: 410)

A term such as 'corporeal substance' does not tell us anything more about the world than a term such as 'body', because if we cannot conceive of the terms corporeal and substance clearly, then conjoining them will not help us to conceive of the term 'body'. So how do we determine the meaning of the 'I' of the cogito? Once Polyander has concluded his exercise in Cartesian doubt, guided by Eudoxus, he realises that 'of all the attributes I once claimed as my own there is only one left worth examining, and that is thought' (Descartes 1984b: 415). That is, the I is determined according to an attribute that is clearly conceived by reason itself.

We can now see how Descartes attempts to solve the problem of philosophical beginnings. Descartes rejects the scholastic approach to philosophy because it presupposes a whole nexus of terms which are not given to reason. To determine what a man is, not only do we have to rely on determinations which are given to us by the senses, but as we proceed in analysing the term, 'man', our enquiry brings in more unknown terms, rather than making the term itself clearer. Descartes therefore rejects the approach of Epistemon in favour of that of Eudoxus. We can already state here a number of the key claims which Descartes makes about the true method of philosophy. First, it accords a 'natural light' to reason whereby reason is the arbiter of truth and falsity. Second, as a consequence of this, it operates internally to reason, excluding the effects of the other faculties on it, since it takes these to be capable of misleading reason. Third, it does not presuppose anything, apart from reason itself. We can also note that Descartes makes Polyander, the 'everyman', conduct the method of doubt, suggesting, as Deleuze notes, that Descartes believes that 'good sense is of all things in the world the most equally distributed' (DR 131/166 and Descartes 1985a: 111). In taking Everyman to be the starting point to his philosophical enquiry, Descartes appears to have developed an alternative to the essentialist approach developed by Aristotle. Rather than presupposing objective facts about the world, reason, when operating according to the purity of its nature, is capable of enquiry. This notion that there is a '*good will on the part of the thinker*' and an '*upright nature on the part of thought*' (DR 131/166) is the first postulate of the image of thought. Deleuze argues that when thought in this context is understood in terms of representation, this belief in the good nature of thought in fact prevents philosophical enquiry. Therefore, an enquiry such as Descartes' relies on an illegitimate presupposition, namely the nature of reason itself:

We would do better to ask what is a subjective or implicit presupposition: it has the form of 'Everybody knows. . .'. Everybody knows, in a pre-philosophical and pre-conceptual manner . . . everybody knows what it means to think and to be . . . As a result, when the philosopher says 'I think therefore I am', he can assume that the universality of his premises – namely, what it means to be and to think . . . – will be implicitly understood, and that no one can deny that to doubt is to think, and to think is to be . . . *Everybody knows, no one can deny*, is the form of representation and the discourse of the representative. When philosophy rests its beginning upon such implicit or subjective presuppositions, it can claim innocence, since it has kept nothing back – except, of course, the essential

– namely, the form of this discourse . . . In fact, *Eudoxus* has no fewer presuppositions than *Epistemon*, he simply has them in another, implicit or subjective form,
'private' and not 'public'; in the form of a natural capacity for thought which
allows philosophy to claim to begin, and to begin without presuppositions. (DR
129–30/165)

While Descartes has avoided the objective presuppositions of reason
(the meanings of terms, etc.), Deleuze's claim is that Descartes' enquiry
is still encumbered by certain subjective presuppositions about the
nature of thought itself.

In order to understand the nature of these subjective presuppositions, and how they might distort philosophy, Deleuze turns to Ludwig
Feuerbach, who 'is among those who have pursued farthest the problem
of where to begin' (DR 319/209). The essay that Deleuze refers to,
Towards a Critique of Hegelian Philosophy, represents a break on Feuerbach's
part with his early enthusiasm for Hegel, but also presents a criticism
of philosophy more generally. To understand this criticism, we need
to look at what Feuerbach thinks philosophy is attempting to do. We
can begin by noting that thinking is an activity: 'Plato is meaningless
and non-existent for someone who lacks understanding; he is a blank
sheet for one who cannot link ideas that correspond with his words'
(Feuerbach 1997: 102). Feuerbach's point is that a philosophical argument is not of value in itself, but only in so far as it is taken up by the
understanding of the person to whom it is addressed. That is why in
Descartes' *Search for Truth*, Eudoxus does not present the argument for
the cogito, but rather leads Polyander to discover the conclusion through
his own reasoning. Implicit in this is the view that philosophical texts do
not impart information, but simply act as a trigger for the reader's own
reason to determine truths for itself. Feuerbach describes the situation as
follows:

For this very reason, what the person demonstrating communicates is not the
subject matter itself, but only the medium; for he does not instil his thoughts into
me like drops of medicine, nor does he preach to deaf fishes like Saint Francis;
rather, he addresses himself to *thinking* beings. The main thing – the understanding of the thing involved – he does not give me; he *gives* nothing at all – otherwise
the philosopher could really produce philosophers, something which so far no
one has succeeded in achieving. Rather he presupposes the faculty of understanding; he shows me – i.e. to the other person as such – my understanding
only in a mirror. (Feuerbach 1997: 105)

If a philosophical text is primarily a means of communication, rather than a demonstration in its own right, then the question arises, under what conditions is thought able to be communicated? In order to make my thinking comprehensible to another, the first point is that I need to 'strip my thought of the form of "mine-ness" so that the other person may recognise it as his own' (Feuerbach 1997: 104). In effect, in putting thinking into language, we eliminate the thinker's 'individual separateness', and present a form of thinking which is 'nothing other than the *realization of the species*' (Feuerbach 1997: 103). That is, philosophical thought abstracts from the particularity of my thinking, and operates by presupposing that which is universal to all thinkers. As Deleuze puts it, '*Everybody knows, no one can deny*, is the form of representation and the discourse of the representative' (DR 130/165). The second point is that in order to present our thoughts, they must be reformulated in a form that is capable of presentation:

And yet, systematic thought is by no means the same as *thought as such*, or *essential* thought; it is only self-*presenting* thought. To the extent that I present my thoughts, I place them in time; an insight that contains all its successive elements within a simultaneity within my mind now becomes a sequence. (Feuerbach 1997: 101)

As it stands, Feuerbach has simply noted that there is a fundamental distinction between thinking and the presentation of thought. This in itself is not a criticism of prior philosophy, but the difficulties emerge when philosophers become prone to a form of paralogism whereby they mistake the successive, abstract representation of thinking for thinking itself. This happens quite naturally, since the way in which we present thinking in a systematic manner is not arbitrary, as 'the presentation of philosophy must itself be philosophical' (Feuerbach 1997: 106). There is thus a tendency to make 'form into essence, the being of thought for others into being itself, the *relative goal* into the final goal' (Feuerbach 1997: 107). We therefore mistake the abstract, communicable element of thought for thinking itself. Deleuze supplements this paralogism with an argument that there is a moral element to systems that mistake the presentation of thought for thought itself, in that to trust in the structure of thinking as communicative implies a fundamental accord between man and the world, and presupposes the belief that 'thought has a good nature and the thinker a good will' (DR 132/167).

Feuerbach's claim that 'every system is only an expression or image of reason' (Feuerbach 1997: 106) can be seen as a forerunner of Deleuze's own claim that representational thinking rests on an 'image of thought', and the aim of Chapter 3 of *Difference and Repetition* is to explore in more detail what this image consists in, and how it is possible to think outside of it. This error of mistaking the image of thought for thinking itself has a number of implications for Feuerbach which are directly relevant for Deleuze's account.

The first implication is that even projects such as those of Descartes and Hegel that attempt to remove all objective presuppositions still make a number of presuppositions in order to operate. As Deleuze notes (DR 129/164), the same criticism that can be raised against Descartes, regarding the equivocation of the empirical and abstract egos, can also be raised against Hegel: both begin with an abstraction. While the notion of pure, indeterminate being is communicable, this is only because communication removes the 'mine-ness' of my relation to the world. In actual fact, 'sensible, concrete, empirical being' (DR 129/164) is prior to the abstraction which Hegel takes as a beginning. As well as abstracting from empirical reality, philosophy which operates according to the image of thought also presupposes the structure of presentation itself. That is, we presuppose 'the form of representation or recognition in general' (DR 131/166). As Feuerbach puts it:

the artist presupposes a sense of beauty – he cannot bestow it upon a person – for in order that we take his words to be beautiful, in order that we accept and countenance them at all, he must presuppose in us a sense of art . . . [Similarly] in order that we recognise [the philosopher's] thoughts as true, in order that we understand them at all, he presupposes reason, as a common principle and measure in us as well as himself. (Feuerbach 1997: 103)

The history of philosophy can from this perspective be seen, not as a progressive extension of our knowledge of the world, but rather as a series of more and more accurate ways of providing a systematic image of the presentation of reason. In this respect, Feuerbach considers Hegel not to have provided the final, presuppositionless, metaphysics, but rather the most accomplished image of reason: 'The systematiser is an artist – the history of philosophical systems is the picture gallery of reason. Hegel is the most accomplished philosophical artist, and his presentations, at least in part, *are unsurpassed models of scientific art sense*' (Feuerbach 1997: 106).

The second implication is that if philosophy simply maps out the image of thought in systematic terms, then it will be incapable of novelty. As Feuerbach puts it, 'the *creation* of concepts on the basis of a particular kind of philosophy is not a real but only a formal creation; it is not creation out of nothing, but only the development, as it were, of a spiritual matter lying within me' (Feuerbach 1997: 102). As we are just dealing with the presentation of what was already implicated in the structure of pre-philosophical thinking, we have a philosophical thought that '"rediscovers" the State, rediscovers "the Church"' during its development (DR 136/172).

The third implication is that philosophy must begin with something that is outside of thought. In *The Search for Truth*, Descartes tries to show that if one thinks through the structure of everyday reason, then one arrives at philosophy. Hegel's *Phenomenology of Spirit* likewise tries to show that speculative philosophy develops immanently from a common sense worldview. These approaches are possible because once the good nature of thought has been assumed, philosophy just becomes the systematic portrayal of a form of reason already implicitly present within common sense. In contrast, if systematic philosophy is simply an expression of pre-philosophical reason, Deleuze argues that philosophy must 'find its difference or its true beginning, not in an agreement with a *pre-philosophical* Image but in a rigorous struggle against this Image, which it would denounce as *non-philosophical*' (DR 132/167). That is, if it is not simply to draw out what is contained in our (rational) common-sense prejudices, it must not begin with reason as we discover it either in its naive or systematic forms. Here, Deleuze is referring directly to Feuerbach's rejection of reason as a foundation for philosophy. In contrast to the Cartesian account, philosophy must begin with a radical encounter with something outside of it:

Demonstrating would be senseless if it were not also *communicating*. However, communication of thoughts is not material or *real* communication. For example, a push, a sound that shocks my ears, or light is real communication. I am only passively receptive to that which is material; but I become aware of that which is mental only through myself, only through self-activity. (Feuerbach 1997: 105)

We will see that Deleuze presents a similar need for an encounter.

What, therefore, is the difference between Deleuze and Feuerbach? While Deleuze's concept of the image of thought is prefigured by Feuerbach, the difference between them emerges when we consider what it is that we encounter that provides a beginning to philosophy. For

Feuerbach, true thinking begins through an encounter with sensuous intuition, which is prior to the abstractions that generate the 'mediating activity of thought for others' (Feuerbach 1997: 102). Here we have something like the opposition between active synthesis and passive sensibility that we discovered in relation to Kant in the last chapter. As we saw, for Kant, the understanding was responsible for active synthesis, and therefore organised the world according to its own categories. The active, synthetic nature of the understanding meant that it rediscovered on an empirical level what it had previously put into the world on a transcendental level. In this sense, we can note that for Kant too, the understanding is incapable of discovering genuine novelty, since sensibility merely provides the material that is organised by the understanding. As we saw, Deleuze accused Kant of assuming that all synthesis was active synthesis, and we can see a similar assumption made here by Feuerbach. In rejecting the active element of reason as unable to provide a genuinely novel beginning to philosophy, he is forced to resort to a purely passive notion of sensibility for his alternative beginning. As Deleuze puts it, 'he supposes that this exigency of a true beginning is sufficiently met by beginning with empirical, perceptible and concrete being' (DR 319/209). Once we have recognised the possibility of a passive synthesis, however, we open the possibility that what is given in sensibility is not the sensible itself, but that which gives rise to the sensible. It is this transcendental which is prior to the sensible that will be the site of an encounter for Deleuze. In order to explore how thought is able to operate outside of the image of thought provided by representation, Deleuze proposes to analyse in more detail how the image of thought operates, developing in parallel an alternative account of thought that takes account of its non-representational origins.

3.3 Descartes and the Postulates of Common Sense and Recognition (132–4/168–70)

What, therefore is the structure of thinking? Deleuze argues that there are eight postulates of representational thought which together allow it to function as a coherent system. As we saw in the previous section, Descartes argues that philosophy emerges through the critical self-examination of our thought. In this sense, Deleuze's account of the image of thought operates on two levels. On the one hand, it is concerned with the presuppositions inherent in prior philosophical systems. On the other, its concern is with the implicit assumptions of everyday thinking from which such formal philosophical structures will be traced. Each of the postulates will therefore have a double structure. We have already seen the first of these, which is the '*cogitatio natura universalis*', the presumption which emerges from a paralogism that the structure of systematic thought is such that it is in accordance with knowledge. The double nature of this assumption is clear in that both Polyander (Everyman) and Eudoxus (sound judgement) both held to it. Thought therefore relies on a good will on the part of the thinker, and a good will on the part of thought itself. We can see this operating in Descartes' *Meditations*. Here, although our knowledge of the world is ultimately guaranteed by God, we only have knowledge of God on the basis of the fact that we can clearly and distinctly conceive of him: 'I now seem to be able to lay it down as a general rule that whatever I perceive very clearly and distinctly is true' (Descartes 1984a: 24). Feuerbach's claim was that such an account is really an account of the structures of communication, rather than the structure of the world.

Feuerbach also claimed that thinking originates with an encounter, and Deleuze supports this claim. At first glance, it appears to be the case that all philosophy deals with that which is beyond thought; that is, philosophy seeks to explain, justify and extend our knowledge of the world. This is particularly clear in the case of Descartes, for whom the *Meditations* are not supposed to be read simply as an account of the nature of God and the self, but also to provide an example of his method, and lay the foundations for Descartes' own account of the natural world. Deleuze's central claim is that while it may appear that an encounter is possible, in actual fact, this possibility is forestalled by the structures of representation. In order to see why this is the case, we need to bring in two more of Deleuze's postulates of the image of thought, and see how they operate in a key section of the *Meditations*. These postulates are 'the postulate of the ideal, or common sense' and 'the postulate of the model, or recognition' (DR 167/207). The example Deleuze uses is the account of the piece of wax from the second of Descartes' *Meditations*. Here, Descartes attempts to reinforce his privileging to the cogito by showing that material objects are not as well known as the self. Descartes gives us the following example:

Let us take, for example, this piece of wax. It has just been taken from the honeycomb; it has not quite yet lost the taste of honey; it retains some of the scent of the flowers from which it was gathered; its colour, shape and size are plain to see; it is hard, cold, and can be handled without difficulty; if you rap it with your knuckles, it makes a sound. In short, it has everything which appears necessary for a body to be known as distinctly as possible. But even as I speak, I put the wax by the fire, and look: the residual taste is eliminated, the smell goes away, the colour changes, the shape is lost, and the size increases; it becomes liquid and hot; you can hardly touch it, and if you strike it, it no longer makes a sound. But does the same wax remain? It must be admitted that it does; no one denies it, no one thinks otherwise. So what was it in the wax that I understood with such distinctness? Evidently none of the features which I arrived at by means of the senses; for whatever came under taste, smell, sight, touch or hearing has now altered – yet the wax remains. (Descartes 1984a: 20)

Descartes' immediate point is that while we might claim that the objects we find around us are more immediately known to us than our own ego, in fact we do not perceive *objects* at all, as is made clear by the fact that all of the perceivable properties of a piece of wax can change while we still continue to see it as the same piece of wax. If it isn't perception that gives unity to objects, then what is it? Descartes continues his analysis by bringing in the following example:

But then if I look out of the window and see men crossing the square, as I just happen to have done, I normally say that I see the men themselves, just as I say that I see the wax. Yet do I see any more than hats and coats which could conceal automatons? I *judge* that they are men. And so something I thought I was seeing with my eyes is in fact grasped solely by the faculty of judgement which is in my mind. (Descartes 1984a: 21)

In this sense, it is the subject that is responsible for unifying the various properties of the object into a coherent object, since the possibility of error shows that the object is not given to us as such. For this reason, even when we are dealing with objects outside of the subject, we are still in a position whereby we only recognise them as objects in so far as they are brought together by the thinking subject into a unity under the form of an object. In this case too, therefore, we can note that we are in a position whereby what is perceived (or what we take to be important in what is perceived) is a function of reason itself. The faculty of the subject that is responsible for unifying the different sense modalities of the subject by relating them to the structure of an object is, for Descartes, common sense, or *sensus communis*. If we look at the example of misrecognition, we can say that what leads us to posit the hats and coats as men is the fact that different sense impressions are all in accordance. This accord leads us to misrecognise them as properties of people. As Deleuze notes, the concepts of common sense and recognition are therefore intimately linked: 'An object is recognised, however, when one faculty locates it as identical to that of another, or rather when all the faculties together relate their given and relate themselves to a form of identity in the object' (DR 133/169).

Common sense in fact refers to two kinds of commonality. On the one hand, it allows different sense modalities to be related to one another, and brought together into a judgement. On this reading, it literally presents what is common to the senses. On the other hand, it is also intimately linked with the 'everybody knows' which was the first postulate of the image of thought. If we return to the work of Merleau-Ponty, we can see that the fact that consciousness is 'forgetful of the perspectivism of my experience' (Merleau-Ponty 1962: 70) in positing objects as the source of my perceptions allows the kind of objective world that makes objective knowledge, and hence communication, possible. Referring directly to Descartes' account in the second meditation of the central role of judgement to perception, Merleau-Ponty writes that:

like the object, the idea purports to be the same for everybody, valid in all times and places, and the individuation of an object in an objective point of time and space finally appears as the expression of a universal positing power . . . I now refer to my body only as an idea, to the universe as idea, to the idea of space and the idea of time. Thus 'objective' thought (in Kierkegaard's sense) is formed – being that of common sense and science – which finally causes us to lose contact with perceptual experience, of which it is nevertheless the outcome and natural sequel. (Merleau-Ponty 1962: 71)

We can further note a distinction between two problematic notions of sense. Common sense provides us with the formal nature of a unified subject to which objects correspond. Good sense, on the contrary is how we actually carve up the world. Thus, common sense is operative in both reality and in dream states, as in both we see worlds that are constituted by objects. To mistake a dream for reality would be a failure of good sense, however, as this would be to illegitimately apply the model of common sense in a given case. Deleuze claims that common sense and recognition form two distinct but strongly interrelated postulates of the image of thought. We recognise something as an object when the same element is presented to each of the faculties (as in the case of the wax example). However, as the wax example shows, recognition is only possible on the basis of the fact that reason presupposes that what it will encounter will be structured in accordance with judgement (an object with properties). Even where good sense fails, common sense is preserved.

The postulates of the good nature of thought, common sense and recognition therefore operate together in order to guarantee that philosophy only produces a restricted vision of the world. The good nature of thought guarantees the communicability of philosophy through a paralogic confusion of the nature of thought and the conditions for the expression of thought. Common sense forces an understanding of the world in terms of unified subjects, whose faculties are in (or at least can be brought into) accord with one another, and recognition posits a world of objects as a correlate to the unified view of the subject. Deleuze's claim is that while each philosophy puts these assumptions into operation in different ways ('No doubt philosophy refuses every particular *doxa* [popular opinion]; no doubt it upholds no particular propositions of good sense or common sense' [DR 134/170]), the essential features of the image of thought that they constitute are at play in the major tradition of philosophy. In order to show this, and to introduce the fourth postulate, the postulate of representation, we need to return to Deleuze's analysis of Kant.

3.4 Kant and the Postulate of Representation (134–8/170–4)

In the previous chapter, we saw that Kant's reliance on the subject as constituting experience prevented him from developing an account of the genesis of representation. Deleuze once again presents an ambivalent relationship to Kant, claiming that he 'seemed equipped to overturn the image of thought' (DR 136/172). I want to come back to the positive (in Deleuze's eyes) aspects of Kant's position in more detail when I discuss the notion of error later in this chapter, but for now, we can note that Kant does not claim as Descartes does that thinking is naturally commensurate with things in themselves. Instead, objects are always given in an intuition of space or time: 'Intuition and concepts constitute, therefore, the elements of all our knowledge, so that neither concepts without an intuition in some way corresponding to them, nor intuitions without concepts, can yield knowledge' (Kant 1929: A50/B74). These two claims lead to the fact that reason no longer has a 'natural right' to correspond to objects, and also to the claim that we will explore later that if reason operates without reference to intuition, then it generates what Kant calls 'transcendental illusions'. In this respect, Kant opposes the Cartesian view that the faculty of reason is, when operating in accordance with its own interests and without the negative influence of the other faculties, free from error. Rather than renounce the image of thought, however, Deleuze claims that Kant simply attempts to determine the bounds of reason, and to delimit its sphere of legitimate employment. In the preface to the *Critique of Pure Reason*, Kant proclaims 'a call to reason to undertake anew the most difficult of all its tasks, namely, that of self-knowledge, and to institute a tribunal which will institute to reason its lawful claims, and dismiss all groundless pretensions, not by despotic decrees, but in accordance with its own eternal and unalterable laws' (Kant 1929: Axi–xii). For this reason, Deleuze claims that Kant's critique 'at most amounts to giving civil rights to thought considered from the point of view of its *natural law*' (DR 136/173). In attempting to show that the object conforms to our forms of cognition, Kant's project can be seen as a radical attempt to formulate a coherent image of thought, with the core of the *Critique* concerning itself with the problem of common sense. While objects may conform to our sensibility, concepts and intuition are different in kind, as the incongruent counterparts argument shows. The central problem of the transcendental deduction can be interpreted along these lines as determining how a common sense can exist between faculties that differ in kind in this way.

The transcendental deduction solves this problem as each of the faculties plays a role in meeting the conditions of possible experience. The procedure involved three syntheses. First, the manifold is 'run through' by the faculty of intuition. In order for it to appear as connected, however, these connections need to be taken up by the imagination, as we need to not simply reproduce past moments, but also to recognise them as reproduced. Finally, to provide coherence to these various moments, they need to be seen as moments related to the same object. This final stage therefore relies on a conceptual determination of the experience as the successive presentation of the same object. The transcendental deduction therefore provides Kant's own model of the first three postulates of the image of thought. The good nature of thought is maintained, albeit only when thinking is related to a manifold of intuition. As we saw in the previous chapter, Kant claims that 'It must be possible for the "I think" to accompany all our representations' (Kant

1929: B131–2). As Kant noted, however, it is not necessary for the 'I think' always to accompany our representations, and we often just find ourselves preoccupied with the world without any explicit reference to ourselves. In fact, for Kant, common sense is not this 'I think', which is rather a result of the operation of common sense at a transcendental level. Common sense is therefore provided by the transcendental unity of apperception. In this sense, Kant differs from Descartes in that for Descartes, common sense is provided by the cogito, whereas for Kant, since the transcendental unity of apperception precedes experience to make it possible, we have what Deleuze calls a 'logical common sense' (DR 137/173) that makes possible the analytical unity of the 'I think'. We can further note that whereas Descartes proceeds from the axiom of the cogito to common sense, and the recognition of the object through judgement, for Kant, common sense and the notion of the object presuppose one another. Thus, as we saw, Kant claims that the subject can only recognise itself as a self if it is able to distinguish itself from its representations. This in turn is only possible if those representations are taken as referring beyond themselves to the object. But the notion of an object is in turn only possible as the result of the synthetic activity of the subject: 'it is the unity of consciousness that alone constitutes the relation of representations to an object' (Kant 1929: B137). Deleuze therefore claims that what Kant has really provided is a corrective to Descartes' project: 'Therefore the real (synthetic) formula of the *cogito* is: I think myself and in thinking myself, I think the object in general to which I relate a represented diversity' (KCP 15–16/14).

We can now bring in the fourth postulate of the image of thought: representation. We have already encountered representation in Chapter 1 of *Difference and Repetition*, where Deleuze classified Aristotle's logic as a type of representation. There, Deleuze claimed that:

There are four principal 'aspects' to reason, in so far as it is the medium of representation: identity in the form of the *undetermined* concept; analogy, in the relationship between ultimate *determinable* concepts; opposition, in the relations between *determinations* within concepts; resemblance, in the *determined* object of the concept itself. (DR 29/37)

These four 'shackles' of representation mapped onto Aristotle's taxonomy of species and genera. They can also be mapped on to the various moments of the transcendental deduction as follows. First, in order to have experience, we need to relate our different representations to a central unity (the identity of the object in the synthesis of recognition). This in turn relies on an analogy between the rules governing our knowledge of objects and the rules governing the structure of objects themselves. Now, in order for these various moments to be related together into a unity, they must have some kind of affinity with one another. This affinity requires that the same properties obtain in the object now and at some moment in the past (if cinnabar were not always red, 'my empirical imagination would never find opportunity when representing red colour to bring to mind heavy cinnabar' [Kant 1929: A100–1]). In order to determine whether a present object is an instance of a type, we therefore need the notion of opposition (red/not-red). Finally, in order to recognise this affinity, we need to be able to determine whether the object presented by a memory and the object presented by perception have *the same* property. As we are dealing with different representations, this is achieved by a comparison that determines whether the representations resemble one another. Thus in order for recognition to function, we require the structures of representation to provide the machinery for recognising that we are dealing with the same object, through the diversity of perceptual experience. We can note further that apart from the identity of the transcendental unity of apperception, which is the fulcrum of Kant's theory of common sense for Deleuze, each of the other operations takes place between faculties (so, for instance, resemblance is a resemblance between representations given to the imagination and intuition), and so provide the notion of communicability between faculties which is the foundation of common sense.

3.5 Plato and the Encounter (138–45/175–83)

The final account of an image of thought given by Deleuze continues to explicate his ambivalent relationship to Plato. As Deleuze notes, in the *Republic*, Socrates also suggests the necessity of an encounter, claiming that 'some reports of our perceptions do not provoke thought to reconsideration because the judgement of them by sensation seems adequate, while others always invite the intellect to reflection because sensation yields nothing that can be trusted' (DR 138/175). This untrustworthiness of sensations does not, for Plato, simply lead to scepticism, but to a thought which moves beyond actual experience, and to a difference between the objects of the various faculties. As we shall see, in this regard, Plato's theory of knowledge appears to mirror Deleuze's own, with anamnesis, or recollection, playing a similar role for Plato as pure memory does for Deleuze and Bergson. In order to structure Deleuze's account of Plato, I want to organise it around three questions. First, what is the encounter with sensation that provokes thought? Second, what is the nature of the thinking that is provoked by the encounter? And third, what is the relationship between the faculties that becomes apparent in this account of thinking? To these questions, I want to add a final question to address why Deleuze ultimately rejects Plato account; namely, why does Plato, in the end, sustain the dogmatic image of thought?

Deleuze begins his discussion of Plato with Socrates' claim that some perceptions summon the understanding to look into them. As Deleuze notes, Socrates does not mean by this those cases where our perceptions of the world do not give us certainty about their objects. He is not interested in those cases where *in fact* there is a limitation on our ability to recognise objects (a failure of good sense), but rather in objections *in principle* to perception (a failure of common sense). His claim will be that some objects possess both properties and their opposites, and it is encounters with these that lead us to think. Socrates presents the contrast that he is seeking to develop with the following cases:

> The ones that don't summon the understanding are all those that don't go off into opposite perceptions at the same time. But the ones that do go off in that way I call summoners – whenever sense perception doesn't declare one thing any more than its opposite, no matter whether the object striking the senses is near at hand or far away. You'll understand my meaning better if I put it this way: These, we say, are three fingers – the smallest, the second, and the middle finger. (Plato 1997b: 523b-c)

Socrates argues that if we look, for instance, at the length of the finger, we will find that it is long or short depending on what we are contrasting that length with. These properties are relative, and depend on other features of the world (other fingers) for their determination. As such, we cannot, even in perfect perceptual conditions, determine whether something is short or long, as it will have both properties, depending on what we compare it to. As each object 'comes into being and passes away' (Plato 1997b: 527b), even properties that are not necessarily relative, such as beauty, will at some moments apply to an object and at other moments no longer apply. Thinking therefore emerges because of an inherent feature of the object: the contradictory status of the properties which we find within it. When the soul encounters an object of this kind, it 'would then be puzzled, would look for an answer, would stir up its understanding, and would ask what the one [object] itself is' (Plato 1997b: 524e). The senses themselves, therefore, 'summon' a form of thinking that does not relate to the sensible, or even to the object that is under the consideration of the sensible. For Deleuze, the nature of this encounter that 'forces us to think' (DR 139/176) will be broader than just sensible properties, and as examples of encounters, he suggests those with 'Socrates, a temple, or a demon' (DR 139/176).

In order to answer the question of what thinking is, Deleuze turns to Plato's account of anamnesis in the *Phaedo*. The *Phaedo* chronicles the last few hours of Socrates' life. Socrates seeks to assuage his friends' fears about his impending death by showing that the philosopher is in fact grateful for death, and its concomitant separation of the soul from the body, 'because the body confuses the soul and does not allow it to acquire truth and wisdom whenever it is associated with it' (Plato 1997a: 66a). Our concern will be not so much with this doctrine, but instead with the doctrine of the Ideas, and the related doctrine of anamnesis. To begin with, there is an extension of the critique of the sensible in the *Phaedo*. If we consider a notion such as equality, we can note that two sticks can appear to be equal in length, or two stones to be equal in size. We can further note that in different circumstances, the length and size of these sets of objects may appear to be unequal. In these cases, we therefore become aware that objects that are equal are not themselves the source of our notion of the Equal, as we think that the Equal itself must always be equal to itself. Similarly, other properties that we encounter in the world, such as justice, or beauty, are not encountered in objects that are purely just, or purely beautiful. Rather, as the world is an imperfect place, these objects amenable to sensation are always deficient cases of justice or beauty. 'Our sense perceptions must surely make us realize that all that we perceive through them is striving to reach that which is Equal but falls short of it' (Plato 1997a: 75b). The implication of this is that as well as the deficient sensory impression of equal or beautiful objects, we are also given by these sensory impressions another object, namely that in relation to which the object is seen to be deficient. Socrates takes this object to be different in kind to a sensory object. It is for this reason that he is dismissive of answers to questions such as 'what is beauty?' or 'what is justice?' in earlier dialogues that define them in terms of empirical objects. Rather, the deficiency of sensory experience relates us to Ideas. At this point, there are two questions we need to address. First, how do we gain access to Ideas, and second, what are Ideas?

In order to experience 'equal' objects as falling short of the true idea of the Equal, or for beautiful objects to fall short of the Beautiful, we need, according to Socrates, to have a prior notion of what the Equal or Beauty themselves are. In order to explain how these two different classes of objects are related, Socrates introduces the example of the lover: 'Well, you know what happens to lovers: whenever they see a lyre, a garment or anything else that their beloved is accustomed to use, they know the lyre, and the image of the boy to whom it belongs comes into their mind' (Plato 1997a: 73d). Thus, on perceiving the imperfect sensory object, the Idea of the object is called to mind. As Socrates notes, this kind of relation between the lyre and the boy is one of recollection, in this case one of a prior moment of sensory experience. In the case of the Equal, however, it is never something that we can experience in the world, as it is presupposed by all cases of experience. In this case, therefore, Socrates argues that the recollection must be a recollection by the soul of a time before it became attached to the body, and thus capable of experiencing the sensory world. In this sense, therefore, knowledge of the essence of equality or beauty – that is, knowledge of the Ideas themselves – must be the recollection of an experience of the Ideas, rather than some kind of extrapolation. What interests Deleuze in this case is that we do not appear to have a 'common sense', as we found in Descartes and Kant, but rather a transmission between two faculties, each of which has an object that is different in kind from the other. As well as the contrary properties we find in sensory experience, we also have, through recollection, knowledge of the Ideas in their purity. As the Ideas are not subject to the effects of becoming, they do not contain contrary properties, and so in this case, we can develop genuine knowledge.

What is the relationship between the faculties that this account presents? To answer this question, we need to return to the *Republic*. In Book VII, Plato gives three different presentations of the relationship between these various faculties: the metaphors of the sun and of the divided line, and the allegory of the cave. We have already seen that we can have knowledge of two kinds of things: sensible objects and the Ideas. According to Plato, we can divide those objects that we can relate to into four groups by dividing a line into four parts: 'It is like a line divided into two unequal sections. Then divide each section – namely, that of the visible and that of the intelligible – in the same ratio as the line' (Plato 1997b: 509d). We therefore have four ways in which we can relate to objects, with some sections of the line longer than others. Moving from the shortest section (and least satisfactory form of relation) to the longest, we first have types of knowledge concerning the visible world: images such as shadows and reflections in water (Plato 1997b: 509e), then visible objects that these shadows and reflections are images of, such as 'the animals around us, all the plants, and the whole class of manufactured things' (Plato 1997b: 510a). Following this, we have the two kinds of knowledge that deal with the intelligible world. The first still proceeds on the basis of images drawn from the visible world, but is not interested in the determinate properties of the image itself. Geometry, for instance, uses images, such as a triangle, to develop general truths about all triangles. It proceeds on the basis of hypotheses and uses images solely as guides. The second intelligible understanding of the Ideas themselves dispenses with any notion of an image of thought, and relates directly to Ideas by means of recollection. Rather than having one object that thinking relates to under different aspects, as in the common sense of Descartes and Kant, we therefore have a whole series of objects. Each of these objects is within the domain of a different faculty of thinking, with imagination and opinion relating to objects of the visible world, and thought and understanding relating to the two classes of object of the intelligible world. These faculties do not converge on one object, but instead simultaneously relate to two separate objects. Thus, to judge that two sticks are equal to one another, we do not simply need the relation of the faculty of opinion to the sticks themselves, but also the relation of the faculty of understanding to the Idea of the Equal, in order to recognise the presence in the visible world of a deficient copy of the Ideas.

For Plato, an encounter with the sensible triggers the recollection of something different in kind from the sensible itself. There is a communication that takes place in terms of difference. This bears a remarkable similarity to the account of the Bergsonian theory of memory that we looked at in the previous chapter (2.4). There, the pure past was brought into relation with the present by the future. In spite of this, there was a fundamental difference in kind between the two moments, as the present was understood in terms of actuality, and the past was understood in terms of virtuality. We can further note that, just as in the case of Deleuze's account of the three syntheses in the previous chapter – where the present and the past were generated in parallel, such that the past was not a past of passed presents – here too we find that what is recollected is something that is never experienced by the actual empirical individual themselves, since it is prior to the soul's connection to the body that we have knowledge of Ideas. Thus, 'transcendental memory . . . grasps that which from the outset can only be recalled, even the first time: not a contingent past, but the being of the past as such and the past of every time' (DR 140/177). Plato's theory of the faculties, with one faculty communicating to another something which cannot be grasped by the first faculty alone (sensibility summoning the Ideas, for instance), thus mirrors the structure of Deleuze's account of the faculties in Chapter 2. Rather than the harmony of the faculties we discover in common sense, we have here a discord of the faculties, which Deleuze sees as opening the way to a novel account of their interrelation. Plato could, therefore, be seen as offering a radically different characterisation of thinking to Descartes and Kant. Ultimately, however, for Deleuze, 'the Platonic determinations cannot be satisfactory' (DR 144/181).

Where does Plato go wrong? 'Everything is betrayed' (DR 142/178) by the metaphorical nature of Plato's theory of the faculties. This betrayal takes the form of arguing that what is recollected, the Ideas, have been perceived, but in another, prior life. The perception of the Ideas is therefore not different in kind from perception of objects in the sensible world. Once this move has been made, the notion of recognition is reintegrated into our account. When we perceive two sticks that are equal in length, we are not presented with a test that 'opposes all possible recognition' (DR 142/178), but merely 'an envelopment that is particularly difficult to unfold' (DR 142/178). It is simply challenging to see the Idea in the empirical instance. Similarly, we no longer have two different forms of each faculty as we found in the notions of active and passive synthesis. Whereas empirical memory, understood as operating in much the way that Kant described, was opposed to Bergsonian transcendental memory by Deleuze, for Plato, there is merely a difference in degree between the operations of the two forms of memory. Recollection of Ideas is now simply recollection of something further removed from the present than any other possible instance could be.

Ultimately, these two failings derive from the fact that rather than enquiring into the being of the sensible and the being of memory, that is, the way in which the objects of these two faculties are structured, Plato takes the sensible and memory each to relate to a being. In this sense, the notion that the faculties relate to objects is reinstated. As we saw in Chapter 1, Deleuze suggests that there are two fundamental distributions: the sedentary and the nomadic. The sedentary understands the world in terms of objects, and understands difference in terms of negation ('this is not that'), whereas the nomadic distribution understands the world as composed of processes. In treating the Ideas as objects, Plato has put into play a sedentary distribution. This essentially means that Plato's conception of reminiscence is static, as opposed to Deleuze's non-objectival, processual conception of difference, which consists in 'introducing time or the duration of time into thought itself' (DR 142/179). In this sense, the four categories of representation can all be found in Plato's model. The encounter is triggered by opposition in the sensible between the contrary properties. In opposition to the sensible world, in which properties possess this oppositional nature, the Ideas are what they are in themselves. That is, the Idea of the Large is absolutely large without also being its contrary. It is thus self-identical. The resemblance of the sensible to the Ideas allows recognition to take place. Finally, Plato compares the Idea of the Good to the sun, which indicates the fact that the transcendental exercise of the faculties is conceived of on the model of the empirical exercise of them (perception of the empirical sun is analogous to perception of the Idea of the Good). Through these various claims, Plato, according to Deleuze, founds representation by making the structure of the object the paradigm case for knowledge.

3.6 The Kantian Sublime and the Discordant Relation of the Faculties (145–6/183–4)

As we have just seen, while Plato appears to give us a model that breaks free from common sense, in actual fact, he preserves its essential features by still understanding our relation to Ideas in terms of judgement. It is the contrary nature of properties in the sensible world (and hence the inability to make non-contradictory judgements about them), that forces us to relate to an atemporal realm where knowledge *is* possible. Instead, Deleuze returns to Kant to find the first instance of a model of the faculties operating apart from common sense, albeit in a section of the third critique which Kant takes to be 'a mere appendix to our aesthetic judging of the purposiveness of nature' (Kant 1987: §23): the analysis of the sublime.

For Kant, situations that engender a feeling of the sublime are those in which we encounter something that shows the limitations of our powers of sensation, such as 'shapeless mountain masses piled on one another in wild disarray, with their pyramids of ice or gloomy raging sea' (Kant 1987: §26). These are situations where we are dealing with objects that exceed the ability of our imagination to understand them as a totality. 'We call that sublime which is absolutely large' (Kant 1987: §25). Now, clearly, it is the case that, *in fact*, the shapeless mountains that we encounter, or the raging sea, are not absolutely large, as there could be larger mountains, and more ferocious storms. For this reason, the objects that generate the feeling of sublimity are not actually themselves sublime, since even the size of the mountains is relative. Rather, the feeling of sublimity is internal, but is elicited by certain objects that are appropriate to its presentation.

Extremely large objects can thus be suggestive of the notion of the infinitely large. When we encounter a 'shapeless mountain mass', while we may be able to determine their height mathematically, through the use of the understanding, we are unable to bring together the object into a single intuition – to see it all at once. Either it is simply too big, and so we apprehend the object through a series of moments that appears to go on to infinity, or else the size of the object means that the parts of the object that we began by apprehending fall away from the imagination before we are able to reach the final elements. On this basis, Kant gives the following characterisation of the sublime:

Nature is thus sublime in those of its appearances, whose intuition brings with them the idea of their infinity. Now the latter cannot happen, otherwise than through the inadequacy of the greatest effort of our imagination in the estimation of an object's magnitude. (Kant 1987: §26)

Now, this discord between the imagination's ability to comprehend the object as a unity and the goal of thinking it as a unity, suggests the presence of another faculty. 'Sublime is what even to be able to think proves that the mind has a power surpassing any standard of taste' (Kant 1987: §25). This power is the power of reason, as it is reason that is capable of thinking the notion of totality. Reason thus 'demands absolute totality as a real idea' (Kant 1987: §25). Here we find the real source of sublimity. The object presented to sensibility is not capable of being absolutely large, as there will always be the possibility of a larger object. What therefore generates the feeling of the sublime is not the object itself, but the fact that the failure of the imagination to synthesise the object into unity points to the fact that reason is capable of thinking a unity that transcends any presentation, thus pointing to our own transcendence of the phenomenal realm. What interests Deleuze in this case is neither the faculties in question, nor the Idea of unity that the encounter with the sublime causes reason to think (and as we shall see in the next chapter,

[4.1] Kant's Ideas of reason are just as much tied to representation as his understanding of the sensible is). Rather, what interests Deleuze here is that even though the faculties of reason and the imagination are shown to be incommensurate with one another, something is nonetheless transferred between them. It is this element itself which brings the two faculties into relation to one another while belonging to neither that Deleuze is interested in. Deleuze puts the point as follows:

> There is, therefore, something that is communicated from one faculty to another, but it is metamorphosed and does not form a common sense. We could just as well say that there are Ideas which traverse all the faculties, but are the object of none in particular. (DR 146/183)

We can see what kind of thing Deleuze has in mind when we look at his account of the three syntheses of time in Chapter 2 of *Difference and Repetition*. As we saw, Deleuze put forward there the claim that memory and habit were different in kind, but could nonetheless communicate with one another, with memory able to inform our practical life through the structure of habit. As we also saw, what allowed the communication between these faculties was not the legislation of one faculty in particular, but rather the field of intensive difference, which in turn was different from either memory or habit, but nonetheless was expressed in terms of the virtual planes of co-existent memory, or the actual succession of impressions. Deleuze here therefore differs from Kant in that Kant associates what is communicated with the Ideas of reason, whereas Deleuze claims that we need to associate the Idea not with any particular faculty, not with, for instance, 'the pure *cogitanda* but rather [with] those instances which go from sensibility to thought and thought to sensibility, capable of engendering in each case, according to their own order, the limit- or transcendent-object of each faculty' (DR 146/183). We will have to wait for the next chapter to see exactly what the nature of these instances is.

3.7 Descartes on the Postulate of the Negative or Error (146–53/184–91)

The postulate of the negative or error is the first of the second set of postulates. These postulates together present a model of language found in the image of thought that emerges from taking the proposition as the primary structure of expression. As we saw in the previous chapter, representation took the subject to be ready-made, and pre-existing the operation of synthesis. It was also the case that the notion of the subject and the notion of an object were interdependent. As we shall see, the four remaining postulates of the image of thought all take knowledge to relate to an already constituted field of objects. These four remaining postulates are: the postulate of the negative, or of error, the postulate of the logical function, or the proposition, the postulate of modality, or solutions, and the postulate of the end, or of knowledge (DR 167/207).

The first of these, the postulate of the negative, or error, is the claim that the failure of thinking must be understood purely in terms of the failure of the structure of recognition, that is, error is purely misrecognition. To see why representation might make this claim, we can return to the example of Descartes. As we have seen, Descartes' aim is to prove certain propositions that are clearly and distinctly perceived, and therefore certain. In order to do so, in the *Meditations*, he instigates the method of doubt: 'reason now leads me to think that I should hold back my assent from opinions that are not completely certain and indubitable just as carefully as I do from those which are patently false' (Descartes 1984a: 12). As Descartes makes clear here, it is *reason* that leads him to introduce the method of doubt, and it is reason that is the arbiter of the success of the operation. In classical scepticism, the method of doubt operates between the faculties to show that none of them can be given primacy, so we may, for instance, use the fact that a stick looks bent in water to show that there is a disparity between reason and the senses, and so neither can be trusted. Descartes' use of scepticism is instead a method for finding those propositions that borrow nothing from any faculty apart from reason. The aim of methodological doubt is therefore to create a space for reason to conduct its enquiries into the structure of the world, since 'deduction or pure inference of one thing from another can never be performed wrongly by an intellect which is in the least degree rational' (Descartes 1985b: 12). If the intellect is incapable of error, however, we have the difficulty of explaining how error can and does occur, particularly given Descartes' contention that we were created by a beneficent and non-deceiving God. Descartes' solution to this central problem of his method is to situate error in the relationship between the faculties. That is, error is simply a failure of good sense. In the *Meditations*, it is the mismatch between the large domain of the will, which has no concern over truth, and the smaller domain of reason which leads to error. Here, the will leads us to assent to claims that go beyond the truths that can be deduced by reason. In this sense, the *Meditations* can be seen as a procedure by which we develop good habits of thought that allow us rationally to pursue an intellectual enquiry without the interference of the other faculties. Descartes' conception of error can be seen to be a corollary of the model of recognition, with error simply being a failure of good sense:

> Does not error itself testify to the form of a common sense, since one faculty alone cannot be mistaken, but two faculties can be, at least from the point of view of their collaboration, when the object of one is confused with *another* object of the other? (DR 148/186)

Thus, to take up Descartes' methodological claim that we might in fact be dreaming, what the imagination presents may be taken to be a real object by reason. In this case, we therefore have a simple case of misunderstanding the nature of the object to which the two faculties refer. The structure of common sense is preserved since the object encountered is amenable to reason (it is an object with properties), but we attribute the wrong properties to it (a failure of good sense), thus misrecognising it and making a false judgement. For Deleuze, thinking does not simply go wrong through the presence of error, but can also be afflicted with 'the terrible trinity of madness, stupidity and malevolence' (DR 149/187). Failures of thinking such as these are understood by Descartes as *de facto* difficulties in thinking that are simply the inessential causes of false judgements. Once we recognise that not everything can be captured within representation, however, another axis of potential failure opens up, namely, when we treat that which is encountered as if it were amenable to the structure of common sense when it is not:

> Stupidity is neither this ground nor this individual, but rather this relation in which individuation brings the ground to the surface without being able to give it form . . . All determinations become bad and cruel when they are grasped only by a thought which invents and contemplates them, flayed and separated from their living form, adrift upon this barren ground. (DR 152/190)

It is not the case that error has always been seen as a failure of good sense caused by the interference of another faculty with reason. For Kant, thinking is discursive, that is, it is *about* something. As we saw in the previous chapter, Kant's claim was that thinking relied on the interrelation between faculties. Now, if this is the case, then for Kant, the faculties themselves *are* capable of falling into error precisely when they operate without reference to the other faculties. Thus, for Kant, reason falls into error when it mistakes its task of unifying knowledge for the possibility that a completely unified system of knowledge could actually be given. This is because some of the conditions of such a system (such as whether the world has a beginning in time or not) go beyond any possible experience, and thus in thinking them, reason no longer relates itself to the other faculties. Nevertheless, Kant argues that without the assumption that all conditions *could* be given, reason would not be able to carry out task of unifying conditions. Reason therefore generates principles called Ideas which, while going beyond experience, nevertheless perform a vital function in allowing us to systematise it. Thus reason is subject to what Kant calls a transcendental illusion that is necessary for its operation but also leads it into error:

> This is an *illusion* which can no more be prevented than we can prevent the sea appearing higher at the horizon than at the shore, since we see it through higher light rays; or to cite a still better example, than the astronomer can prevent the moon from appearing larger at its rising, although he is not deceived by this illusion. (Kant 1929: A297/B355)

As we shall see in the next chapter, while Kant's theory of Ideas and transcendental illusion is an important advance for Deleuze, representing something 'radically different from the extrinsic mechanism of error' (DR 150/188), it ultimately fails to overturn the image of thought of representation.

3.8 The Postulate of the Proposition (153–6/191–5)

Even if the image of thought takes truth and falsity to be the defining characteristics of language, it still needs a further characteristic: sense. As Deleuze notes, 'Teachers already know that errors or falsehoods are rarely found in homework . . . Rather, what is more frequently found – and worse – are nonsensical sentences, remarks without interest or importance, banalities mistaken for profundities, ordinary "points" confused with singular points, badly posed or distorted problems – all heavy with dangers, yet the fate of us all' (DR 153/191). Deleuze's discussion of the nature of sense is very compressed, largely because it reiterates the much more sustained account given in *The Logic of Sense*, but we can grasp the fundamental features of this account by looking at Bertrand Russell's account of significance:

> An assertion has two sides, subjective and objective. Subjectively, it 'expresses' a state of the speaker, which may be called a 'belief', which may exist

without words, and even in animals and infants who do not possess language. Objectively, the assertion, if true, 'indicates' a fact: if false, it intends to 'indicate' a fact, but fails to do so. There are some assertions, namely those which assert present states of the speaker which he notices, in which what is 'expressed' and what is 'indicated' are identical; but in general these two are different. The 'significance' of a sentence is what it 'expresses'. Thus true and false sentences are equally significant, but a string of words which cannot express any state of the speaker is nonsensical. (Russell 1940: 171)

Russell here is making a distinction between the truth value of a proposition (whether it is true or false), and the meaning of a proposition. Truth or falsity determine whether something is successfully indicated (in Russell's terms) or designated (in Deleuze's terms) by a proposition. Designation is simply a relation whereby either the structure of the proposition mirrors a state of affairs in the world (and hence is true), or does not (and hence is false). For Russell, truth and falsity cannot capture the significance, or sense, of a proposition, because what a proposition expresses is not a correspondence between a state of affairs and a proposition, but rather the beliefs of the speaker who asserts the proposition. While whether a proposition succeeds in indicating a fact or not depends on the truth or falsity of a proposition, since the sense of a proposition depends on the psychological beliefs of the speaker, its significance or lack thereof is not dependent on truth or falsity. A proposition can still 'make sense', even though it is false. Thus, we have to be able to separate sense from truth.

Deleuze sees Russell's kind of account as essentially providing a transcendental model of the conditions of the possibility of a proposition being true or false. In other words, it is an account of what counts as a significant proposition. Nonetheless, Deleuze claims that this kind of model of sense suffers from the same difficulties as Kant's transcendental model of experience. We can note the following similarities between the two accounts. First, sense is abstract and broader than the propositions it relates to: 'the condition [sense] must retain an extension larger than that which is conditioned [the true or false]' (DR 153/191). As Russell notes, 'we may say that whatever is asserted by a significant sentence has a certain kind of possibility' (Russell 1940: 170). That is, whereas designation aims at an actual state of affairs, sense for Russell operates according to possible states of affairs. Something is significant if it *could* be the case. Second, and a consequence of this, sense merely repeats the structure of the proposition at this higher level. Whereas Kant's categories have structural parallels with the functions of judgement, the sense of a proposition actually is itself a proposition. In the case of Russell's model, the sense of the proposition, 'x is the case' is the statement, 'I believe x is the case'. In this manner, the sense of a proposition does not explain what makes a proposition true or false, in that sense is understood in propositional terms, and therefore already presupposes the true and the false. Sense for Russell is therefore much like common sense, in that it guarantees the fact that all significant propositions we encounter will either be true or false, just as common sense guaranteed that all states of affairs would be amenable to judgement. Finally, 'The true and the false are supposed to remain unaffected by the condition which grounds the one only by rendering the other possible' (DR 153/192). That is, sense does not explain the genesis of the true and the false, but merely conditions them, just as Kant fails by not providing a truly genetic transcendental account. We can see the difficulty of this account if we try to give some kind of grounding to sense. Deleuze specifies two ways in which we might do this: 'We are then in a strange situation: having discovered the domain of sense, we refer it only to a psychological trait or a logical formalism' (DR 153/191–2). That is, we might take the latter case, and simply specify sense in terms of the proposition itself, but this just involves repeating the proposition at a higher level without explaining it. Otherwise, we might try to find the root of the sense of propositions. As the sense of a proposition is itself another proposition, then, Deleuze notes, we quickly fall into a regress, as we attempt to determine the sense of the sense of the proposition, and so on. Either this regress is infinite, or we stop with a 'first proposition of consciousness' (DR 155/194), such as Descartes' cogito, thus leading us back into the difficulties of common sense with which we began the chapter. As we can see, Russell takes up this Cartesian solution when he notes that expression and indication are identical in reflective belief statements.

In order to avoid the kind of regress that threatens the Russellian model of sense, Deleuze instead proposes a difference in kind between the transcendental and empirical operations of sense: 'from this point of view, sense is the veritable *loquendum*, that which in its empirical operation cannot be said, even though it can be said only in its transcendental operation' (DR 155/193). While it is 'easier to say what sense is not than to say what it is', (DR 155/193), Deleuze makes clear in this section that it is 'like the Idea which is developed in the sub-representative determinations' (DR 155/193). We will deal with this notion of the Idea in the next chapter, but for now, we can note that what will give sense to propositions is something that is different in kind from the propositional, responsible for the constitution rather than simply the conditioning of truth ('truth is a matter of production, not of adequation' [DR 154/192]), and no wider than that which it conditions.

3.9 The Postulate of Modality or Solutions (156–64/195–204)

Deleuze therefore turns to an alternative to the proposition as an account of sense: If sense cannot be given in terms of a proposition, can it be given in terms of a question? It is clearly the case that we can see a proposition as in some way expressing a question, and it is also the case that a question differs from a statement, in that it is not itself true or false. The extent to which we are able to understand the ground of the proposition as different in kind from it will depend on how we understand questioning, however. If we take Deleuze's example of a government referendum (DR 158/197), then it is clearly the case that the question or problem that is addressed by the referendum is primarily understood in terms of the solution or solutions that are the outcome of the vote. In this case, we are therefore once again in the situation whereby sense appears to be defined in terms of a simple widening of the proposition through the addition of possibility: the question is simply a way of expressing a number of different propositional possibilities ('yes' or 'no'). Deleuze's reference to Aristotle's *Topics* makes this point clearly:

The difference between a problem and a proposition is a difference in the turn of phrase. For if it be put in this way, 'Is two-footed terrestrial animal the definition of man?' or 'Is animal the genus of man?' the result is a proposition; but if thus, 'Is two-footed terrestrial animal the definition of man or not?' and 'Is animal the genus of man or not?' the result is a problem. Similarly too in other cases. Naturally, then, problems and propositions are equal in number; for out of every proposition you will make a problem if you change the turn of phrase. (DR 158/196)

In Aristotle's case, the problem is simply a syntactical modification of the proposition. As such, it is parasitic on the structure of the propositional solutions that appear to emerge from it. We can further note that the value of a problem is understood in terms of the possibility of its being solved. 'When, however, a false problem is "set" in a science examination, this propitious scandal serves only to remind families that problems are not ready-made but must be constituted and invested in their proper symbolic fields' (DR 158–9/197). Here, what makes the problem false is purely the fact that it does not have any (propositional) solutions. We therefore encounter the seventh postulate of the image of thought, that 'truth and falsehood only begin with solutions or only qualify responses' (DR 158/197). While truth characterises propositions, it is the case that problems can go wrong not simply in not designating a state of affairs, but in aspects that cannot be captured by the notion of truth. They can circumscribe too narrow or too broad a domain to capture properly the point at issue. In these cases, they are false through overdetermination or indeterminacy, regardless of whether they generate true propositions. Empirical truth therefore is not an adequate way to capture the nature of problems. We could, at this point, reject the notion that sense could be understood in terms of problems. Deleuze instead argues that the difficulty is the way in which problems are formulated within the image of thought. We have already seen the reason for this: as with Russell's notion of sense, the notion of the problem is defined simply in terms of possibility. Likewise, when we look at the notion of a referendum, it presents a problem that can be specified purely in terms of a circumscribed domain of possible solutions. A problem in this sense can be seen as simply a disjunction of propositions, one of which is true. As such, it fails to escape from the image of thought.

As we have seen, Kant at first glance appears to provide something of an exception to this conception of the problem by introducing the notion of transcendental illusion. Kant's claim is that reason's task of systematising knowledge leads it to introduce what are known as transcendental Ideas. These are concepts of unconditioned totality that arise naturally when reason goes beyond the bounds of experience, and provide a focal point (*focus imaginarius*) for reason. As such, reason generates false problems not simply in the sense of problems with no true solutions, but as necessary moments in its operation. In introducing the Idea in the *Critique of Pure Reason*, Kant explicitly claims to take up the Platonic notion of the Idea as 'something which not only can never be borrowed from the senses but far surpass the concepts of the understanding . . . inasmuch as in experience nothing is ever met with that is coincident with it' (Kant 1929: A313/B370). As modes of thinking of totality, the Ideas emerge when reason considers all possible relations between our representations. There are thus three transcendental Ideas for the three forms of relations that encompass everything: the relation to the subject, the relation to objects, and the relation to all things:

All transcendental ideas can therefore be arranged in three classes, the first containing the absolute (unconditioned) unity of the thinking subject, the second the absolute unity of the series of conditions of appearance, the third the absolute unity of the condition of all objects of thought in general. The thinking subject is the object of psychology, the sum-total of all appearances (the world) is the object of cosmology, and the thing which contains the highest condition of the possibility of all that can be thought (the being of all beings) the object of theology. (Kant 1929: A334/B391)

Precisely in so far as these concepts go beyond experience, Kant calls them problematic concepts. As we shall see in the next chapter, in Kant's conception of them, transcendental Ideas have many of the properties that Deleuze wants to attribute to problems, and he asserts that 'not only is sense ideal, but problems are Ideas themselves' (DR 162/201). For Kant, the Ideas are regulative concepts. They are a projection that allows us to systematise knowledge, and they allow us to introduce concepts into our system of knowledge that cannot be found in nature. Ultimately, therefore, for Deleuze they sustain the image of thought precisely at the moment when reason goes beyond experience. We can see this in the fact that the Ideas of reason, God, the self and the world all have structures that are amenable to judgement, whilst referring to objects that fall outside of any possible empirical experience. They are therefore a means of bringing into the image of thought that which is recognised to fall outside of it. Further, they play a regulative role rather than a truly genetic role. As we saw, when sense was seen as being a merely a condition of the proposition, rather than as that which generates it, it was possible to separate sense and the proposition from one another. This is what gave rise to the 'puerile' examples that Deleuze takes to be responsible for the image of thought. Instead, what is needed is a model that recognises the intrinsic relationship between representations and their non-representational ground. Rather than being interested in what regulates the image of thought, Deleuze is interested in those structures that underlie it. In this way, sense is what makes possible the proposition. Similarly, the Idea is what makes possible the structure of recognition that we encounter in the image of thought. The two processes operate concurrently, just as the passive syntheses operated underneath active syntheses.

3.10 Conclusion: The Postulate of Knowledge (164–7/204–8)

There is one final postulate of the image of thought, and with it, one final reversal of Platonism. This is the postulate of knowledge. If problems are defined in terms of solutions, then our engagement with problems will be determined by the solutions they engender. That is, we engage in problems in order to develop a better understanding of the world through propositional solutions. The image of thought thus privileges knowledge as itself the solution to problems. Once problems themselves are not simply characterised in terms of propositions, the situation becomes more complex. For Plato, knowledge is a relation to the Ideas. For Deleuze, the relation to Ideas is also important, but these Ideas are no longer to be understood in terms of propositions, but rather in terms of problems. This reversal means that what is important is the engagement with problems, which Deleuze calls learning, rather than the solutions that they engender, as knowledge. As such, the supposed result of learning, knowledge, is simply a by-product of what is primary: a relationship of each faculty to its transcendental ground. As Deleuze puts it:

it is knowledge that is nothing more than an empirical figure, a simple result which continually falls back into experience; whereas learning is the true transcendental structure which unites difference to difference, dissimilarity to dissimilarity, without mediating between them; and introduces time into thought. (DR 166–7/206)

Chapter 4 will give an account of the nature of learning, and with it, an account of the transcendental structure of the Idea that makes learning possible.

Chapter 4. Ideas and the Synthesis of Difference

4.1 Introduction: Kant and Ideas (168–71/214–17)

Chapter 4 of *Difference and Repetition* opens with two intertwined discussions: of Kant's theory of Ideas, and of the calculus. In the last chapter, we saw how Deleuze was opposed to Kant's philosophy since it provided an account of the faculties that merely repeated the structures of common sense at a higher level. We also saw in Deleuze's discussion of sense that if problems are seen as merely replicating solutions (albeit with the addition of the concept of possibility), then they are unable to provide an account of the genesis of experience, but can at best show

how it is conditioned by the faculties operating on a transcendental level. I want to begin, therefore, by looking at Kant's notion of the Idea, to see why Deleuze thinks that this notion is a key innovation of the Kantian system, but why ultimately it is unable to provide a genetic account for the structure of representation. As we shall see, Deleuze takes the calculus to offer an alternative to the Kantian model. In the previous chapter, Deleuze hinted at the possibility of a 'thought without image' (DR 167/208). Chapter 4 deals with this possibility more explicitly, answering the question, 'how does it operate in the world?' (DR 167/208).

In the last chapter (3.7) we saw that, for Kant, knowledge requires a connection between different faculties. While this relationship allows us to make judgements about the world, clearly knowledge involves something more than just particular judgements – it also requires these particular judgements to be organised into a coherent system of knowledge. This is the role of reason (3.9), which 'does not *create* concepts (of objects) but only orders them, and gives them that unity which they can have only if they be employed in their widest possible application, that is, with a view to obtaining totality in various series' (Kant 1929: A643/B671). In order to unify knowledge, reason requires the idea of total unity, as a focal point for its enquiries. Now, this total unity cannot actually be given in experience, and serves merely as a '*focus imaginarius*' (Kant 1929: A644/B672) that allows reason to perform its function. In this sense, reason is subject to a natural illusion that the end point of all of the understanding's rules for conceptualising the world is 'a real object lying outside of the field of empirically possible knowledge' (Kant 1929: A644/B672). This is what gives rise, according to Kant, to the transcendental illusion that reason is capable of fully determining its objects of knowledge, and Deleuze will put forward an analogous claim that it is this that makes us believe that everything can be captured by representation. As Deleuze notes, these Ideas play a necessary regulative role for Kant that allows reason to carry out the task of unifying knowledge, even if a final unification is not possible. Much of Deleuze's concern in the previous chapter was with developing a notion of a problem that wasn't defined in terms of the truth or falsity of its solutions. Since Kant's notion of an Idea goes beyond experience, and hence specifies an object that simply cannot be given, Kant calls the status of the Idea 'problematic'. An Idea refers to an object that can be thought but not known, and so 'it remains a *problem* to which there is no solution' (Kant 1929: A328/B384). Kant goes further, and notes that it would be wrong to say that each of these

Ideas is 'only an idea' since our inability to determine these Ideas does not mean that they do not relate to objects. In this sense, the Idea appears to fulfil Deleuze's requirements for a notion of a problem that is real, an 'indispensible condition of all practical employment of reason' (Kant 1929: A328/B385), but is not reliant on the empirical content of experience itself (the field of solutions). While Deleuze will take up many of the features of this account, ultimately he will argue that Kant has failed to properly escape from the image of thought Deleuze presented in Chapter 3. In order to demonstrate this, he introduces three categories: the indeterminate, the determinable and the determined.

First, the Idea itself is undetermined. That is, the object of the Idea cannot be presented in a determinate form in intuition. Taking, for instance, the Idea of God, which Kant considers to be the ground of all appearances, it is clear that we cannot know it, because the grounds of appearance are not themselves appearances: 'Outside of this field, [the categories] are merely titles of concepts, which we may admit, but through which we can understand nothing' (Kant 1929: A696/B794). It is nonetheless a concept that we can determine to some extent by analogy with our own empirical intelligence. In doing so, however, we only determine it '*in respect of the employment* of our reason *in respect to the world*' (Kant 1929: A698/B726). That is, the concept of God is determinable (we can specify what properties inhere in it) by analogy to the empirical world, but on condition that we only use this Idea to allow us to unify our understanding of the world further (by seeing the world *as if* it were created for an intelligible purpose, for instance). Furthermore, the Idea is also present in empirical objects, in so far as we consider them to be completely determined. If we are going to consider empirical objects as being completely specifiable in terms of intelligible properties, Kant claims that we need the Idea of God. In order to specify something completely in terms of the properties that it has, we need some kind of account of all properties it is possible for an object to possess, so that we can determine which of each pair of properties (the property and its contrary) inheres in the object. 'The Ideal is, therefore, the archetype (*prototypon*) of all things, which one and all, as imperfect copies (*ectypa*), derive from it the material of their possibility, while approximating to it in various degrees' (Kant 1929: A578/B606). Now, as Deleuze notes, these three moments of the Idea together could be used to make up a genetic account of actualisation. The Idea as undetermined provides a moment which differs in kind from the actual, and hence falls outside of its categories. As determinability, it is a moment whereby the object of the Idea becomes capable of sustaining predicates, and hence being determined as an actual object, and as determined, it provides a moment whereby it takes on the actual properties the object has. The three moments of the Idea therefore could provide an account as to how the ground of appearances expresses itself within the world of appearance itself. It would thus provide an account of how a problem finds expression in empirical solutions without having to understand the problem itself in empirical terms, as the Idea remains indeterminate in relation to that in which it is expressed, while nonetheless determining it.

In order for this model to account for the movement from the problem to its empirical solution, all three moments would have to be intrinsic parts of the Idea. As Deleuze notes, however, for Kant, 'two of the three moments remain as extrinsic characteristics' (DR 170/216). That is, the way in which we understand the determinability and the determined nature of an Idea such as God is solely in relation to already existing empirical states of affairs. We do this purely in order to allow reason to pursue its interests in systematising our knowledge of the world, and not in order to explore the conditions for the constitution of the world itself. The Idea 'is not a constitutive principle that enables us to determine anything in respect of its direct object, but only a merely regulative principle and maxim, to further and strengthen *in infinitum* (indeterminately) the empirical employment of reason' (Kant 1929: A680/B708). In this sense, while Ideas at first appear to offer us a way to think of problems in a way which is not dependent on solutions, Kant's account ultimately only allows us to make use of them in so far as they are thought by analogy with and in relation to empirical objects. The problem of the Kantian Idea is still understood in terms of the solutions it gives rise to. What is needed, therefore, is an account that intrinsically relates Ideas to the empirical world, while allowing them to maintain their difference in kind, rather than Kant's merely extrinsic and regulative account.

4.2 Ideas and the Differential Calculus (170–82/217–30)

Although determinability and determination are extrinsic determinations of Ideas on the Kantian model, Deleuze argues that we can develop a notion that intrinsically incorporates all three moments of the Idea by turning to the differential calculus as a model of thinking: 'Just as we oppose difference in itself to negativity, so we oppose dx, the symbol of difference [*Differenzphilosophie*] to that of contradiction' (DR 170/217).

In order to see why the calculus is important for Deleuze, it's necessary to outline in general what the calculus is. A first approximation is that the calculus is a field of mathematics dealing with the properties of points on curves (Boyer 1959: 6). As Boyer notes, this concern with properties of points on curves is similar to a concern with the properties of a body in motion, such as its velocity at a given moment in time. If we wanted to determine the average velocity of a body in motion, we would determine this by finding a ratio between two quantities, the distance that the body has travelled in the time period (s), and the time period itself (t). We could represent this, for instance, in the following form: average velocity $= \Delta s / \Delta t$, that is, the difference in displacement over the period divided by the difference in time (with Δ symbolising difference). This would give us an average velocity in terms of metres per second, or miles per hour. While this might be effective for average velocities, the problem emerges when we want to determine the velocity of the body at a particular moment in time. When we are talking about a particular moment, we are no longer talking about average velocity, but rather now about instantaneous velocity. If a body is moving at constant speed, then the average and instantaneous velocities of the body will coincide, but if a body is accelerating or decelerating, however, then its instantaneous velocity will be constantly changing, and so we cannot determine it based on its average velocity.

Leibniz's solution to this dilemma was to suggest that if we take the average velocity of the body over a time, beginning with the point we are trying to determine the instantaneous velocity for, and slowly decrease the slice of time we are using to divide the distance travelled, the average velocity will approach the instantaneous velocity. That is, the smaller the segment of time over which we determine the average velocity, the closer it will be to the instantaneous velocity at a point. If we extend this idea, and determine the average velocity over an infinitesimally small stretch of time, then, because this stretch of time is for all intents and purposes 0, the average velocity will actually equal the instantaneous velocity. Now, what we have been dealing with here is a relation between two quantities, distance and time. One of the main concerns of mathematics is with relations more generally, and the calculus in fact provides a way of accounting for relations between varying quantities in general, that is, for all kinds of continuous curves. We represent curves in terms of mathematical equations, and so the differential calculus is a procedure we can apply to mathematical equations. In this respect, the equation that generates the curve is known as the primitive function. When we apply the calculus to the equation of a curve, we get what is known as the derivative, which is an equation that gives us the gradient of the curve at each point (in the example of the body in motion, the velocity at each point). For the average velocity between two points, we used the symbol $\Delta s/\Delta t$, where Δs indicates an arbitrary distance, and Δt represents the stretch of time the body takes to travel that distance, but the calculus is not concerned with average velocities, which rely on finite differences, but with infinitesimal differences, otherwise known as differentials. In order to represent infinitesimal differences, Leibniz introduces the symbolism dy/dx. As we saw in Chapter 1, relations for Aristotle were defined in terms of negation. The differential calculus provides the possibility of developing a theory of relations that relies on reciprocal determination of the elements, dy and dx. Deleuze claims that 'there is a treasure buried in the old so-called barbaric or pre-scientific interpretations of the differential calculus' (DR 170/217). This treasure is covered over by two mistakes: 'it is a mistake to tie the value of the symbol dx to the existence of infinitesimals; it is equally a mistake to refuse it any ontological or gnoseological value in the name of a refusal of the latter' (DR 170/217). In order to understand why we might make these two mistakes, we need to look further at what the term, dx, signifies. Now, as we saw, dx represents for Leibniz an infinitesimal distance between two points. When we want to use this to determine instantaneous velocity, however, we encounter a contradiction. To see this, we can turn to the account of the infinitesimal of L'Hôpital, one of the earliest popularisers of the calculus:

> *Postulate I.* Grant that two quantities, whose difference is an infinitely small quantity, may be taken (or used) indifferently for each other: or (which is the same thing) that a quantity, which is increased or decreased only by an infinitely smaller quantity, may be considered as remaining the same. (L'Hôpital 1969: 314)

This postulate is needed because dx must be seen as having a determinate value in order to form a ratio, dy/dx, but also has to have no magnitude ($=0$) in order to capture the gradient at a point, rather than across a length of the curve. Clearly, this is a fundamental difficulty, since the consistency of mathematics is threatened by taking a variable simultaneously to have and to lack a magnitude. In this sense, it appears that Deleuze is right in holding it to be a mistake to give the differential a sensible magnitude, even if this were infinitely small, and modern readings of the calculus concur, presenting an interpretation of the calculus in terms of a concept of limits that does away with the need to give anything beyond a formal meaning to the differential. Deleuze, however, holds that this reading is also a mistake. In providing an alternative reading of the calculus, Deleuze returns to the metaphysical readings of the eighteenth and nineteenth centuries. The three figures he presents, Bordas-Demoulin, Maimon and Wronski, all held that the contradiction in the mathematical account of the differential did not entail that the differential itself was contradictory, but rather that a proper understanding of it involved a metaphysical interpretation that brought in resources not available within mathematics itself. I want now to present a brief summary of how Deleuze takes up these different readings in order to present an alternative to the Kantian notion of the Idea. Each of these figures takes up a different moment of the world of appearances. Bordas-Demoulin's account is concerned with quantities. As a follower of Descartes, he takes matter to be continuous, rather than made up of discrete atoms. In this regard, he is interested in the way in which the calculus allows us to provide an account of these continuous magnitudes. Maimon is concerned with qualities, such as the colours of objects. As such, he is interested in how these qualities are reciprocally determined, and how we are to understand the changes in quality of objects. Finally Deleuze's discussion of Wronski develops an account of potentiality in terms of the calculus, that is, the moments in the development of an object where its nature itself changes.

The first figure Deleuze introduces is Bordas-Demoulin, 'a Plato of the calculus' (DR 170–1/217). Bordas-Demoulin asks how we can represent mathematical universals as they are in themselves. He claims that Descartes, for instance, does not represent the concept of circumference in itself, but only this or that particular circumference. Descartes' procedure is, according to Bordas-Demoulin, to present the algebraic equation for a circle, $x^2 + y^2 - R^2 = 0$. If we drew the graph of this equation, then for a specific value of R, all of the solutions to the equation would together give us a circle, centred on the point $(0, 0)$ of the Cartesian coordinate system. Why does this Cartesian definition not give us the true definition of a circle? Bordas-Demoulin puts the point as follows:

In $x^2 + y^2 - R^2 = 0$, I can assign an infinity of indifferent values to x, y, R, but nevertheless I am obliged to always attribute to them one, that is, one determinate value, and by consequence to express a particular circumference, and not circumference in itself. This is true for equations of all curves, and finally for any variable function, so called because they give a continuous quantity and its symbol. It is the individual curve or function which is represented, and not the universal, which, accordingly, remains without a symbol, and has not been considered mathematically by Descartes. (Bordas-Demoulin 1843: 133)

In relation to particular circles, algebra functions like the Russellian notion of sense, or the Kantian notion of a condition, in that the variables, x, y, R simply stand in for particular values. It gives us an account of what circumference is in general, but this account can only be 'cashed out' by choosing specific values to put into the equation. Ultimately, therefore, we simply define the structure of this or that particular circumference, rather than circumference itself. In order to develop an account of what circumference is in itself, we need to remove these references to the particular terms, and this is achieved by using the differential calculus, 'whose object is to extract the universal in the functions' (Bordas-Demoulin 1843: 54). When we differentiate a function, we receive another function that no longer gives us the precise values of the function, but instead, the variation of the function. Moreover, because this function is constituted in terms of dy and dx, which cannot be assigned a value (they are strictly 0 in regard to y and x), we no longer have a function that can be understood simply in terms of possible values of variables. For Bordas-Demoulin, therefore, dx does not represent a variable that can be given different particular values, but rather a radical break with understanding structure in actual terms. 'Applied to $x^2 + y^2 - R^2 = 0$, [the calculus] gives $ydy + xdx = 0$, an equation that does not express any particular circumference, but circumference in general, dx, dy being independent of all determinate or finite magnitudes' (Bordas-Demoulin 1843: 134). What Deleuze wants to take from this is the idea that the differential is simply inexpressible in terms of quantity, and so is inexpressible in terms of the primitive function. Nevertheless, if we reverse the operation of differentiation by integrating a function, we get the formulae for particular, actual circumferences. The differential is not simply different from the primitive function, but we can also see that it has an intrinsic relationship with it: 'If in, $ydy + xdx = 0$, one still encounters the finite magnitudes y, x, this is because in quantity, no more than in substance, can the universal isolate itself completely and form a separate being' (Bordas-Demoulin 1843: 134). We thus have a situation that parallels the account of Plato that Deleuze has given in the last chapter. An empirical concept, such as that of circumference, carries within it its Idea, the differential, in comparison with which it falls short. Whereas for Plato the Idea was ultimately understood by analogy with empirical objects (the use of analogy in Plato's theory of memory), the differential allows Bordas-Demoulin to present a difference in kind between the Idea and its instantiations. In emphasising the degree to which the differential is immanent to the primitive function while different in kind from it, Bordas-Demoulin chooses another figure as a model of the metaphysics of the calculus who might be even better suited to Deleuze's account: 'According to this metaphysics [of the calculus], one might say, by way of comparison, that the God of Spinoza is the differential of the universe, and the universe, the integral of the God of Spinoza' (Bordas-Demoulin 1843: 172).

The second figure Deleuze introduces is Salomon Maimon, who Deleuze claims to be the Leibniz of the calculus. Maimon, for Deleuze, uses the calculus to overcome what he takes to be Kant's 'reduction of the transcendental instance to a simple conditioning and the renunciation of any genetic requirement' (DR 173/220). Deleuze's reading of Maimon derives almost entirely from Guéroult's *The Transcendental Philosophy of Salomon Maimon*, so I will concentrate on that reading here. We can see Maimon's basic project as problematising the Kantian account of the *a priori* through the reintroduction of a form of Humean scepticism, whilst simultaneously adding a pre-critical element to the Kantian project through introducing a Leibnizian genetic account of the production of space, time and intensity. Just as Bordas-Demoulin took the differential to provide the universal for particular mathematical figures, Maimon takes the differential to be the source of a construction, this time of the phenomenal world. We can begin by recalling that Kant's fundamental problem is finding a way to relate faculties that are different in kind. Kant's concern is to guarantee knowledge, and so he isn't concerned with the reasons why we possess faculties that differ in kind, but is purely interested in how these faculties can be related to one another in order to produce knowledge. Maimon instead wants to investigate the genetic conditions of phenomena. In his *Philosophical Dictionary*, he makes the following comment on the relationship of reason to the object of intuition:

Reason demands that one must not consider the given in an object as something of a pure unalterable nature, but merely as a consequence of the limitation of our faculty of thinking. Reason demands of us therefore an infinite progression through which that which is thought is perpetually increased, the given, however being decreased to an infinitesimal. (Maimon 1791: 169)

Rather than seeing what is given as merely the passive matter of the faculty of intuition, Maimon sees it simply as that which the intellect cannot think. If we did not have a limited faculty of thought, but instead had an infinite understanding, the entirety of what is for us given would be thought, and so the given itself would disappear. To this extent, Maimon's account is rather like Leibniz's, with the given empirical object being a confused form of perception of the true nature of things. Whereas for Leibniz, the difference between the thought of a finite being and an infinite being was a difference in degree (a greater intellect would have no need to perceive conceptual relations under the confused form of space), for Maimon there is a difference in kind between the two kinds of thinking. As we have seen, the infinitesimal cannot be given a sensible interpretation without contradiction. Nonetheless, when we relate two infinitesimals to each other in a differential function (dy/dx), we derive a formula that does have a sensible interpretation (the formula for the gradient of the points on a curve). The differential is thus like the Kantian noumenon, which can be thought, but cannot be presented in intuition. Maimon takes this mathematical interpretation of the differential, and gives it a transcendental interpretation, so the differential, dx, becomes a symbol of the noumenal grounds for the synthesis of phenomena:

These differentials of objects are the so-called *noumena*; but the objects themselves arising from them are the *phenomena*. With respect to intuition = 0, the differential of any such object is $dx = 0$, $dy = 0$ etc.; however, their relations are not = 0, but can rather be given determinately in the intuitions arising from them. (Maimon 2010: 32)

An infinite understanding is able to think these differential relations, and thus to think the object in its totality without intuition. In this sense, as Deleuze notes, for Maimon, 'the particular rule by which an object arises, or its type of differential, makes it into a particular object; and the relations of different objects arise from the relations of the rules by which they arise or of their differentials' (Maimon 2010: 33). Since the differential gives us a rule that governs the infinite relations of the object, however, the finite intellect is unable to think it all at once. In this respect, as opposed to thinking the object *a priori* according to the rules governing the way it arises, it can only think of it as given, that is, through sensible intuition. Thus, rather than the extrinsic relation between the faculties, Maimon shows how intuition emerges through the finite intellect's inability to think the relations of differentials all at once. Instead of thinking the object as a completed synthesis, it must be thought as a synthesis in process, as an 'arising' or 'flowing'. Now, as Guéroult makes clear, the fact that we cannot simply think the object means that we become subject to a transcendental illusion:

> The imagination is thus never conscious of anything other than representations; it therefore has, inevitably, the illusion that all of the objects of consciousness are representations; it is led by this to also consider the original object or the complete synthesis as a representation. (Guéroult 1929: 66)

It is this illusion that leads us to see problems in the same terms as solutions. We can therefore see in Maimon two different modes of thinking. One that operates in terms of intuition, and provides a philosophy of conditioning, and another that provides a genetic model of thought that attempts to trace the genesis of the given back to its differential roots.

We can now present the alternative theory of the Idea. Rather than seeing it as a relation between three moments, two of which are extrinsic, the differential calculus relates the three moments intrinsically. It is undetermined in that the differential, dx, cannot be given in intuition. When it is put into a relation, such as dy/dx, it becomes determinable, as it specifies the complete range of values the function can take. Finally, it is determined in terms of specific values that the function takes at particular moments (the instantaneous velocity of a particular point in time in our prior example). Whereas the infinite understanding thinks the curve as a whole, we can only think the process of generation of the curve, equivalent to the actual evolution of the object in intuition. As Guéroult puts it, 'the differential is, then, the noumenon (that which is simply thought by the intellect), the source of phenomena (which appear in intuition)' (Guéroult 1929: 60).

The final figure Deleuze introduces is Wronski. The mathematician, Joseph-Louis Lagrange, tried to show that we could give an algebraic interpretation of the calculus, representing it as an infinite series of terms using his notion of functions. In the introduction to his *Theorie des Fonctions Analytiques*, he makes the claim that 'the Analysis which is popularly called transcendental or infinitesimal is at root only the Analysis of primitive and derived functions, and that the differential and integral

Calculi are, speaking properly, only the calculation of these same functions' (Lagrange, quoted in Grattin-Guinness 1980: 100–1). Lagrange's claim that the calculus can be understood purely in terms of algebra would, if successful, remove the need for the kind of 'barbaric' interpretation that Deleuze puts forward, since we would no longer need to give a metaphysical interpretation of the differential. It is to save the possibility of a 'barbaric' interpretation that Deleuze introduces Wronski. As with the other thinkers of the calculus discussed in this chapter, Wronski holds that there is a fundamental distinction between the differential and normal quantity:

It is this important transcendental distinction that is the crux of the metaphysics of Calculus. – In effect, the finite quantities and indefinite quantities, that is to say, infinitesimal quantities, belong to two entirely different, even heterogeneous, classes of knowledge: the finite quantities relate to the objects of our cognition, and infinitesimal quantities relate to the generation of this same cognition, so that each of these classes must have knowledge of proper laws, and it is obviously in the distinction of these laws that the crux of the metaphysics of infinitesimal amounts is found. (Höené Wronski 1814: 35)

Now, while Lagrange believes that he has escaped from the need to introduce infinitesimals by resorting to the (algebraic) indefinite, which can be understood purely in algebraic terms, Wronski's claim is that the indefinite itself cannot be understood without the infinitesimal. To bring the infinitesimal into the domain of cognition, it has to be presented in an intuition, which can be done purely as an indeterminate quantity. The indeterminate quantity that is at the centre of Lagrange's method is thus, for Wronski, still reliant on the differential.

In claiming that Lagrange's method still relies on the differential, Wronski does not deny that, precisely because it is derived from it, it is still correct. In fact, Lagrange's method produces a series of differentials which allow us to distinguish between two kinds of points on the line: singular points and ordinary points. If we remember our initial example of the calculus, relating distance to time gave us the velocity of a body. If we differentiate this equation once more, we will obtain a relationship between velocity and time, which is the acceleration of a body. Points on this curve, such as where it is flat, indicate singular features of the movement of the body, such as in this case the point at which it is travelling at constant motion. In more abstract curves, points where the gradient is $0/0$, or is null or infinite, define points where the nature of the curve changes. Potentiality thus defines the points at which the nature of the relationship between the terms radically changes.

We can tie these three moments together to develop an account of the Idea where its three moments, the indeterminate, the determinable and the determined, are intrinsic to it. As we saw when we looked at Bordas-Demoulin, the differentials themselves, dy and dx, are completely undetermined with respect to representation, and hence to the field of solutions. Nonetheless, when brought into relation with each other, they give us an equation that *is* determinable. This equation gives us the rates of change of a function at each point in time (or more correctly, for any value of x). Such an equation, as Wronski shows, contains singular points that determine the points on the curve where its nature radically changes. That is, by specifying a value of x, we can determine the rate of change at any point. Specifying a value of x, therefore determines the Idea. We therefore have a particular determined value (intuition), a determinable equation that subsumes it (the concept), and a field of differentials themselves which engenders both the determinable and determination. The differential, as problem, therefore contains the solution intrinsically, rather than simply being interpreted in terms of it. While this account may seem abstract for now, as we shall see in the following four sections, we can develop concrete examples of the Idea that operate according to this schema.

The remainder of Deleuze's discussion of the differential calculus draws the consequences from this understanding of the calculus as Idea. As Deleuze notes, 'the interpretation of the calculus has indeed taken the form of asking whether infinitesimals are real or fictive' (DR 176/223). As Wronski's account makes clear, however, this question has traditionally been interpreted in terms of whether differentials can be an object of (representational) cognition, or are fictions. Once we recognise that they are of a different order to what they engender, 'the first alternative – real or fictive? – collapses' (DR 178/225). Likewise, Deleuze notes that the alternative between seeing the calculus as operating in terms of an infinitesimal, or modern finitist interpretations that seek to dispense with the infinitesimal, is equally invalid. Deleuze's claim is that both of these interpretations are ways of describing magnitudes, but as these magnitudes operate within the domain of representation, neither of these terms is adequate to the differential. Finally, as we have seen, on Deleuze's reading, the emphasis is not on the primitive function, but on the differential, dx, as constitutive of the primitive function.

As such, it is concerned with problems, rather than solutions. In this sense, Deleuze claims that rather than talking of a metaphysics of the calculus, we should talk of a dialectics of the calculus, dialectic meaning 'the problem element in so far as this may be distinguished from the properly mathematical element of solutions' (DR 178/226). The work of the mathematician, Abel, is therefore important to Deleuze, because he developed a method for determining whether a problem has a solution without resorting to actually solving the problem itself.

We have already seen how the three moments of the Idea are intrinsically, rather than extrinsically, connected in the calculus, and Deleuze reiterates and summarises his discussion in the following passage:

> Following Lautman's general theses, a problem has three aspects: its difference in kind from solutions; its transcendence in relation to the solutions that it engenders on the basis of its own determinant conditions; and its immanence in the solutions which cover it, the problem being the better resolved the more it is determined. Thus the ideal connections constitutive of the problematic (dialectical) Idea are incarnated in the real relations which are constituted by mathematical theories and carried over into problems in the form of solutions. (DR 178–9/226)

Each of these three moments is present in the calculus as a method of intrinsically relating two structures that are different in kind from one another. The calculus thus provides a model for an account of the genesis of determinate quantity from something different in kind where each of its moments is intrinsically connected with the others.

4.3 Ideas and the Wider Calculus (178–84/226–32)

Deleuze notes that 'differential calculus obviously belongs to mathematics, it is an entirely mathematical instrument. It would therefore seem difficult to see in it the Platonic evidence of a dialectic superior to mathematics' (DR 179/226). When we looked at Plato's simile of the divided line (3.5), we saw that Plato held mathematics to be the second highest form of knowledge, below knowledge of Ideas themselves. It seems equally clear that Deleuze wants to provide an account of the world, not just of the field of mathematics. In fact, once we recognise that problems are of a different order to solutions, we can note that mathematics is a way of representing solutions – 'what is mathematical (or physical, biological, psychical or sociological) are the solutions' (DR 179/227). These domains do not apply to problems themselves, but only to problems as *expressed* in relation to (and within) solutions. The calculus is itself a way of providing symbols of difference, and as such, it is still propositional, and tied to a specific domain. Since what these symbols refer to cannot be represented, however, the calculus points beyond itself to the problem itself. 'That is why the differential calculus belongs entirely to mathematics, even at the very moment when it finds its sense in the revelation of a dialectic which points beyond mathematics' (DR 179/227). What is important about the calculus is that it presents an account of how undetermined elements can become determinate through entering into reciprocal relations. As relations exist in domains outside of mathematics, the differential calculus 'has a wider universal sense in which it designates the composite universal whole that includes Problems or dialectical Ideas, the Scientific expression of problems, and the Establishment of fields of solution' (DR 181/229).

As we have seen, Ideas are formed from the differential relations of their elements. In this sense, Deleuze claims that 'Ideas are multiplicities' (DR 182/230). They are the reciprocal relationships of elements that in themselves are indeterminate. Now, when we are dealing with a spatial multiplicity, we talk about multiplicity in terms of a structure possessing many elements. In this sense, we can call it an adjectival notion of multiplicity. The 'many' in this case is a way of describing elements that can be in a sense indifferent to being given the classification, 'many'. They are determinate before they form a group. On the contrary, with differentials, they become determinate precisely by being reciprocally determined. Rather than multiplicity being an adjective that describes a group of substances, Deleuze claims that '"Multiplicity", which replaces the one no less than the multiple, is the true substantive, substance itself' (DR 182/230). As we have just seen, in order to conceive of the multiplicity in this way, we can't see it in terms of self-standing elements. Now, at least on a first reading of Kant, experience for him was experience of objects, which *are* self-standing elements. Thus the notion of a multiplicity in Deleuze's terms cannot be found within Kantian experience. In fact, Deleuze gives three criteria for the emergence of Ideas. First, 'the elements of the multiplicity must have neither sensible form nor conceptual signification, nor, therefore, any assignable function' (DR 183/231). That is, they must be determined through their relationships with one another, rather than prior to it. Second, 'the elements must in effect be determined, but reciprocally, by reciprocal relations which allow no independence to subsist' (DR 183/231). As Deleuze notes, 'spatio-temporal relations no doubt retain multiplicity, but lose interiority'. That is, the elements are not intrinsically related to one another, but are simply related by occupying a certain space together. On the other hand, 'concepts of the understanding retain interiority, but lose multiplicity' (DR 183/231). When we determine a concept (man is a rational animal, for instance), we do so by subsuming it under another. As such, while they are intrinsically connected, they form a unity, rather than a multiplicity. Finally, 'a differential *relation*, must be actualised in diverse spatio-temporal *relationships*, at the same time as its *elements* are actually incarnated in a variety of terms and forms' (DR 183/231). That is, if the Idea is to provide some kind of explanation of the structure of the world, it must be applicable to more than one situation; it must capture relations in more than one domain. All of these features can be found in the differential calculus, but to explain how this account functions more generally, Deleuze provides three examples of Ideas in non-mathematical fields: atomism as a physical Idea, the organism as a biological Idea, and social Ideas.

4.4 First Example: Atomism as a Physical Idea (184/232–3)

The first example Deleuze gives of an attempt to develop a wider calculus is that presented by the atomists, notably Epicurus in his *Letter to Herodotus* and Lucretius in his *De Rerum Natura*. What Deleuze presents in this section is essentially a synopsis of his longer treatment in his essay, 'The Simulacrum and Ancient Philosophy', published as an appendix to *The Logic of Sense* (LS 253–79/291–320). Epicurus claims that the universe is composed of two kinds of entities: atoms and void. While the atoms vary in size, they are all below the threshold of perception. Since resistance slows bodies down, and there is no resistance within the void, the atom's 'passage through the void, when it takes place without meeting any bodies which might collide, accomplishes every comprehensible distance in an inconceivably short time'. They move 'quick as thought' (Epicurus 1926: 37). These atoms have shapes, and the structure of the visible world is explained by their combination into compound structures. Atoms in these compound structures appear to move at a perceptible rate, but this is simply due to the fact that as their directions differ, the atoms 'vibrate', leading to a perceptible average motion. Given that it is 'essential that atoms be related to other atoms at the heart of structures which are actualised in sensible composites', we need to ask what allows this relation to take place. Lucretius gives the following account of how atoms enter into relations with one another:

> In this connection, I am anxious that you should grasp a further point: when the atoms are being drawn downward through the void by their property of weight, at absolutely unpredictable times and places they deflect slightly from their straight course, to a degree that could be described as no more than a shift of movement. If they were not apt to swerve, all would fall downward through the unfathomable void like drops of rain; no collisions between primary elements would occur, and no blows would be effected, with the result that nature would never have created anything. (Lucretius 2001: 40–1)

It is through this swerve (*clinamen*) that atoms come into contact with one another. Deleuze's analysis of this situation begins with the claim that since the void provides no resistance, it is not the case that the atoms simply have an undefined location. Rather, moving at the speed of thought, they are strictly speaking 'non-localisable'. In this sense, they operate much like the differential, dx, in that they are undetermined, lacking one of the key characteristics of 'sensible form'. Second, they can only be given in sensibility though a reciprocal relation formed between them, just as it is only through the differential relation dy/dx that differentials become determinate. In the case of atomism, this reciprocal relation is provided by the *clinamen*, which allows a collection of atoms to take on sensible significance. Finally, as the atoms are capable of forming diverse relationships amongst themselves, they can be 'actualised in diverse spatio-temporal *relationships*' (DR 183/231). Atomism therefore appears to meet Deleuze's criteria for the Idea. In fact, however, Deleuze claims it fails to exemplify the Idea fully, because the atom is still too tied to sensible determinations. Epicurus' account of its nature is based on an analogy with sensible bodies: 'We must suppose that the atoms do not possess any of the qualities belonging to perceptible things, except shape, weight and size, and all that necessarily goes with shape' (Epicurus 1926: 31).

4.5 Second Example: The Organism as Biological Idea (184–5/233–4)

Deleuze's second example of the Idea is derived from a nineteenth-century debate over the nature of the organism. This was the debate as to whether comparative anatomy should understand the structure of organisms in terms of what are known as analogies or in terms of homologies. For traditional (and pre-evolutionary) comparative anatomy, the names of the parts of animals are, to a certain extent, derived analogically from other animals, archetypally with man. On a model dating back to Aristotle, we define what an organ is by looking at the functional role it plays in allowing the organism to perpetuate itself. Parts are thus defined by their relationship to the whole. The importance of this relationship is made clear by one of the most important comparative anatomists of the nineteenth century, Georges Cuvier, who claims that 'it is in this dependence of the functions and the aid which they reciprocally lend one another that are founded the laws which determine the relations of their organs and which possess a necessity equal to that of metaphysical or mathematical laws' (Cuvier, quoted in Coleman 1964: 67). When the function or form of the parts differ, however, a different term must be assigned to the part in question. Thus, although there is a similarity between the fins of a fish and the arm of man, on a teleological account, the functional and structural differences mean that different terms must be applied to each. This teleological account proves itself to be problematic in terms of evolutionary theory, since evolution often involves the change of function of the same structure between different creatures.

Now, one of the key conceptual developments that made the theory of evolution possible was Geoffroy St. Hilaire's positing of homologies between different parts of organisms. Rather than seeing an organism as defined by the form or function of parts, Geoffroy, a contemporary of Cuvier, saw it as defined by the relations between parts. By focusing on relations rather than functions, Geoffroy was able to provide an account that explains one of the key results of evolutionary theory – that the *same* structure can change its function in different organisms (fins becoming arms, for instance). Geoffroy didn't relate organisms to one another directly to generate his account of homologies, but rather posited a transcendental structure of an ideal organism that other organisms were instantiations of (he called his approach 'transcendental anatomy').

Deleuze's interpretation of Geoffroy's work rests on what he calls Geoffroy's dream, 'to be the Newton of the infinitely small, to discover "the world of details" or "very short distance" ideal connections beneath the cruder play of sensible and conceptual differences and resemblances' (DR 185/233). He claims that what Geoffroy is aiming at with his emphasis on connections is a field of differential elements (the ideal correlates of the bones) forming specific types of relations (the connections which are central to Geoffroy's account). On this basis, Deleuze claims that Geoffroy's transcendental anatomy functions like an Idea, with its three characteristics. The elements of the Idea 'must have neither sensible form nor conceptual signification', and transcendental anatomy fulfils this requirement due to the fact that what is important is not the sensible properties of the bones, which vary in different creatures, but their relations. Second, 'these elements must be determined reciprocally', which means that what is central is not the bones themselves, but the connections they hold with other bones, what Geoffroy calls the 'unity of composition'. Third, 'a multiple ideal connection, a differential *relation*, must be actualised in diverse spatio-temporal *relationships*, at the same time as its *elements* are actually incarnated in a variety of *terms* and forms'. Deleuze emphasises that homologies do not exist directly between actual terms, 'but are understood as the actualisation of an essence, in accordance with reasons and at speeds determined by the environment, with accelerations and interruptions' (DR 184/233). That is, we discover a homology between two creatures by recognising that the actual parts of both organisms are actualisations of the same transcendental essence, the unity of composition, rather than by an analogical correlation of actual terms, as in comparative anatomy. As Deleuze notes, this approach finds its parallels in genetic theory, where genes gain their significance from their relations to one another. In fact, genetics represents an advance over Geoffroy's account in that for him the transcendental correlates of bones, according to Deleuze, 'still enjoy an actual, or too actual, existence' (DR 185/233–4). The Idea in this case therefore allows us to determine in what way diverse phenomena (different organisms) are related to one another.

4.6 Third Example: Are there Social Ideas, in a Marxist Sense? (186/234–5)

The third domain Deleuze considers is the social domain, where he takes up a structuralist reading of Marx. Marx is traditionally understood as a historicist philosopher, and a disciple of Hegel. Just as in the *Phenomenology of Spirit* Hegel tries to show that new relations between subjects and objects would arise from the contradictions in their predecessors, the Marxist project, on this reading, would be to show how different social structures emerged from the internal contradictions of their predecessors. Since what generates a new set of social and economic relations is a prior set of such relations (the inherent contradictions in

Feudalism immanently determining the transition to capitalist economic relations, for instance), Marx's philosophy is essentially a philosophy of history. Deleuze here takes up Althusser's claim that, at least for the later Marx, there is a radical break with Hegel, meaning

that basic structures of the Hegelian dialectic such as negation, the negation of the negation, the identity of opposites, 'supersession', the transformation of quantity into quality, contradiction, etc., *have for Marx (in so far as he takes them over, and he takes over by no means all of them) a structure different from the structure they have for Hegel*. (Althusser 2005: 93–4)

In fact, the division of history into periods, for Althusser, is secondary to Marx's analysis of productivity in terms of modes and relations of production.

What is central to Marx's analysis, according to Althusser, is the mode of production, conceived of as a certain combination between the means of production (land, for instance), and the agents of production (itself divided into direct agents, such as workers, and indirect agents, such as managers). Althusser's claim is that what is fundamental to Marx's analysis is not man himself (or even man alone, as this would be to exclude the means of production), but rather the relations between these terms themselves:

The true 'subjects' (in the sense of constitutive subjects of the process) are therefore not these occupants or functionaries, are not, despite all appearances, the 'obviousnesses' of the 'given' of naïve anthropology, 'concrete individuals', 'real men' – but the definition and distribution of these places and functions. The true 'subjects' are these definers and distributors: the relations of production (and political and ideological social relations). But since these are 'relations', they cannot be thought within the category subject. (Althusser and Balibar 2009: 180)

What are these relations? Althusser argues that it would be a mistake to see them as ones of domination and servitude, for instance, although such structures may result from these relations. Rather than dealing with visible relations, such as exploitation, he is concerned with the structural relations that underlie these surface phenomena:

The relations of production are structures – and the ordinary economist may scrutinize economic 'facts': prices, exchanges, wages, profits, rents, etc., all those 'measurable' facts, as much as he likes; he will no more 'see' any structure at that level than the pre-Newtonian 'physicist' could 'see' the law of attraction in falling bodies, or the pre-Lavoisierian chemist could 'see' oxygen in 'dephlogisticated' air. Naturally, just as bodies were 'seen' to fall before Newton, the 'exploitation' of the majority of men by a minority was 'seen' before Marx. (Althusser and Balibar 2009: 181)

Althusser's account, therefore, is that surface phenomena, such as 'juridical, political, ideological' (DR 186/234) structures emerge in order to support the underlying structures of relation between roles of workers and means of production. In what sense does Althusser's reading of Marx relate to Deleuze's conception of the Idea? First, we can note that the elements of his analysis have no conceptual significance outside of their relations. What Althusser is discussing is the way in which roles relate to the means of production. If we separate these from one another, they cease to have any significance: 'Whatever the social form of production, labourers and means of production always remain factors of it. But in a state of separation from each other either of these factors can be such only potentially' (Marx, quoted in Althusser and Balibar 2009: 175). Second, these potential elements become significant by being related to one another. Land only becomes a means of production by being related to a worker, who becomes determined as a worker precisely through this relation. Finally, this structure can be actualised in diverse spatio-temporal relations. Depending on how the elements are related, different actual structures and relations, and hence different forms of society, will of necessity come into existence to sustain the underlying mode of production. Thus,

to obtain the different modes of production these different elements do have to be combined, but by using specific modes of combination or '*Verbindungen*' which are only meaningful in the peculiar nature of the result of the combinatory (this result being real production) – and which are: property, possession, disposition, enjoyment, community, etc. (Althusser and Balibar 2009: 176)

The Idea, in the Marxist sense, thus allows us to get away from the anthropomorphic and historicist study of surface structures, and hence to develop a science of society.

4.7 The Relations of Ideas (186–7/235–6)

How then do Ideas relate to one another? Deleuze claims that 'Ideas are varieties that include within themselves sub-varieties' (DR 187/235).

This claim emerges from two previous observations. First, as we have already seen, a differential function can itself be differentiated. As one of the key features of Ideas is that they are differentiated, they too can be further differentiated to give Ideas of Ideas. Second, as we have seen, Ideas are related to the domain in which they are solved. This implies that the same Idea can be expressed in different actual situations, depending on what kind of solution we are looking for. In fact, there are three 'dimensions of variety', the first of which is the 'vertical dimension' (DR 187/235). This depends on what the elements and relations we are concerned with are. Depending on whether we conceive of the elements as atoms, bones or relations of production, the solution we arrive at will be expressed in the fields of physics, biology or social theory respectively. While we have here different 'orders', these orders are still interrelated, in that Ideas of physics can be 'dissolved' in higher order problems such as those of biology, and likewise social theory will find itself 'reflected' in the structure of the individuals that compose it. The second, 'horizontal' dimension deals with 'degrees of a differential relation within a given order' (DR 187/235). As we saw in 4.2, by repeatedly differentiating an equation, we can find 'singular' points along a curve where the nature of the curve changes. Now, the same Idea can give rise to Ideas with different singular points. Deleuze gives the example of conic sections to explain this concept. In geometry, we can generate a curve by cutting a cone with a plane, just as if we cut a cylinder in half, we would find, on the surface of the cut (the section), a circle. Now, if we take a section of a cone, depending on the angle to the cone at which we take the section, we will have a different type of curve:

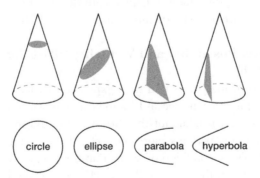

Figure 2: Conic sections

Each of these curves has different singular points (points where the gradient is 0, null or infinite), despite the fact that all of the curves are created from the same fundamental shape. In a non-mathematical field, we can note that Geoffroy's comparative anatomy relies on the fact that the same structure is to be found in the relations between the bones of all animals. Nevertheless, the singular points will vary within species, so the same bones that attach the jaw to the skull in fish are found in the inner ear in mammals. Deleuze explains the final dimension of variety, that of depth, with an example from the mathematical theory of groups. He gives the example of 'the addition of real numbers and the composition of displacements' in this context (DR 187/236). As the structuralist mathematical collective, Bourbaki, noted, the addition of real numbers and the composition of displacements traditionally belong to two very different fields of mathematics, since one involves discrete units, and one continuous measurement:

> quite apart from applied mathematics, there has always existed a dualism between the origins of geometry and of arithmetic (certainly in their elementary aspects), since the latter was at the start a science of discrete magnitude, while the former has always been a science of continuous extent; these two aspects have brought about two points of view which have been in opposition to each other since the discovery of irrationals. (Bourbaki 1950: 221–2)

Bourbaki note, however, that underneath the surface structures of the specific axioms of these different branches of mathematics, we can discern structures that occur in both branches, provided the elements of each branch are understood in a sufficiently undefined manner. Thus, certain relations may hold between elements that are obscured by further specifying their nature. Underneath the structures of geometry and arithmetic are deeper structures which they both share.

4.8 Essence, Possibility and Virtuality (186–8/235–7, 208–14/260–6)

Given the claim that Ideas find their expression in actual entities, we might be tempted to consider an Idea to be a kind of essence of a thing. Deleuze, however, is adamant that 'Ideas are by no means essences' (DR 187/236), or, perhaps more precisely, that we can call an Idea an essence 'only on condition of saying that the essence is precisely the accident, the event, the sense' (DR 191/241). This claim is inseparable from his claim that Ideas 'perplicate' or interpenetrate one another (DR

187/236). At several points in his analysis, Deleuze likens the Idea of colour to white light (DR 182/230, 206/258), and the Idea of sound to white noise (DR 206/258). This is a reference to a discussion by Bergson of essence in his essay, 'The Life and Work of Ravaisson'. In this text, Bergson considers the question of determining what different colours have in common, and hence, how we are to think, philosophically, the notion of colour. In effect, we are therefore asking the question 'what is X?' for colour, the question Deleuze takes to be 'the question of essences' (DR 188/236). Now, according to Bergson, there are two ways of answering this question. The first is the traditional answer to the question of essences provided by Aristotle. In order to determine the essence of something, we abstract from it those properties that are inessential (or accidental), to arrive at purely those properties that every individual in the class has. Thus, 'we obtain this general idea of colour only by removing from the red that which makes it red, from the blue what makes it blue, from the green what makes it green' (Bergson 1992: 225). If we try to answer the question 'what is colour?' by this means, we end up with a concept that is abstract and empty, as we have proceeded 'by gradual extinction of the light which brought out the differences between the colours' (Bergson 1992: 225).

The alternative is what Deleuze takes up with his concept of perplication. Bergson suggests that rather than proceeding by abstraction, we proceed by

taking the thousand and one different shades of blue, violet, green, yellow and red, and passing them through a converging lens, bringing them to a single point. Then appears in all its radiance the pure white light which, perceived here below in the shades which disperse it, enclosed above, in its undivided unity, the indefinite variety of multicoloured rays. (Bergson 1992: 225)

Such an account can only be an analogy, as light is still seen in this case too much along the lines of actual phenomena, but it clarifies the interpenetrative notion of the Idea. Just as the conjunction of the two terms of the differential relation allow us to specify all of the points on a curve, the differentials of the Idea together specify all of the possible states of affairs that a given system can exhibit. Rather than achieving this by excluding what is non-essential, it does so by positively specifying the genetic conditions for each of these states. In this sense, for Deleuze, the Idea does not so much contain the essence of a state of affairs, as the grounds for the totality of possible accidents a system can exhibit. Depending on how the elements are related to one another, different states of affairs will be generated.

Clearly, if an Idea is to be understood as forming a multiplicity of interpenetrating elements, then it cannot have the same nature as states of affairs. Elements in states of affairs are determined in an opposite manner to the interpenetrative structure of perplication, namely by determining their limits (what they are not). Furthermore, we can see that just as problems were immanent to their solutions, the genetic conditions for states of affairs (Ideas) are simultaneous with states of affairs themselves. Thus, for Epicurus, atoms co-existed with the sensible objects that they constituted, and for Althusser, the mode of production co-existed with the actual relations that it determined. We thus have two series that differ in kind: actual events that occur within the world, and the ideal events of 'sections, ablations, adjunctions' that engender them (DR 188/237).

I want to jump ahead somewhat now, to introduce the related discussion of the Idea and possibility. We have already seen that the Idea can give rise to different actual situations; so, for instance, Geoffroy's unity of composition provides the rules for generating the anatomical structure of different animals, and Marx's mode of production gives the structure underlying different real social organisations. Deleuze defines the structure of the Idea as being *virtual*. Now, Deleuze introduces three claims about the nature of the virtual that need to be explored. It is 'real without being actual, differentiated without being differenciated, and complete without being entire' (DR 214/266). I want to go through these different claims, contrasting them with the structure of possibility, which appears at first glance to be a closely aligned concept. In fact, Deleuze claims that 'the only danger in all this is that the virtual could be confused with the possible' (DR 211/263).

What does it mean to say that the virtual is real without being actual? If we return to the notion of possibility, we can ask, what happens when something which is merely possible is realised? We can begin by following Kant in noting that there is no difference in structure between a possible object and a real object: 'A hundred real thalers do not contain the least coin more than a hundred possible thalers' (Kant 1929: A599/B629). Rather, the difference is purely in the existential status of the two objects. In order to distinguish a hundred real thalers from a hundred possible thalers, we need to note that the former exist whereas the latter do not. Possibility is therefore distinguished from actuality in terms of existence. Now, the virtual is instead 'Real without being actual, ideal without being abstract' (DR 208/260). Throughout this chapter, we have seen that Ideas are different in kind from actual states of affairs, just as differentials differ from actual numbers. In this sense, we do not need to distinguish possibility from actuality in terms of reality, as they can be distinguished by this difference in kind itself. More than this, however, the virtual is real to the extent that it provides the structure responsible for the genesis of the qualities we find in actual entities. 'The reality of the virtual is structure' (DR 209/260). It provides a complete account of the structure of the actual state of affairs that results from it, and is no less a real part of the object than the actual object itself. In this regard, Deleuze notes that it is 'complete without being entire' (DR 214/266). Deleuze's point is that the virtual does not rely on any reference to the actual, although in fact it is always found to be associated with the object which it engenders. In this sense, it escapes from the limitation of possibility we discussed in the previous chapter. There, we saw that the concept of possibility could not give us the sense of an object, because it merely reduplicated it at a higher transcendental level of analysis. As such, a possible object is not complete, since it is dependent on the notion of a real object to which we add the concept of non-being. The completeness of the virtual is thus what allows us to understand it as giving the sense of a proposition, even though it is not whole, since 'every object is double' (DR 209/261).

Finally, the virtual is differentiated without being differenciated. That is, it operates according to an entirely different procedure of determination to that of the possible. As Deleuze puts it, 'one [the possible] refers to the form of identity in the concept, whereas the other designates a pure multiplicity in the Idea which radically excludes the identical as a prior condition' (DR 211–12/263). We saw that Chapter 1 of *Difference and Repetition* deals at length with the claim that in order to determine something through the properties it possesses, we need some kind of concept of identity. This is because we describe an object by ascribing predicates to a subject (we differenciate it). The other procedure of determination generates structural properties by bringing into relation with each other elements which are in themselves undetermined (they are differentiated, in the sense of the differentials we looked at in 4.2). Deleuze characterises these two modes of organisation in terms of Leibniz's distinctions between the clear and confused, and the distinct and obscure. We saw in Chapter 1 that Leibniz's understanding of the world ultimately traces it back to the notion of possibility, as God chooses the best of all possible worlds. Nevertheless, in his claim that perception of spatio-temporal objects is a confused perception of conceptual relations, we have an important insight into the relationship between virtuality and actuality. In the *New Essays on Human Understanding*, Leibniz puts forward the claim that perception of objects is based upon microperceptions below the threshold of the senses. In support of this theory, he gives the following analogy:

> To give a clearer example of these minute perceptions which we are unable to pick out from the crowd, I like to use the example of the roaring noise of the sea which impresses itself on us when we are standing on the shore. To hear this noise as we do, we must hear the parts which make up this whole, that is the noise of each wave, although each of these little noises makes itself known only when combined confusedly with all the others, and would not be noticed if the wave which made it were by itself. (Leibniz 1997: 54)

Deleuze interprets this passage as presenting 'two languages which are encoded in the language of philosophy and directed at the divergent exercise of the faculties' (DR 214/266). On the one hand, we have the language of the roaring noise of the sea. This is the language of the clear-confused. It is clear, in so far as I am able recognise the roar of the sea as a whole and take it up as an object, but it is confused as I only do so in so far as I do not take account of the elements (the waves) which together determine it as an object. On the other hand, we have the language of the waves themselves, which is the language of the virtual, and of the distinct-obscure. If, on the contrary, we focus on the noise of the waves themselves, the waves are perceived distinctly, as we grasp the differential relations that make up the noise as a whole, but also obscurely, since our focus on these particular relations precludes our comprehension of the 'white noise' of the sea as a whole. In contrast to Descartes' notion of clear and distinct ideas, Deleuze's claim is that 'the clear is confused by itself, in so far as it is clear' (DR 254/316). It is this radical divergence between the two languages of philosophy that allows us to give the sense of a proposition, or the conditions of experience, without simply falling into a banal reiteration of the structure of actuality.

4.9 Learning and the Discord of the Faculties (188–97/237–47)

Now that we have an account of Ideas, we can return to two themes Deleuze introduces in Chapter 3 of *Difference and Repetition*: learning (3.10) and the relationship of the faculties (3.6). To explain why we need Ideas in order to learn, we can once again return to Plato and his conception of the hypothesis. When we looked at the simile of the divided line, we saw that Plato suggested two kinds of intelligible knowledge: mathematics and knowledge of the forms. He defines the difference between these two in the following terms:

In one subsection, the soul, using as images the things that were imitated before, is forced to investigate from hypotheses, proceeding not to a first principle but to a conclusion. In the other subsection, however, it makes its way to a first principle that is not a hypothesis, proceeding from a hypothesis but without the images used in the previous subsection, using forms themselves and making its investigation through them. (Plato 1997b: 510b)

The first form of thinking, that uses images, is mathematical thinking, as it is found in fields such as geometry (Euclid's *Elements* would be the archetypal example). In this case, thinking proceeds deductively to a conclusion. The strength and the limitation of a deductive argument, however, is that its conclusion does not contain anything that is not implicitly assumed in its premises. The most it can do is simply make explicit what we have assumed at the outset. For this reason, it is essential to know that the premises of one's argument are true, since it is from these that the argument gains its content, and validity. Philosophy traditionally, according to Deleuze, has therefore attempted to show that we can convert hypotheses into categorical statements by arguing from premises that are absolutely certain, either by invoking the Ideas, or by, in Descartes' case, positing certain concepts that are clear and distinct, and hence indubitable. Now, as we have seen, Plato understands the Ideas by analogy with objects of empirical recollection, and Descartes' clear and distinct ideas are fully transparent to consciousness. In both cases, therefore, we remain within the domain of consciousness and the proposition.

Deleuze opposes this kind of procedure to 'vice-diction', which, instead of moving between two propositions directly, moves from a proposition to an Idea and then to a solution. He sums up the two stages of the process of vice-diction as: 'the determination of the conditions of the problem and . . . the correlative genesis of cases of solution' (DR 190/239). The two examples Deleuze gives of learning in this context, learning to swim and learning a foreign language (DR 192/214), are both favourite examples of Bergson. Bergson's formulation of the swimming example is as follows:

> If we had never seen a man swim, we might say that swimming is an impossible thing, inasmuch as, to learn to swim, we must begin by holding ourselves up in the water and, consequently, already know how to swim. Reasoning, in fact, always nails us down to the solid ground. But if, quite simply, I throw myself into the water without fear, I may keep myself up well enough at first by merely struggling, and gradually adapt myself to the new environment: I shall thus have learnt to swim. So, in theory, there is a kind of absurdity in trying to know otherwise than by intelligence; but if the risk be frankly accepted, action will perhaps cut the knot that reasoning has tied and will not unloose. (Bergson 1998: 192)

Here we see the contrast between the two methods of learning. On a propositional account, learning to swim appears impossible, because thinking operates simply by drawing out what is already implicit in the axioms of thought. If I do not already know how to swim, I can never know. Deleuze's rather abstract analysis of the process of learning to swim or learning a language is that we do so by 'composing the singular points of one's own body or one's own language with those of another shape or element, which tears us apart but also propels us into a hitherto unknown and unheard-of world of problems' (DR 192/241). In order to escape the deductive sterility of the proposition, therefore, he claims that thinking needs to raise itself to the level of the Idea. The first stage of vice-diction is therefore that of finding other relevant cases that together specify the problem we are faced with, 'fragments of ideal future or past events' (DR 190/239). By 'discovering the adjuncts', Deleuze means this procedure of finding equivalent cases that emerge from the problem. As the Idea is an interpenetrative multiplicity, these elements must be combined to generate the Idea corresponding to the problem, just as the shades of light were passed through the convergent lens in Bergson's example. Once we have the Idea of the problem, we can attempt to find those singular points of the Idea where it engenders solutions that are different from the present state of affairs. Deleuze gives the example of Lenin's thought, which would involve the extraction from the present state of affairs of the Idea of the economic (abstract modes of production), and then the generation of a solution that involves a different conjunction of singularities (just as selecting a different plane of a conic section will give us a different curve). Thus, we move from the present society to the problematic genetic principles that give rise to it, and then back to an alternative solution, or form of society. In a similar way, we do not look at the relations between parts of animals directly, as they may have different functional roles, but instead relate each to the others through the transcendental rules for their production. Thinking thus does not go from proposition to proposition. Rather, thinking becomes creative by tracing back propositions to the non-propositional field of problems that engender them.

Learning does not have to involve simply moving from one empirical state to another via an Idea. It can also involve investigating Ideas themselves. So how do we relate to Ideas? Well, first, we can note that although we have been applying the terminology of problems and solutions to situations where the solution is understood in terms of knowledge (or learning), Deleuze's conception of problems and solutions is much broader than this. We will come back to this point later, but for now, we can note that even 'an organism is nothing if not the solution to a problem, as are each of its differenciated organs, such as the eye which solves the light "problem"' (DR 211/263). In this sense, as we have already seen, Ideas are not the pure concern of reason, but in fact, each faculty is concerned with them, in so far as it is capable of a transcendent exercise. We can see that each of the faculties themselves is a solution to a problem:

Take, for example, the linguistic multiplicity, regarded as a virtual system of reciprocal connections between 'phonemes' which is incarnated in the actual terms and relations of diverse languages: such a multiplicity renders possible speech as a faculty as well as the transcendent object of that speech, that 'metalanguage' which cannot be spoken in the empirical usage of a given language, but must be spoken and can be spoken only in the poetic usage of speech coextensive with virtuality. (DR 193/242–3)

In this case, the faculty of speech is rendered possible by the virtual multiplicity, which gives the rules for actual speech production. If we relate the structure of speech to the Idea, we can see that it contains each of its moments. The phonemes are undetermined, but able to enter into determinable relations. These relations describe the expressiveness of the language. In turn, an individual speech act corresponds to the integration of this field of expressions. There is a reciprocity here, however, since the multiplicity is constituted in terms of the differential relations between phonemes because it is related to the field of a given language ('each dialectical problem is duplicated by a symbolic field in which it is expressed' [DR 179/227]). So the constitution of the faculty of speech (the solution) in turn determines the virtual multiplicity (problem) relative to it. 'The transcendental form of a faculty is indistinguishable from its disjointed, superior, or transcendent exercise' (DR 143/180). In this sense, each of the faculties is an Idea as well as a relation to an Idea.

We have already seen that each faculty communicates violence to the others, to the extent that they communicate in terms of objects that differ in kind. Thus, the object of sensation differed in kind from the object of memory, but yet was able to enter into a relationship with it. What is it that allows these faculties to communicate? Well, once we recognise that each of the faculties has its own transcendent object, because their objects are 'express[ed] technically in the domain of solutions to which they give rise' (DR 179/227), it becomes simple to explain how they can communicate with one another, yet still be distinct. On an empirical level, each faculty is distinct, as each has its own set of objects (both transcendent and empirical). While each of the faculties contains a difference between empirical and transcendental exercises, this is only the first degree of difference. The 'second degree' of difference is where each of these faculties is in turn the solution to the problem of pure difference:

This harmonious Discord seemed to us to correspond to that Difference which by itself articulates or draws together. There is thus a point at which thinking, speaking, imagining, feeling, etc., are one and the same thing, but that *thing* affirms only the divergence of the faculties in their transcendent exercise. (DR 193–4/243)

Each faculty is therefore the expression of an Idea, Difference itself being the Idea of an Idea. In this way, each of the faculties is both the same as, and different from, the others (what Deleuze calls para-sense as opposed to common sense, because it escapes the structure of representation). While all of the faculties relate to Ideas, it is still the case that thought is in some sense superior to the other faculties. If we take speech, then we can see that it is constituted in terms of phonemes. The elements that constitute thought, however, are Ideas themselves. Thought is thus the Idea of Ideas, and relates the other faculties. Thus, 'while the opposition between thought and all forms of common sense remains stronger than ever, Ideas must be called "differentials" of thought, or the "Unconscious" of pure thought' (DR 194/244).

4.10 The Origin of Ideas (195–202/244–52)

We are now in a position to ask what the origin of Ideas themselves is. Deleuze begins by noting that what we have encountered so far is a reorientation of the nature of a problem. Rather than a problem being seen as a purely subjective matter, we have seen that exploring the nature of the problem is a properly ontological or metaphysical matter. Thus, as he has noted, the organism can be seen as a solution to a problem. In fact, the question-problem complex is 'the only instance to which, properly speaking, Being answers without the question thereby becoming lost or overtaken' (DR 195/244).

What, therefore, is the relationship between a problem and a question? Deleuze presents his answer in the following manner: 'Problems or Ideas emanate from imperatives of adventure or from events which appear in the form of questions' (DR 197/247). Such an imperative would be the kind of encounter that we discussed in the previous chapter, paralleling Socrates' discovery of the incommensurability of his categories of thought (the large, the small) with the purely relative determinations found within the world of becoming. Rather than operating in terms of contrary properties, however, the encounter for Deleuze is tied to the eruption into the field of representation of a moment of intensity. In the discussion of the fractured I in Chapter 2 (2.6), we saw that representation was subject to a natural illusion that the 'I' had a substantive nature. Deleuze's claim was instead that the 'I' could be traced back to a pre-individual field of intensive difference. As we saw in relation to Blanchot however (2.12), this illusion to which representation is prone is perpetually threatened by the disruptive influence of intensity. For this reason, Deleuze makes the claim that 'Ideas swarm in the fracture, constantly emerging on its edges, ceaselessly coming out and going back, being composed in a thousand different manners' (DR 169/216). These encounters with intensity raise the faculties to a transcendental operation, and hence allow them to engage with Ideas. Questions map this relationship between the encounter with intensity and the problematic unground responsible for it. As such, 'questions express the relation between problems and the imperatives from which they proceed' (DR 197/247). So far, therefore, the account provided by Deleuze parallels the Platonic account quite closely. Whereas for Plato, Deleuze claims, this process leads to a ground in an apodictic principle, for Deleuze, it instead leads to an unground in the problem. This difference between grounds and ungrounds ultimately simply relates to the fact that apodictic principles have the same structure as the system of propositions they ground (they are amenable to the structure of judgement). On the contrary, the problem differs in kind from the solutions it engenders. As such, it cannot ground solutions by providing a principle that we know to be true, because truth is a function of judgement, and the problem is different in kind to judgements. Thus, rather than a ground, it serves as an 'unground', destabilising the vision of the world as amenable to judgement in its entirety. Rather than invoking 'the moral imperative of predetermined rules' (DR 198/248), Deleuze instead therefore invokes the notion of the dice throw and decision:

> It is rather a question of a throw of the dice, of the whole sky as open space and of throwing as the only rule. The singular points are on the die; the questions are the dice themselves; the imperative is to throw. Ideas are the problematic combinations which result from throws. (DR 198/248)

The imperative is the problematic instance within the state of affairs (the throw), that points beyond itself, through the question (the dice itself), to the problem that engenders the state of affairs and the problematic instance itself (the combination on the die). The Ideas result from this process as the result of our going beyond the state of affairs to find its conditions. The remaining moment of the analogy to explain is the significance of the points on the dice themselves. We can explain this by introducing the moment of decision. As we saw in the first case of learning, we move to the sub-representational level by combining 'adjunct fields', or similar cases, to reach the problem (in Bergson's example, we relate walking to swimming). Now, depending on which cases we combine to form the problem, our understanding of it will differ. How we relate together different encounters, and which encounters we relate, will give a different emphasis to the problem (a different set of singularities), and hence to our Ideas. If the relation of different adjunct fields gives us different Ideas, then how is it that a given throw is able to 'affirm the whole of chance' (to provide an objective Idea) (DR 198/248)? When we looked at the example of the conic section (4.7), we saw that depending on how we took a section on the cone, we would derive a different curve, and with it, a different set of singularities. Each of these curves was, nonetheless, an objective characterisation of the cone. In a similar way, each enquiry gives us an objective problem, but these are not exclusive, since different enquiries will take a different section of the cone, and hence derive different singularities.

This is the reason why in spite of each throw being an objective constitution of the problem, 'there are nevertheless several throws of the dice: the throw of the dice is repeated' (DR 200/251). In this sense, there is no ultimate characterisation possible, as there would be with knowledge, but rather a whole series of questions, each of which generates its own field of singularities. Each philosophical enquiry therefore puts forth its own question, on the basis of an imperative, which constitutes its own field of singularities. Remaining true to the encounter does not, therefore, lead us to one apodictic principle, but rather to an objective organisation of a problem. Just as each conic section gives us a different curve, each question gives us a different distribution of singularities. But as each conic section also repeats the structure of the others, each question is also a repetition, albeit a repetition that differs, not just in terms of solutions, but also in terms of its Ideas: 'Repetition is this emission of singularities, always with an echo or resonance which makes each the double of the other, or each constellation the redistribution of another' (DR 201/251). At this point, Deleuze notes an affinity with Heidegger's emphasis on the question, while also cautioning that the emphasis on one single question risks covering over the real structure of the dice throw:

Great authors of our time (Heidegger, Blanchot) have exploited this most profound relation between the question and repetition. Not that it is sufficient, however, to repeat a single question which would remain intact at the end, even if this question is 'What is being?' [*Qu'en est-il de l'etre?*]. (DR 200/251)

4.11 The Origin of Negation (202–4/253–5, 206–8/257–60)

We have seen that from the beginning of *Difference and Repetition*, Deleuze has claimed that the existence of the negative is an illusion. Now that we have the theory of Ideas, we can give a fuller account of the origin of negation, which will once again rest on a confusion between seeing transcendental problems and empirical solutions. As Deleuze writes, 'There is a non-being which is by no means the being of the negative, but rather the being of the problematic. The symbol for this (non)-being or ?-being is 0/0' (DR 202/253). The problematic is therefore non-being in the sense that it is not extensive being, in the same way that the differential was not actual (it did not have a magnitude) without on that basis not existing (it was, in Wronski's terms, an intensive quantity). As we have seen, Deleuze takes problems to be interpenetrative multiplicities which determine all possible actual states of the object. In this sense, the problem does not contain any negation. Learning and solving problems involve a move from the actual state of affairs to the Idea and back again to a different possible solution. They thus involve differentiation to determine the Idea followed by differenciation to reach an alternative solution. Now, as Deleuze notes, 'the negative appears neither in the process of differentiation nor in the process of differenciation' (DR 207/258). We can see that differentiation does not lead us to posit the negative, as differentiation involves contracting together actual states of affairs to form an affirmation. Similarly, differenciation is the process whereby we extract a state of affairs from the Idea, and as such is also an affirmation of the Idea. How does negation therefore occur? Once again, Deleuze's answer is that it is the result of taking the problem to be structured like a proposition. To make this clear, we can turn to another example from Bergson:

> If I choose a volume in my library at random, I may put it back on the shelf after glancing at it and say, 'This is not verse.' Is this what I have really seen in turning over the leaves of the book? Obviously not. I have not seen, I never shall see, an absence of verse. I have seen prose. But as it is poetry I want, I express what I find as a function of what I am looking for, and instead of saying, 'This is prose,' I say, 'This is not verse.' In the same way, if the fancy takes me to read prose, and I happen on a volume of verse, I shall say, 'This is not prose,' thus expressing the data of my perception, which shows me verse, in the language of my expectation and attention, which are fixed on the idea of prose and will hear of nothing else. (Bergson 1998: 221)

In this case, we have a simple failure of expectations, in so far as our characterisation of the problem fails to conform to the nature of the problem itself. '"That is not the case" means that a hypothesis passes over into the negative in so far as it does not represent the currently fulfilled conditions of a problem, to which, on the contrary, another proposition corresponds' (DR 206/257). Determining the nature of the problem is a part of learning, and so, 'a problem is always reflected in *false problems* while it is being solved, so that the solution is generally perverted by an inseparable falsity' (DR 207–8/259). Once we understand the problem itself in terms of propositions, however, the negation, which really just captures the incomplete grasp of the problem, becomes an ontological feature of the world. If we understand a problem as just a collection of cases that are possible solutions, then, 'each of these hypotheses [becomes] flanked by a double negative: whether the One is, whether the One is not . . . whether it is fine, whether it is not fine' (DR 202/253). Because the problem is now understood in the same terms as the solution, we cannot help but give a genuine existence to the negation that appears to subsist in the solution.

> Now, if Mons. Jourdain heard me, he would infer, no doubt, from my two exclamations that prose and poetry are two forms of language reserved for books, and that these learned forms have come and overlaid a language which was neither prose nor verse. Speaking of this thing which is neither verse nor prose, he would suppose, moreover, that he was thinking of it: it would be only a pseudoidea, however. (Bergson 1998: 221)

As Deleuze notes, at the heart of the issue is the claim that opposition and limitation are interchangeable (DR 203/253), or in other words, that negation (this is not that) is the way in which something is determined. It should be noted that the issue here is not one of whether negation actually exists, but of the determination of the problematic, regardless of whether this determination is taken to be real or logical. Central to this critique is therefore a different theory of determination that operates through the reciprocal determination of differentials, rather than determining objects (either real or conceptual) through limitation and negation. Negation thus only appears when we understand all determination as determination through opposition: 'Forms of the negative do indeed appear in actual terms and real relations, but only in so far as these are cut off from the virtuality which they actualise, and from the movement of their actualisation' (DR 207/258).

4.12 Actualisation (214–21/266–74)

If we understand the grounds of actual objects to be some kind of possibility, then clearly we will have no problem explaining why the actual object has the properties that it has, since these would be already mapped out in the structure of the possible. In actual fact, however, this turns out to be a drawback of this kind of account, since, if the only difference between the possible and the actual is the fact of existence, then it becomes difficult to explain the *development* of the possible into the actual. 'We are forced to conceive of existence as a brute eruption, a pure act or leap which always occurs behind our backs and is subject to a law of all or nothing' (DR 211/263). For Deleuze, there is no problem explaining *that* development takes place, but he needs to show how the distinct-obscure structure of the virtual becomes actualised in the clear-confused structure of actual relations. This is accomplished by a process called dramatisation, which involves the folding of spaces, and processes operating at differential rates. In Chapter 4, Deleuze sketches out this process from the perspective of the Idea. As we shall see in the next chapter, however, an account in terms of the Idea alone is inadequate, and a full account will require an understanding of the role that intensity plays.

As we have seen, Deleuze is interested in the conditions of production of actual objects and relations. In discussing the process of actualisation, he focuses on the science of embryology, which also deals with the genesis of forms and relations. When we look at an egg, we see that it develops from a completely undifferenciated form into one encompassing the various qualities that characterise its species. As we saw with Geoffroy's transcendental anatomy, his claim was that only by looking at the unity of composition governing two animals, and the way this is actualised, can we determine how different parts were actualised in different organisms. Deleuze notes that we can equally make this point about the egg itself: 'Take a division into 24 cellular elements endowed with similar characteristics: nothing yet tells us the dynamic process by which it was obtained $-2 \times 12, (2 \times 2) + (2 \times 10)$, or $(2 \times 4) + (2 \times 8) \dots$?' (DR 216/268). In fact, Deleuze uses embryology to provide a more general model of actualisation. He delineates the various stages of the process as follows: 'The world is an egg, but the egg itself is a theatre: a staged theatre in which the roles dominate the actors, the spaces dominate the roles and the Ideas dominate the spaces' (DR 216/269). 'Spaces' here does not refer to actual spaces that we might measure, but rather to what Deleuze calls 'spatio-temporal dynamisms' (DR 214/266).

When we look at the development of a cell into an organism, we can note that the cell itself appears to have none of the properties we would associate with the organism it develops into. If we are to understand its development, we cannot see it as a 'heap' of atoms and molecules, since this would obscure the nature of the processes that the embryo undergoes. Rather, Deleuze suggests, in line with work in embryology, that we should see the embryo as developing through a series of transformations of its surfaces that simultaneously constitute the parts of the organism. Thus, we can view the development of the organism as involving 'the augmentation of free surfaces, stretching of cellular layers, invagination by folding, regional displacement of groups' (DR 214/266). This process is governed by a 'kinematics' specified by the Idea. As Deleuze notes, this kinematics differs from the possible movements of the developed organism, as the embryo is capable of transformations that are simply not possible for a developed organism. What Deleuze is suggesting here is that we are confronted with a process that cannot be understood in terms of cause and effect operating on a collection of atoms. Rather, the appropriate model is that of a drama, or in Ruyer's terms, a sociology of development, where we understand the interactions between the elements in terms of the roles that they play, or the relations that they hold with other elements within the embryo:

There is definitely, we shall see, a possible sociology of organic forms and their development, provided we give the word 'society' its true meaning, and don't understand by 'society' a simple juxtaposition of individuals. A society in general always implies that the individuals that compose it follow a series of themes of coordination, and they know how to play their 'roles' in various stimuli-situations; 'roles' that do not arise automatically, like the effect of a cause, the sole spatial situation of the individual in the social whole. We cannot dispel the mystery of differenciation by making it the effect of differences in situation produced by equal divisions. These differences are of stimuli and not of causes. (Ruyer 1958: 91)

These dynamisms are not purely spatial, however, and Deleuze takes up Geoffroy's suggestion that the differences between organisms can be understood by the relative speeds of the different processes that operate within the embryo. As such, the embryo constitutes its own time, which is defined by the differential relations of these processes. In fact, as Deleuze suggests, because we are talking about relationships between distances and time, at the level of the spatio-temporal dynamism, we cannot separate the dimensions of space and time themselves:

Consider the following example, concerning sterility and fecundity (in the case of the female sea-urchin and the male annelid): *problem* – will certain paternal chromosomes be incorporated into new nuclei, or will they be dispersed into the protoplasm? *question* – will they arrive soon enough? (DR 217/270)

Thus, the process operates at a level prior to the constitution of the extensive field of space and time. Furthermore, this process operates on two levels simultaneously. We have the generation of the organism as an instance of a species (what Deleuze calls the element of qualitability), and on the level of the parts (the element of quantitability [DR 221/274]). Differenciation is therefore a process that generates both the extensive characteristics of the organism (its size) and the qualities it possesses. The process of cellular development therefore plays the same role in the world as integration of differentials plays in the sphere of mathematics. In both cases, they explain how we are able to move between two states that are different in kind. In the final chapter of *Difference and Repetition*, Deleuze will look at this account from the perspective of intensity, to give an account of how Ideas are 'dramatised', or played out in a field of intensity.

Chapter 5. The Asymmetrical Synthesis of the Sensible

5.1 Introduction

The final chapter of *Difference and Repetition* shares much in common with Chapter 2. There, we saw Deleuze arguing that representation tended to falsify our understanding of time by relating it to the structures of common sense. Deleuze instead presented an account of time that grounded (or rather, ungrounded) it in a field of intensive difference. Chapter 5 turns to the nature of space. Deleuze notes that difference *is* connected to intensity in the branch of science known as energetics, or thermodynamics. As we shall see, Deleuze's claim is that because thermodynamics sees the world in terms of systems that are already constituted (good sense and common sense), it is subject to the transcendental illusion that differences in energy or intensity tend to be cancelled out. This is what leads to Boltzmann's famous hypothesis that the end of the universe will be a form of 'heat death', where all of its energy is homogeneously distributed, thus making any kind of order impossible. For this reason, Deleuze focuses in this chapter on the role of intensity in constituting systems and the space that they occupy. Recognising this moment gives us a more positive account of intensity. In the process, Deleuze clarifies how the differential model of Ideas that we looked at in the last chapter can be related to the field of intensive difference that Deleuze introduced in opposition to Aristotelian metaphysics.

5.2 Thermodynamics and Transcendental Illusion (222–9/280–8)

Deleuze opens Chapter 5 with a discussion of thermodynamics. As the name suggests, thermodynamics deals fundamentally with the properties of heat. As a modern science, it originated with Carnot's publication of his *Reflections on the Motive Power of Fire* in 1824. Carnot's aim in this paper was to explore the relationship between temperature and the efficiency of engines. His main discovery was that the efficiency of even an ideal frictionless engine was dependent on the difference between its hottest and coldest parts: the greater the difference, the greater the efficiency. Thermodynamics as a discipline emerged prior to the general acceptance of atomic theory, and as such makes few assumptions about the composition or specific mechanisms in operation within the systems it considers. This means that it can be applied to a variety of different types of systems, and as Deleuze suggests, its agnosticism as regards the actual processes of heat transfer means that it is relatively easy to take its specific physical claims as providing 'local manifestations of a transcendental principle' (DR 223/281). In this section, I want to explore Deleuze's engagement with thermodynamics by looking at three questions. First, what is the transcendental principle that thermodynamics embodies? Second, why does this transcendental principle reinforce rather than overturn good sense? And third, why does Deleuze consider this transcendental principle to be a transcendental illusion?

The transcendental principle of thermodynamics rests on the second law of thermodynamics. This is, in Clausius' formulation, the claim that 'heat does not pass from a body at low temperature to one at high temperature without an accompanying change elsewhere' (Atkins 2010: 42). Now, this statement rests on a central insight by Carnot that, when we look at a system, the work that the system is able to do is not dependent on the heat entering the system, but rather on the *difference* between the temperature entering the system and the temperature leaving the system. Thus, if we wished to improve the efficiency of, say, a steam engine, we could do this either by increasing the temperature of the steam that powers it, or alternatively we could reduce the temperature of the environment surrounding the generator (although only the first of these alternatives is in general really practical). The important implication of this is that what allows work to be done by a system is not intensity (temperature in this case), but rather difference in intensity (and in fact Deleuze makes the stronger claim that 'intensity is difference' [DR

223/281]). Carnot's work shows that if the input and output energies of an engine were equal, the efficiency of the engine would drop to zero. Thus, difference is fundamentally implicated in 'everything which happens and everything which appears' (DR 222/280). In line with Deleuze's distinction between the transcendental and the empirical, Deleuze draws from this the principle that 'every phenomenon flashes in a signal-sign system' (DR 222/280). Just as the difference in the intensity of temperature gives rise to work, Deleuze's claim is that more generally, differences in intensity manifest themselves as qualities in the phenomenal world. If this were the final result of thermodynamics, then clearly it would provide a model of physics commensurate with Deleuze's metaphysics. Deleuze claims, however, that thermodynamics betrays its own principle of difference through the introduction of entropy, and the concomitant equalisation of differences.

If we return to Carnot's engine, we can see that useful work cannot be done with total efficiency by the engine (except in the impossible situation of a difference between absolute zero and an infinite temperature). What happens to the heat that isn't converted into work by the engine? Well, this energy is introduced into the output reservoir as heat (just as a steam engine heats the environment as well as moving the train). Thus, in the process of doing work, the system reduces the difference between the two temperatures. It is possible to reverse this process within the system itself by doing work (a refrigerator, for instance, is able to reduce the temperature of objects placed within it), but this work itself will not be totally efficient. We can see this in the case of the refrigerator if we take into account its environment. In order to create a temperature differential, it requires a flow of energy from outside of it. So while the refrigerator allows heat to flow from bodies at low temperature to bodies at higher temperatures, this is only as a result of an interaction with its environment whereby energy is supplied to it by equalising a temperature differential elsewhere (the power station, for instance). In this case, a temperature differential is maintained in the system because the system exchanges heat with its environment (it is what is known as an open system); but if we look at the universe as a whole as a system, we can see that in this case, there is no further environment with which it can exchange energy (it is a closed system). Now, given the first law of thermodynamics, which states that there is a fixed quantity of energy in the world, then, over time, as various processes in the universe do work, more energy will be lost as heat as a result of inefficiency. Eventually, the differences in intensity that make work possible will themselves be equalised by this loss of heat, leading to what Boltzmann called the 'heat death' of the universe, as it becomes a homogeneous field of constant temperature. This, according to thermodynamics, is what gives the 'arrow of time' a direction: time only moves in one direction because certain processes are irreversible.

Deleuze relates this result to the structures of good sense and common sense. As we saw, common sense refers to the indeterminate structures of the subject and the object. Now, we never actually encounter indeterminate objects, but rather a field of objects, each with diverse properties. It was good sense that related these various properties together into a hierarchy, such as the tree of Porphyry, affirming their ordered relation to the object as an instance of an object in general. Here, thermodynamics provides a physical instance of this process. If the properties of objects are defined by differences in intensity, then thermodynamics shows that over time, these differences, and hence the properties they sustain, will be cancelled out. The heat death of the universe, with its model of total homogeneity, is the final affirmation of the true nature of the world as grounded in indeterminate subjects and objects, despite the transient appearance of diversity that appears to signal otherwise.

> [Good sense] ensures the distribution of that difference in such a manner that it tends to be cancelled in the object, and because it provides a rule according to which the different objects tend to equalise themselves and the different Selves tend to become uniform, good sense in turn points towards the instance of a common sense which provides it with both the form of a universal Self and that of an indeterminate object. (DR 226/285)

Thus, organised systems tend to fall into disorder over time as the intensive differences that allow structure and useful work to take place give way to a disordered field lacking in any organising differences in intensity.

Finally, why is this model considered by Deleuze to be a transcendental illusion? As Deleuze notes, the theory of thermodynamics is a partial truth, but it becomes a transcendental illusion when we attach 'the feeling of the absolute to [this] partial [truth]' (DR 226/284). This partial truth operates within the framework of 'forms of energy which are already localised and distributed in extensity, or extensities already qualified by forms of energy' (DR 223/281). As such, it assumes the differences in intensity as already given as preformed. What is missing from the thermodynamic model is an account of the genesis of these intensive differences in the first place, and their localisation in particular regions of extensity (space). As Deleuze puts it, 'perhaps good sense even presupposes madness in order to come after and correct what madness there is in any prior distribution' (DR 224/283). Stewart and Cohen argue similarly in their study of complexity theory that the classical model of thermodynamics works well for the kinds of systems its inventors were interested in (Stewart and Cohen 2000: 258). These situations were where we have an individuated, isolated system that is brought into interaction with another system (the engine being brought into relation with its environment, or in Boltzmann's classic example, the mixing of two gasses). In these cases, the amount of disorder increases because the number of systems has reduced, just as 'a children's party with ten children is far more chaotic than two parties with five each' (Stewart and Cohen 2000: 258). If we move away from the mechanical models of the nineteenth century, we find that frequently systems are not just put into relation to their environment, but are also capable of isolating themselves from this environment. Life, for instance, is a process of individuation whereby new systems emerge, and with this emergence, decrease the amount of entropy present in the world:

The features that are of interest when studying steam engines, however, are not particularly appropriate to the study of life . . . For systems such as these, the thermodynamic model of independent subsystems whose interactions switch on and off is simply not relevant. The features of thermodynamics either don't apply, or are so long-term that they don't model anything interesting. (Stewart and Cohen 2000: 259)

While thermodynamics provides an account of processes affecting pre-constituted systems, qualities and extensities, it does not account for the emergence of these systems, qualities and extensities in the first place. Much of the remainder of the chapter will attempt to show how intensity is central to this process of constitution.

5.3 Merleau-Ponty and Depth (229–32/288–91, 241–4/302–5)

If we are to explain the constitution of systems, Deleuze claims, then we cannot do so *within* space or extensity. Rather, we need to explain the genesis of space as well as the systems it contains. We have already seen in Chapter 2 that for Kant the intuition of time was given *to* a subject.

As such, an account of the emergence of the subject within time was rendered impossible. Deleuze makes a similar point here about space. So long as space is seen purely as an 'anticipation of perception' (DR 231/291), the subject will be seen as given. With the subject comes the constituted realm of qualities, as well as 'the high and the low, the right and the left, the figure and the ground' (DR 229/288) as structures that show themselves for a subject. In Chapter 2, Deleuze introduced the notion of a passive synthesis, that is, a synthesis that constituted a subject rather than presupposing one. Just as there were three syntheses of time, so there are three spatial syntheses. When we looked at the notion of entropy in the previous section, we noted that the system of differences of intensities constituted an arrow of time. This arrow moved from particular, ordered systems to generalised, disordered systems. This directionality from the particular to the general forms a rough analogue of the first temporal synthesis of habit. The second spatial synthesis will give an account of how a horizon of intensive depth constitutes the qualities and localised intensities presupposed by thermodynamics. This synthesis can be equated with the synthesis of memory. Finally, just as there was a third synthesis of time in terms of the pure intensity of the eternal return, there is a third spatial synthesis of pure depth as intensity. In this section, I want to go through the second and third of these syntheses.

In section 1.11, we saw how for Merleau-Ponty, forgetfulness of the perspectivism of our experience led us to posit a world of objects. Within this world, objects were understood in terms of their relationships with other objects, that is, the distances they held to their surroundings. As such, we cannot explain the nature of constituted objects without also explaining the possibility of these distance relations: we need an explanation of space. In this regard, Merleau-Ponty's analysis of depth is central. As he notes, traditionally depth has been considered to be different from the other dimensions of height and breadth. Whereas those dimensions are directly perceivable by us, depth is imperceptible. If we take a naive view of painting, we can see a painting as presenting a number of signs that allow us to reconstruct a three-dimensional space on the basis of the two dimensions given by its surface (lines that converge to a point in the painting are used to recreate lines that remain parallel in space itself, more boldly coloured objects are taken to be closer to the viewer, etc.). On this reading, which Merleau-Ponty notes is the foundation of Renaissance painting (Merleau-Ponty 1964: 174), depth would be a construction on the basis of extensive magnitudes that *are* visible to us.

'Depth is a *third* dimension derived from the other two' (Merleau-Ponty 1964: 172). Merleau-Ponty's claim about this form of understanding of depth is that, while it recognises the perspectival nature of our experience, this perspectivism ultimately sees perspective as a subjective feature of our representations of an objective and pre-existing spatiality:

> What I call depth is in reality a juxtaposition of points, making it comparable to breadth. I am simply badly placed to see it. I should see it if I were in the position of a spectator looking on from the side, who can take in at a glance the series of objects spread out in front of me, whereas for me they conceal each other – or see the distance from my body to the first object, whereas for me this distance is compressed into a point . . . For God, who is everywhere, breadth is immediately equivalent to depth. (Merleau-Ponty 1962: 255)

While representation attempts to derive the field of depth from the two given dimensions, thus characterising depth itself as an axis of extended space, Merleau-Ponty reverses this procedure. That is, rather than seeing depth as derived from the given dimensions, he sees it as that by which the given dimensions of extensity are given to us. Depth is not merely breadth seen from another angle, but rather is something different in kind that, by making possible a field of autonomous but interrelated objects, also makes possible the system of extensive distances taken as foundational by representation.

> Once depth is understood in this way, we can no longer call it a third dimension. In the first place, if it were a dimension, it would be the first one; there are forms and definite planes only if it is stipulated how far from me their different parts are. But a *first* dimension that contains all the others is no longer a dimension, at least in the ordinary sense of a *certain relationship* according to which we make measurements. Depth thus understood is, rather, the experience of the reversibility of dimensions, of a global 'locality' – everything in the same place at the same time, a locality from which height, width, and depth are abstracted, of a voluminosity we express when we say that a thing is *there*. (Merleau-Ponty 1964: 180)

As Merleau-Ponty notes, this primordial depth here is no longer simply a 'container' for objects and qualities which are found within it. A consequence of this is that the genesis of quality and the genesis of space can no longer be seen as two separate projects: 'We must seek space and its content *as* together' (Merleau-Ponty 1964: 180). In 'Eye and Mind', he makes the claim that the enigma of depth is one of the primary inspirations of modern painting, and takes the work of Paul Klee and Paul

Cézanne as exemplary of the new project of showing 'how the things become things, how the world becomes world' (Merleau-Ponty 1964: 181).

This process by which a primordial depth is expressed in the form of qualities and extensions is, for Deleuze, the second spatial synthesis. 'Depth as the (ultimate and original) heterogeneous dimension is the matrix of all extensity, including its third dimension considered to be homogeneous with the other two' (DR 229/288). In a move that goes beyond Merleau-Ponty, he equates this non-extensive depth with intensity ('Depth is the intensity of being, or vice-versa' [DR, 231/290]). Now, we can note that while in the first thermodynamic synthesis, intensity was localised, in this second synthesis, intensity is rather that which allows localisation to take place – it is a horizon that allows things and qualities to be constituted. It is therefore responsible for four features of the spatial world: *extensio*, as the individual distances between objects; the *extensum*, as the three dimensions of space themselves (the frame of reference for the *extensio*); *qualitas*, as the milieu of intensive differences recognised by thermodynamics as responsible for the appearance of qualities; and *quale*, as these qualities themselves. Just as there were three temporal syntheses, here there are three spatial syntheses. The third synthesis of time was the pure form of time, prior to its expression in habit or memory. Deleuze describes the third spatial synthesis as 'space as a whole, but space as an intensive quantity: the pure *spatium*' (DR 230/289). While the second synthesis provides an account of the process by which intensity as depth generates the three dimensions (the explication of extensity), Deleuze notes that the fact that depth is different in kind from the dimensions it constitutes means that it is 'definable independently of extensity' (DR 230/289). The third spatial synthesis therefore goes beyond Merleau-Ponty's phenomenological account by considering intensity independently of this process of the constitution of perspective.

Just as Deleuze equated the third synthesis of time with the eternal return (2.8), in so far as it presented us with the pure field of intensity that gave rise to the two modes of temporality, the third spatial synthesis is also equated with the eternal return. Once again, as we saw in Chapter 2, Deleuze makes the point that the eternal return is not to be seen as something like the Platonic doctrine of an actual circularity of time, with a concomitant replication of a prior state of affairs. Rather than the eternal return being the claim that 'things revolve' (DR 241/302), depth is precisely what is responsible for the constitution of things, and hence must be prior to them. Thus, 'things must be dispersed within difference, and their identity must be dissolved before they become subject to eternal return and to identity in the eternal return' (DR 241/302). If we are to think the unground from which things emerge, this unground cannot be thought in terms of things without leading to an infinite regress.

These three syntheses therefore explain why for Deleuze the increase in entropy proposed by thermodynamics is a transcendental illusion. Thermodynamics notes that intensive differences that we find already constituted and located in a spatial milieu tend to equalise themselves, but such an account only gives us half the picture. What is missing is the account given by the second and third syntheses whereby the extensive magnitudes thermodynamics presupposes, and with them the systems of intensive differences, are constituted. This presupposition that extensity is already constituted in effect rules out any consideration of these syntheses, thus leading to the transcendental illusion that intensive difference can only be equalised, but not constituted. The thought of depth is the thought of the eternal return because it is the thought of a field of intensity that is not cancelled by the laws of entropy. In fact, Deleuze claims that the eternal return is the thought of that which gives rise to the laws of nature, mirroring his analysis of repetition we looked at in the introduction (0.2). In the next section, we will address an issue brought up by this third synthesis. While we may have an understanding of intensity operating within extensive space (the difference in temperature between two locations, for instance), what does Deleuze mean by intensity defined independently of extension?

5.4 The Three Characteristics of Intensity (232–40/291–300)

So what are the characteristics we find in intensity? We can see that the kind of spatio-temporally localised intensity dealt with by thermodynamics differs from extensity. Whereas adding two extensities just gives us an area equal in size to the two original areas, combining two liquids at different temperatures leads them to instead reach an average temperature, for instance. Similarly, intensity understood prior to its location in extensity will have different characteristics to extensity itself. Deleuze's presentation here focuses on the difference in the way elements relate to one another in intensity and extensity, and the nature of the elements themselves, but his aim is to show that the nature of the *extensum* and the *spatium* as a whole are radically different. While his presentation focuses on the mathematics of cardinal and ordinal numbers, in the background of this discussion is Bergson's account of two multiplicities. Deleuze claims that intensity has 'three characteristics' (DR 232/291). These are that it 'includes the unequal in itself' (DR 232/291), it 'affirms difference' (DR 234/293), and it 'is an implicated, enveloped, or "embryonised" quantity' (DR 237/297). In this section, I want to go through these three characteristics.

In what sense does intensity 'include the unequal in itself'? To explain this point, I will follow the analysis provided by DeLanda (2002: 73–4). As we have seen, one of the key differences between intensive and extensive quantities is that the latter can be added without changing their nature. As Deleuze notes, this difference reflects one of the key features of extensive magnitudes: that they can be measured numerically, and that these measurements are comparable (or commensurate) with one another. Now, if we look just at the natural numbers (0, 1, 2, 3 . . .), we find that frequently we come across magnitudes that cannot be expressed in these terms. For instance, provided we remain with the natural numbers, we cannot divide 7 by 2, as the result is not itself a natural number. The obvious solution to this difficulty is to introduce another order of numbers that does allow us to relate these two quantities to each other, in this case, fractions. Similarly, we will discover that fractions do not allow all quantities to be related to one another, leading to the instigation of a new order of numbers: real numbers (such as √2 or π). In each case, we have an incommensurability between quantities that cannot be cancelled within the order of numbers themselves, but only by instigating a new order of numbers. As Deleuze notes, as well as proceeding from natural numbers to fractions and real numbers, we can also ask if there is an order from which natural numbers themselves proceed. Now, we can make a distinction between cardinal numbers (one, two, three . . .) and ordinal numbers (first, second, third . . .). Whereas cardinal numbers can be constructed out of basic numerical units, and so we can construct identities between them (for instance, that the difference between one and three is equal to the difference between two and four), ordinal numbers just give us a sequence without requiring that the difference between the elements is the same in each case (thus, the difference between first and third does not have to be the same as the difference between second and fourth). Now, in a technical sense, we *can* talk about distance in relation to ordinal numbers, in that they form an ordered sequence, but these distances are not metric or measurable distances as they would be for cardinal numbers. Without ordinal numbers presupposing a basic metric unit, the kinds of operations we can perform with cardinal, natural numbers cannot be performed, meaning that we cannot produce equalities within this domain. Rather, it is only by the addition of a common measure between numbers (and thus the conversion of ordinal numbers to cardinal numbers) that we can begin to talk about equalising quantities: 'In fact, ordinal number becomes cardinal only by extension, to the extent that the distances enveloped in the *spatium* are explicated, or developed and equalised in an extensity established by natural number' (DR 233/292). We can note that, in these cases, we have a model that parallels the account of intensity we have seen so far. An uncancellable difference (intensity) gives rise to a new domain (extensity) within which that difference is cancelled. 'Here, however, we rediscover only the duality between explication and the implicit, between extensity and the intensive: for if a type of number cancels its difference, it does so only by explicating it within the extension that it installs. Nevertheless, it maintains this difference in itself in the implicated order by which it is grounded' (DR 232/292). Whereas in the thermodynamic model, difference is cancelled *within its own domain,* leading to the idea of the heat death of the universe, for Deleuze difference can only be equalised in a constituted realm, leaving it unequalised in its original domain. Now, while we have been discussing the relationships between numbers, these relationships presuppose different conceptions of space. As cardinal numbers are constituted from elements that are absolutely identical with one another, they presuppose an extensive space. Bergson makes the point as follows:

And yet [numbers] must be somehow distinct from one another, since otherwise they would merge into a single unit. Let us assume that all the sheep in the flock are identical; they differ at least by the position which they occupy in space, otherwise they would not form a flock. But now let us even set aside the fifty sheep themselves and retain only the idea of them. Either we include them all in the same image, and it follows as a necessary consequence that we place them side by side in an ideal space, or else we repeat fifty times in succession the image of a single one, and in that case it does seem, indeed, that the series lies in duration rather than in space. But we shall soon find out that it cannot be so. For if we picture to ourselves each of the sheep in the flock in succession and separately, we shall never have to do with more than a single sheep. In order that the number should go on increasing in proportion as we advance, we must retain the successive images and set them alongside each of the new units which we picture to ourselves: now, it is in space that such a juxtaposition takes place and not in pure duration. (Bergson 1910: 77)

Thus, Deleuze follows what he takes to be Bergson's claim that 'space [is] a condition of number, even if only an ideal space, the time that arises in the ordinal series arising only secondarily, and as spatialized time, that is to say as space of succession' (L 00/00/70).

The second claim Deleuze makes is that intensity affirms difference. Whereas the first claim aimed to show that intensity couldn't be understood in terms of extensity, this second claim is that it also cannot be understood as a quality. Now, in order to support this claim, he argues that whereas qualities are understood in terms of negation, intensity, while it is characterised by difference, is not also characterised by negation. As we saw in Chapter 1, within the Aristotelian notion of definition, a difference presupposes negation. That is, when we wanted to talk about the essence of man, we did so by attributing a property to him called a difference. This difference allowed us to divide the genus into two opposed classes: the rational and the non-rational. Negation was thus fundamental to the process of definition, and to the specification of properties. We can sum up this characterisation of difference with the claim that if x differs from y, x is not y. As we saw in Chapter 1, this constraint on the concept of difference was not inherent to difference itself, but only difference thought in terms of extensity. Scotus' intensive conception of difference avoided the need to define it in terms of negation. We can, in effect, note that the introduction of negation into difference rests on the need to see contrary properties as not inhering in the same object, or occupying the same 'space'. Since intensity is prior to the emergence of both objects and (extensive) space, these restrictions do not apply to it. As Deleuze points out, even if we do look at intensity as it occurs within extensive space, we do not find the strict absence of intensity: 'It is said that in general there are no reports of null frequencies, no effectively null potentials, no absolutely null pressure, as though on a line with logarithmic graduations where zero lies at the end of an infinite series of smaller and smaller fractions' (DR 234/294). Thus, whereas negation can be applied to properties, we never actually discover the negation of an intensity, but only its difference from other intensities. Deleuze here supports Plato's insight that the fact that objects can possess contrary properties presents a shock capable of leading to thinking. Rather than seeing these contrary properties as leading us to contemplation of a timeless realm of Ideas, Deleuze argues that they refer us to a field of intensive difference responsible for the change in qualities we find in the world around us. What makes the qualities in becoming contradictory is that they actualise an underlying intensive difference, and it is this difference that provides the real opening to thought.

Finally, as a third characteristic, 'intensity is an implicated, enveloped, "embryonised" quantity' (DR 237/297). This third characteristic is derived from the previous two. We have seen that cardinal numbers are divisible. Deleuze makes the claim in a lecture on Bergson that this is because, since they are a collection of equal units, dividing them is simply an intellectual operation:

> The divisibility of the unit; for a number is a unity only by virtue of the cardinal colligation, that is to say the simple act of the intelligence that considers the collection as a whole; but not only does the colligation bear on a plurality of units, each of these units is one only by virtue of the simple act that grasps it, and on the contrary is multiple in itself by virtue of its subdivisions upon which the colligation bears. It's in this sense that every number is a distinct multiplicity. And two essential consequences arise from this: at once that the one and the multiple belong to numerical multiplicities, and also the discontinuous and the continuous. The one or discontinuous qualifies the indivisible act by which one conceives one number, then another, the multiple or continuous qualifying on the contrary the (infinitely divisible) matter colligated by this act. (L 00/00/70)

Qualities, on the other hand, are not divisible. It makes no sense to talk of dividing rationality, or animality, for instance. Now, intensity is not like quality, in that it *can* be divided. It is not composed of equal elements, however, but is rather a sequence of asymmetrical relations, such as we find with the ordinal numbers (it is asymmetrical in that second is defined by being 'in between' first and third, but first and third are not 'in between' second). Thus, 'a temperature is not composed of other temperatures, or a speed of other speeds' (DR 237/297). If an intensive multiplicity is not simply constituted from pre-existing elements, then division is true division, leading to a change in the nature of what is divided. Here we can turn to Bergson's alternative form of multiplicity. For Bergson (at least at this stage of his philosophical development), this alternative form of organisation is that which we find in our conscious states, although for Deleuze this mode of organisation is not simply a feature of our perception of the world, but rather of the world itself. As we can see, Bergson's account of the perception of a melody presents clearly the way in which dividing non-extensive multiplicities leads to a change in their nature:

> Pure duration is the form which the succession of our conscious states assumes when our ego lets itself live, when it refrains from separating its present state from its former states. For this purpose it need not be entirely absorbed in the passing sensation or idea; for then, on the contrary, it would no longer endure. Nor need it forget its former states: it is enough that, in recalling these states, it does not set them alongside its actual state as one point alongside another, but forms both the past and the present states into an organic whole, as happens when we recall the notes of a tune, melting, so to speak, into one another. Might it not be said that, even if these notes succeed one another, yet we perceive them in one another, and that their totality may be compared to a living being whose parts, although distinct, permeate one another just because they are so closely connected? The proof is that, if we interrupt the rhythm by dwelling longer than is right on one note of the tune, it is not its exaggerated length, as length, which will warn us of our mistake, but the qualitative change thereby caused in the whole of the musical phrase. We can thus conceive of succession without distinction, and think of it as a mutual penetration, an interconnexion and organization of elements, each one of which represents the whole, and cannot be distinguished or isolated from it except by abstract thought. (Bergson 1910: 100–1)

The two different notions of multiplicity can be mapped onto the extensive and intensive in a relatively straightforward manner:

> Therefore there are two types of multiplicity: one is called multiplicity of juxtaposition, numerical multiplicity, distinct multiplicity, actual multiplicity, material multiplicity, and for predicates it has, we will see, the following: the one and the multiple at once. The other: multiplicity of penetration, qualitative multiplicity, confused multiplicity, virtual multiplicity, organized multiplicity, and it rejects the predicate of the one as well as that of the same. (L 00/00/70)

These two forms of multiplicity can be related to the *extensum* (extensity in general), and the *spatium* (the field of intensive difference as a whole). The three spatial syntheses show how these two multiplicities are related. The final question to be addressed is how the intensive multiplicity is related to the Idea. In answering this question, we will also have to deal with the problem of individuation, or the emergence of the subject from an a-subjective field of intensity.

5.5 Individuation (244–56/305–19)

At this point, we are ready to ask two interrelated questions. The first relates to the two forms of multiplicities we have just encountered. Intensity is explicated in extensity, but as we have just seen, these two structures differ in kind. How, therefore, does the intensive explicate itself into a world of extensions and properties? Second, Chapter 5 has provided a characterisation of the world as intensity. What is the relationship between intensity and the Ideas that Deleuze introduced in the previous chapter?

Answering this second question will allow us to also develop an answer to the first. We have already seen a case of a virtual multiplicity interacting with an individuated intensive system in the second chapter, where memory, which was virtual, interacted with an actual, intensive system governed by habit. In Chapter 5, Deleuze approaches the question of this interaction from a different perspective. His account is relatively straightforward, and I want to begin to explore it by once again taking up his claim that 'the world is an egg' (DR 251/313). When we looked at the structure of the Idea in the previous chapter, we saw that one of the examples Deleuze gave was of Geoffroy's unity of composition (4.5). Geoffroy's intention in developing this structure was to provide a way of comparing different animals in terms of the way in which they actualised a universal set of relations between bones. Thus, the form of actual creatures differs depending on how the non-metric relationships between parts were given determinate magnitudes in extensive space. The anatomical structures of a giraffe and a bison can both be mapped onto the same unity of composition if we only consider the relationships between bones, and put to one side the sizes of the bones themselves as expressed in extensity. The Idea therefore is in some sense determinative of the structure of the organism. At this point, we encounter a potential danger in our account of the development of the form of the organism. If we see the unity of composition as determinative of the form of the organism, we risk merely reiterating the structure of the organism at a transcendental level. By doing so, we remove the essential characteristic of the Idea that it is different in kind from the structure it generates. Deleuze cites DNA as the modern formulation of the Idea of the organism, in that it presents a field of elements that are different in kind from the characteristics we find in the organism to which it relates. Despite the fact that DNA differs in structure from the structure of the organism, there is still a temptation to understand it in terms of those structures. Thus, as the biologist Susan Oyama writes, 'though we all know that there are no hooves or noses in the genes, the accepted formulation is that the genes that are literally passed on make hooves and noses in ontogenesis' (Oyama 2000: 43). Seeing a direct relationship between the Idea and the extensive form that it determines in fact rests on the same model of synthesis we saw in Kant's philosophy. The Idea here would be akin to the active subject that manipulates passive extensive matter into form, and the differenciation of the Idea would be the simple expression of its structure. To turn to Oyama once again, we can see that this model of active synthesis is indeed widespread in genetic theory:

The discovery of DNA and its confirmation of a gene theory that had long been in search of its material agent offered an enormously attractive apparent solution to the puzzle of the origin and perpetuation of living form. A material object housed in every part of the organism, the gene seemed to bridge the gap between inert matter and design; in fact, genetic *information*, by virtue of the meanings of *in-formation* as 'shaping' and as 'animating,' promised to supply just the cognitive and causal functions needed to make a heap of chemicals into a being. (Oyama 2000: 14)

Deleuze himself notes that seeing Ideas as solely responsible for the constitution of the world is a potential misstep in the philosophy of difference that we are prone to:

In fact any confusion between the two processes, any reduction of individuation to a limit or complication of differenciation, compromises the whole of the philosophy of difference. This would be to commit an error, this time in the actual, analogous to that made in confusing the virtual with the possible. Individuation does not presuppose any differenciation; it gives rise to it. (DR 248/308–9)

Instead of the structure of the organism being governed by the operation of Ideas on passive extensity, Deleuze instead argues that it is governed by the interplay between the Idea and the field of intensity: 'Individuation is the act by which intensity determines differential relations to become actualised, along the lines of differenciation and within the qualities and extensities it creates' (DR 246/308).

The process by which intensity generates extensity is governed by a fourfold structure which Deleuze describes as 'differentiation-individua-tion-dramatisation-differenciation' (DR 251/313). As the first category suggests, differentiation is the moment of the calculus, in particular, the wider calculus of the Ideas that we looked at in the previous chapter. At this level, we are not dealing with anything resembling the kinds of entities we encounter in sensibility, hence Deleuze refers to this moment as being structured by 'pre-individual singularities' (DR 246/308). The second moment is the moment of intensity. As we saw, intensity is understood as a difference between two potentials. It is this difference between potentials which allows work to be done in the thermodynamic model of intensive quantities. To return to the example of the cell, we not only have the nucleus, which contains the genetic material, but also the cytoplasm, which appears to be a homogeneous field. Nonetheless, we find that the cytoplasm contains chemical gradients that determine differences between points within the egg. These differences set up potentials similar to the differences in temperature which allow the thermodynamic engine to function. This field of potentials is what Deleuze calls the 'field of individuation': 'An intensity forming a wave of variation throughout the protoplasm distributes its difference along the axes and from one pole to another' (DR 250/312). The interaction of these two moments Deleuze calls 'dramatisation'. If we return to the archetypal model of the Idea, colour, we can see that the Idea can be actualised in a variety of forms, each of which excludes the actualisation of other forms. If we actualise the Idea of colour, it will have to take the form of a particular colour. Similarly, if we actualise the Idea of the unity of composition, we will get a particular animal. It is the field of intensities which determines which form is actualised by determining the speed of development of various parts of the organism according to the distribu-tion of intensities within the egg. Thus, the field of intensity determines how the relations between elements are determined in extensity. As Deleuze noted in Chapter 4, this process of dramatisation relies on movements by the embryo that are topological – that is, understood in non-metric rather than metric terms. While these movements are possi-ble within the intensive field of constitution, they are not possible within the constituted field of extensity: 'Embryology already displays the truth that there are systematic vital movements, torsions and drifts, that only the embryo can sustain: an adult would be torn apart by them' (DR 118/145). While it might be claimed that DNA differs from the unity of composition, in that it specifies one particular form or species, in fact, we can note that here too, the milieu in which the genetic material expresses itself is fundamental to the form generated:

Development seems to involve dynamics as well as chemical computation. When the developing frog embryo turns itself inside out during gastrulation, it looks just like a viscous fluid, flowing in an entirely natural manner. Some of the information required to make this process work may be specified by the laws of fluids, not by DNA. Brian Goodwin sees development as a combination of natural free-flow dynamics and DNA-programmed intervention to stabilize a particular dynamic form. Why should nature waste effort programming the shape of the organism into DNA if the laws of physics will produce it free of charge? It's like programming into DNA the fact that salt crystals must be cubical. For example, the eye – a shape that puzzled both Darwin and his detractors – is dynamically very natural. Rudimentary eyes can occur naturally without any special DNA coding. Natural selection can then refine the rudimentary eye into something more sophisticated, but it is the dynamics that gives selection a head start. (Stewart and Cohen 2000: 294)

The process of dramatisation gives us the final moment: differenciation. The result of the process of dramatisation is the extensive form. We should note, however, that the intensive does not become extensive, but rather gives rise to it. To that extent, dramatisation is concomitant with differenciation.

We have already seen that Deleuze makes the claim that the world is an egg. This claim can be taken in two senses. The first is that the milieu of individuation is not circumscribed by the boundary of the egg. In fact, we can note that the *spatium* (the complete field of intensity) is not made up of discrete elements. As such, the field as a whole is responsible for the differenciation of each entity, although most moments of intensity will have a negligible effect in each case. The second sense is that all phenomena can be understood on the model of the egg. If we return to the opening of Chapter 1, for instance, we find the example of lightning: 'Lightning . . . distinguishes itself from the black sky but must also trail it behind, as though it were distinguishing itself from that which does not distinguish itself from it. It is as if the ground rose to the surface, without ceasing to be ground' (DR 28/36). Here, a difference in electrical potential between the cloud and the ground (individuation) leads to a process of equalisation of charge (differentiation) along a path of least resistance (dramatisation), leading to the visible phenomenon (differenciation). Intensity expresses itself as extensity without itself ceasing to be intensity. There are of course differences in the process of differenciation of biological, physical and social Ideas, but in each case, it is by being brought into relation with a field of intensity that the Idea becomes actualised.

We can now see why Deleuze makes the claim that 'it is not the individual which is an illusion in relation to the genius of the species, but the species which is an illusion – inevitable and well founded, it is true – in relation to the play of the individual and individuation' (DR 250/311). As we saw in Chapter 1, species are defined by the addition of differences to an indeterminate subject. By progressively specifying the properties of an individual, we gradually limit the logical possibilities of what something can be, determining the nature of man, for instance, by addition of the properties material, animate, sensitive and rational, to substance. Given that different individuals clearly do belong to different species, we might be tempted to claim that this hierarchy of terms is what determines the nature of the individual. Thus, we saw that even though DNA differs in kind in structural terms from the organism to which it relates, there was a strong temptation to see it as straightforwardly encoding the kinds of properties Porphyry's tree relied upon: 'there is a tendency to believe that individuation is a continuation of the determination of species, albeit of a different kind and proceeding by different means' (DR 247/308). Once we recognise that individuation does not simply operate on homogeneous, or at best, recalcitrant, matter, but relies on the particular potentialities within the egg, then we can no longer see it as a process of active synthesis relying on the attribution of universal qualities to a particular subject. Rather, differences are always individual, to the extent that they are determined by the reciprocal interplay of Ideas and intensity. They only give rise to these generalised properties once we draw together these individual differences according to their resemblances within the structure of representation. Now, one final point to consider is that if the individuality of the intensive field is responsible for differences being individual, then it cannot be the case that the same intensive field exists in different eggs. If that were the case, then we *could* talk about there being a real existence to species, although this would derive from the intensive field, rather than the Idea. It therefore has to be the case that each egg possesses a different set of intensive potentials:

The form of the field must be necessarily and in itself filled with individual differences. This plenitude must be immediate, thoroughly precocious and not delayed in the egg, to such a degree that the principle of indiscernibles would indeed have the formula given it by Lucretius: no two eggs or grains of wheat are identical. These conditions, we believe, are fully satisfied in the order of implication of intensities. (DR 252/314)

This condition is met by the fact that intensity is not constructed from pre-existing equal units, as extensity is. Rather, Deleuze's claim that 'the world is an egg' makes explicit that the entire *spatium* is implicated in the potentialities of each individual egg, although different aspects of it are implicated to different degrees. As each occupies a different position in the *spatium*, each expresses the *spatium* differently.

At this point, we can note the fundamental difference between Ideas and intensity. When we looked at Descartes' method at the opening to Chapter 3, we saw that Descartes based his method on clear and distinct ideas. The lack of separation between these two terms is, for Deleuze, a fundamental failing of representation:

the weakness of the theory of representation, from the point of view of the logic of knowledge, was to have established a direct proportion between the clear and the distinct, at the expense of the inverse proportion which relates these two logical values: the entire image of thought was compromised as a result. (DR 253/315)

Now, as we saw in the previous chapter (4.8), the terms clear and distinct do not need to be associated with one another. If we consider the noise of the sea, we can conceive of it clearly, in that we can recognise it. Nonetheless, we do not perceive the differences which make it up (the noise of the individual drops of water that make it up and are below our threshold of perception). In this case, our perception of the noise of the sea is both clear and confused. If we instead focus on the noise of the individual waves, we can conceive of these distinctly, even though we cannot form a clear idea of them as they are too small to perceive. Thus, in this case, we either focus on the waves, which are distinct, but obscure, or the sea, which we perceive clearly but confusedly. Similarly, the pure Idea, is distinct, in that it is completely determined. Nonetheless, in so far as it is only in relation to a field of intensity that it can determine *how* it relates to an actual organism (whether it will instantiate a bison or a giraffe), it is obscure. Conversely, intensity expresses some relations clearly only at the expense of other aspects of the Idea which, while still present in the organism, are only present confusedly, on the basis of the domination of certain intensive potentialities. Thus, the process of differenciation can be seen as the movement from a distinct-obscure Idea to a clear-confused field of intensity. Likewise, the thinker, as an individual, is an intensive field. The thought he expresses, however, is the distinct-obscure of the Idea. What gives unity to the thinker is this intensive nature. Just as we cannot divide an intensity without changing its nature, a thinker cannot give up their unity without ceasing to be the particular thinker that they are. Nonetheless, as we saw in Chapter 2, everything thinks. Thus, the death of the thinker is not the end of thought, but merely a change in thinking's nature.

5.6 The Other (256–61/319–25, 281–2/351–2)

In the last few sections, Deleuze's concern has been to explore the processes of individuation and differenciation. A natural question to ask is, where do we locate the individual? We have already seen in our analysis of Feuerbach that the 'I' is a structure of the species (a claim implicit in Descartes' attempt to replace the Aristotelian definition of man with the 'I think') (3.2). As species are a transcendental illusion that emerge after the individual, the 'I' cannot be the seat of the individual. Similarly, the Self – when it is defined as Deleuze does here as 'the properly psychic organism, with its distinctive points represented by the diverse faculties which enter into the comprehension of the I' (DR 257/320) – cannot be identified with the individual, as in this case we are dealing with a representation of the psychic system. In both cases, therefore, we are dealing with a representation of the individual, rather than the individual themselves. Rather than these structures, which are defined in terms of universal properties and extensions, we find the individual in the field of intensity that gives rise to these representational structures. It is the field of intensity, in relation to the Idea that is expressed within it, that forms the basis for the individual: 'These Ideas, however, are expressed in individuating factors, in the implicated world of intensive quantities which constitute the universal concrete individuality of the thinker or the system of the dissolved Self' (DR 259/322).

At the close of Chapter 5, Deleuze introduces the last philosophical theme of *Difference and Repetition*: the Other. As we saw in Chapter 1 (1.11), Deleuze takes up Merleau-Ponty's account of the forgetfulness of our perspective. Now, one of the key moments in this account was the presence in the world of the Other. It was the Other that gave us an infinite number of possible perspectives of the object, thus leading us to take the object, as a given extensive object with properties, as essential, and our own perspective as inessential. Similarly, it was the Other that made us fail to recognise the intensive quality of depth. Rather than seeing depth as the ground for the other dimensions, the presence of the Other allows us to see it 'as a possible length' (DR 281/352), i.e., what is depth for us is simply length from another point of view. Thus, it is the Other that presents us with the field of extended objects and properties, and allows us to develop the language to express 'our commonalities as well as our disagreements with the other' (DR 261/324).

The Other is therefore a precondition for representation, but how does our understanding of the Other develop? Deleuze's claim is that once we note that both the I and the Self are bound up with extensity, representation needs to explain how there can still be a development of the psychic system itself. This process of individuation cannot be attributed to either the self or the I, as these are both extensive or qualitative moments. Rather, the process of individuation is attributed to something seemingly outside of the system of the psyche: to the Other. While the self is seen as something given (the Cartesian cogito), the Other cannot be reduced to a set of properties. Rather, 'the Other cannot be separated from the expressivity which constitutes it' (DR 260/323). When we look at, to use Deleuze's example, a terrified face, we see this face as expressing a world that is terrifying for the subject. Just as extensity differs in kind from intensity, the terrified face differs in kind from the terrifying world it expresses. As such, the Other presents an analogue for the process of individuation. There is a key difference, however. Whereas the intensive is in principle inaccessible to representation, the world expressed in the face of the Other is understood by the psyche as only *de facto* inaccessible. It is merely the same world viewed from another perspective. Rather than providing an understanding of individuation, the Other allows representation to occlude the process of individuation, and thereby establish a world of pre-existing qualities and extensities. It's worth noting at this point that Deleuze is here talking about the Other as a structure within the psyche itself, rather than a particular individual, and in fact, Deleuze leaves space for the possibility of a genuine encounter with others (see DR 139/176 on the encounter with Socrates, for instance). Nonetheless, the role of the philosopher is still one of the renunciation of the 'everybody knows', and with it, the Other:

departing from the subjects which give effect to the Other-structure, we return as far as this structure in itself, thus apprehending the Other as No-one, then continue further, following the bend in sufficient reason until we reach those regions where the Other-structure no longer functions, far from the objects and subjects that it conditions, where singularities are free to be deployed or distributed within pure Ideas, and individuating factors to be distributed in pure intensity. In this sense, it is indeed true that the thinker is necessarily solitary and solipsistic. (DR 282/352)

The Two Prefaces

After *Difference and Repetition* (xv–xxii/xiii–xx)

I want to conclude this guide by taking Deleuze's advice and turning last to the two prefaces to *Difference and Repetition*. The first preface is to the English edition, which was written in 1986, eighteen years after the book's publication in France. The second accompanied its original publication. In this final section, I want to consider briefly how Deleuze's view of *Difference and Repetition* changed after its publication.

In the later preface, Deleuze draws a distinction between his intentions in writing his earlier works, where he 'stud[ied] the arrows or the tools of a great thinker, the trophies and the prey, the continents discovered' (DR xv/xiii), and *Difference and Repetition*, his first attempt at 'doing' philosophy. As such, whilst *Difference and Repetition* is permeated by the history of philosophy, it is the history of philosophy as '*collage*' (DR xix/xx) which provides the material for Deleuze's positive philosophy. As well as presenting a transition in Deleuze's philosophical development, in 1968, Deleuze believes that *Difference and Repetition* is a work on the cusp of a new approach to philosophy more generally, and a concomitant new mode of philosophical expression: 'The time is coming when it will hardly be possible to write a book of philosophy as it has been done for so long: "Ah! the old style ..."' (DR xxi/xx). The original preface is replete with assertions about the dangers of invoking pure differences, and claims about what philosophy *should be* (rather than what it is). These changes were necessary, as Deleuze noted eighteen years later, because 'the majority of philosophers had subordinated difference to identity or to the Same, to the Similar, to the Opposed or to the Analogous' (DR xv/xiii). If philosophy was to continue (and Deleuze is clear that any notion of an end of philosophy is simply 'idle chatter' [WP 9]), a new mode of expression needed to be found. Does *Difference and Repetition* supply this new mode of expression?

In the later preface, Deleuze makes that claim that 'All that I have done since is connected to this book, including what I wrote with Guattari' (DR xv/xiii). In this guide, we have seen that *Difference and Repetition* provides a critique of judgement, together with a positive metaphysics of intensity. It is the critique that is taken up by Deleuze in his later works. For this reason, Deleuze claims that 'it is therefore the third chapter which now seems to me the most necessary and the most concrete, and which serves to introduce subsequent books up to and including the research undertaken with Guattari where we invoked a vegetal model of thought: the rhizome in opposition to the tree, a rhizome-thought instead of an arborescent thought' (DR xvii/xv). In spite of the importance of *Difference and Repetition*, in many of Deleuze's later reflections on it we can detect a certain ambivalence in his attitude. In a preface written in 1990 to Jean-Clet Martin's book on Deleuze's thought, Deleuze writes, 'it seems to me that I have totally abandoned the notion of simulacrum, which is all but worthless' (TRM 362). What is indicative in this comment is a rejection of the more positive project of *Difference and Repetition*. The simulacrum is a key moment in Deleuze's efforts to overturn Platonism, and with it, the model of judgement, but in the process, Deleuze develops a mirror image of Plato's own philosophy, even if, as with Lewis Carroll's looking glass, 'everything is contrary and inverted on the surface, but "different" in depth' (DR 51/62). Thus, at the very moment when, in *Difference and Repetition*, Deleuze appears to break with classical philosophy, he finds himself operating within those same structures:

For my part, when I was no longer content with the history of philosophy, my book *Difference and Repetition* still aspired nonetheless toward a sort of classical height and even toward an archaic depth. The theory of intensity which I was drafting was marked by depth, false or true; intensity was presented as stemming from the depths (and this does not mean that I have any less affection for certain other pages of this book, in particular those concerning weariness and contemplation). (TRM 65)

Deleuze's reflection here clarifies his later attitude to *Difference and Repetition*. While it cleared the ground for the new task of philosophy, *Difference and Repetition* is still a work in the 'old style' which at the time he thought he had left behind. As such, *Difference and Repetition* itself is a text which Deleuze might assign to the history of philosophy. Perhaps rather than seeing *Difference and Repetition* as the beginning of a new phase in Deleuze's development, it might be better to see *Difference and Repetition* as the last (at least until his late book on Leibniz) of his great works on the history of philosophy, and a work itself of the history of philosophy. It is in his later collaborations with Félix Guattari that Deleuze draws out the implications of *Difference and Repetition*, in order to attempt to develop a philosophy that thinks in terms of 'multiplicities for themselves' (TRM 362) rather than 'difference in itself'. There, Deleuze replaces the logic of genealogical enquiry and selection with a thinking in terms of the rhizome and horizontal connections. As he puts it in conversation with Claire Parnet: 'In my earlier books, I tried to describe a certain exercise of thought; but describing it was not yet exercising thought in that way . . . With Félix, all that became possible, even if we failed' (D 16–17/13). Not everyone follows Deleuze in moving beyond *Difference and Repetition* however, and we can also note that its hybrid nature, as a text in the 'old style' that opens onto the later work, is also its strength. *Difference and Repetition* provides a point of transition, but also a point of engagement for those who wish to critique Deleuze, and for those who wish to deploy his own critique within the debates between more traditional philosophical approaches.

2. Study Aids

Glossary

Actualisation: the process whereby Ideas are incarnated in actual terms. (4.12, 5.5)

Clear-Confused: A Leibnizian expression Deleuze uses to characterise the structure of the actual. We can either understand the world in terms of the pre-individual singularities that constitute it, in which case we understand it distinctly (we understand its basic determinations) but obscurely (our analysis is not on the level of how the world is actually given to us), or we can understand it as constituted, in which case we understand it clearly (our analysis is in terms of the given), but confusedly (our analysis does not separate out the genetic factors responsible for the nature of the given). These two languages are mutually exclusive. (4.8)

Cogito: An argument (*Cogito Ergo Sum:* I think, therefore, I am) used by Descartes for the existence of a thinking substance. Also often used to describe the thinking substance itself. (2.6, 3.1)

Common Sense: A faculty that connects together determinations of different faculties by relating them to an abstract object. Deleuze holds this to be the second postulate of the dogmatic image of thought. (3.3)

Dark Precursor: The 'differenciator of difference' that relates together disparate series, thus producing fields of individuation. (2.8)

Depth: Merleau-Ponty's term for the horizon that allows the visible (perspectival) world to be constituted. Deleuze understands this in terms of intensity, and also posits pure depth as the *spatium*. (5.3)

Determination: A property belonging to an object that allows us to distinguish it from other objects.

Difference: Difference is *represented* in terms of negation (x differs from y if x is not y). *Difference and Repetition* presents the project of discovering another kind of affirmative difference that constitutes representational difference. (0.7)

Differenciation: the process whereby the pre-individual distinct-obscure determinations of the Idea become incarnated in actual individuals. (4.12, 5.5)

Differentiation: A mathematical procedure for determining the tangent of a curve. Also, the process of determining the pre-individual elements that constitute a particular individual. (4.2)

Distinct-Obscure: see Clear-Confused.

Dramatisation: The process whereby Ideas find expression in an individuated field of intensity. (5.5)

Extensity: A space of measurable (metric) magnitudes (our classical model of actual space, for instance), or a given measurable magnitude. (5.4)

Extensum: The whole of extensity. (5.3)

Faculty: A mental power to be able to relate to a certain kind of experience, or to relate to a particular aspect of an object (the faculty of speech, the faculty of taste, or the faculty of reason, for instance). (3.3–3.6, 4.9)

Fractured I: Deleuze's characterisation of the self which represents itself as a clear-confused unity that is (un)grounded in a distinct-obscure abyss. (2.6)

Good Sense: A systematic organisation of determinations of objects (for instance, the tree of Porphyry) that is presupposed by the dogmatic image of thought. (3.3, 3.7, 5.2)

Idea: For Kant, a structure that allows reason to systematise knowledge. For Deleuze, a structure that governs the constitution of the actual. (4.1–4.12)

Illusion, transcendental: For Kant, a transcendental illusion is an object that is not given in experience, but must nonetheless be posited in order for reason to systematise our knowledge. It leads us into error if we follow thought's natural tendency and assume that it can be known, rather than just thought. For Deleuze, the main transcendental illusion we suffer from is that for something to be determined is for it to have the structure of a representation, thus ruling out the possibility of non-conceptual difference. (3.4, 3.7, 4.1, 4.2, 5.2, 5.5)

Individuation: The establishment of a relation of resonance between intensive series, leading to the establishment of a field of individuation. (5.5)

Intensity: In terms of thermodynamics, this refers to an intensive property, such as temperature or pressure that allows work to be performed. In Deleuze's terms, it is a non-metric field of differences that differs in kind when divided. (5.4)

Judgement: In logical terms, the attribution of a determination or property to an object. (1.1)

Larval subject: A systematic collection of passive syntheses which together constitute a self. (2.3)

Multiplicity: A variety. This can either be an actual multiplicity, which is made up of a set of elements subsumed under a unity (the one and the many), or a virtual multiplicity, where the unity is constituted by the elements themselves. (5.4)

Nomadic Distribution: A conception of the foundations of the world of representation that sees those foundations as having a different kind of structure to the world itself. (1.6)

Passive Synthesis: A process whereby elements are drawn together and organised that constitutes, rather than presupposes, a self. (2.2)

Problem: Deleuze describes two kinds of problems. The first, drawn from solutions, cover over difference. (3.9) The second are different in kind from their solutions, and give rise to the actual. Problems are objective structures, and occur in amongst others, psychological, biological and social milieus. (4.1, 4.10)

Question: The question emerges from an encounter (an imperative), and relates thought to Ideas. For Plato, the question is, 'What is x?', for Deleuze, the key questions are 'how many', 'how', 'in which cases'? (4.10)

Repetition: Deleuze introduces two forms of repetition. 'Bare' repetition is our normal conception of repetition, whereas 'clothed repetition' is different in kind from this form of repetition, and is responsible for it. (0.4)

Representation: A way of characterising the world, relying on the concepts of identity, analogy, opposition and resemblance, that attempts to guarantee the subordination of difference to identity. (0.5, 1.1, 3.4)

Sedentary Distribution: A conception of the foundations of the world of representation that sees those foundations as having the same kind of structure as the world itself. (1.6)

Simulacrum: An image that does not rely on a prior identity. (1.11, 1.12)

Spatium: The field of intensity taken as a whole. (5.3, 5.4)

Univocity: The claim that the being of everything is said in the same sense. (1.3–1.7)

Virtual: A type of organisation associated with the distinct-obscure, a multiplicity formed by reciprocally determining elements that gives the conditions for experience. (4.8)

Further Reading

The variety of thinkers Deleuze refers to in *Difference and Repetition* is overwhelming. The aim of this section is to give some of the key reference points Deleuze relies on in the various sections, as an aid to further reading. The list is not comprehensive by any means, and largely tracks the reading of *Difference and Repetition* given in this book. Similarly, I have only listed texts available in English. The vast majority of these texts are thought provoking pieces in their own right, however, and I would advise the reader to spend time reading them beyond the bounds of their relevance to *Difference and Repetition*. I have also listed some other texts on Deleuze that might be of use in approaching *Difference and Repetition*. While there is much excellent scholarship on Deleuze's philosophy, here I want to focus on those texts which concern themselves principally with *Difference and Repetition* itself.

Other Commentaries on *Difference and Repetition*

Keith Ansell Pearson (1999) is an excellent study of Deleuze's attempt to rework many of the fundamental concepts of biology. While Ansell Pearson's analysis is thematic, and his aim is not to give an account of the whole of *Difference and Repetition*, the sections on Freud, Weismann, the eternal return, and modern biology are well worth reading.

Levi Bryant (2008) provides a thoughtful reading of *Difference and Repetition*, reading it in relation to Deleuze's early works more generally, and focusing on Deleuze's attempt to use Kant to develop an augmented Bergsonism.

Manuel DeLanda (2002) gives a coherent, albeit idiosyncratic reading of *Difference and Repetition*. DeLanda reads Deleuze almost exclusively in terms of his engagements in science.

Joe Hughes (2009) provides a very readable introduction to *Difference and Repetition*, taking a different line to the one taken here. Hughes sees Deleuze as developing a theory of experience, reading him primarily in relation to Kant, Husserl and Heidegger.

James Williams (2003) approaches *Difference and Repetition* thematically, and provides a strong, consistent interpretation of the book. It is one of the few books on Deleuze to attempt to assess the veracity of his arguments.

Further Reading by Section
Introduction: Repetition and Difference
0.2) The limitations of science are a theme running through Bergson's work, but, see in particular Bergson 1998: 1–23.

0.3) Deleuze is here referring to Kant 1998. Deleuze's detailed analysis of the need for analogy in Kant's moral philosophy can be found in KCP 33–35/28–30.

0.4) Kierkegaard 1983 is the principal source for Deleuze's reading of Kierkegaard – on the fact that Abraham falls outside of the universal, see in particular the sections on Preliminary Expectoration (25–53) and Problema I (54–67). For the impossibility of physical repetition, see 148–54, and for spiritual repetition, Letters from the Young man (188–215), particularly 13 January (212–13).

0.6) The key source for the debate about the nature of space is Leibniz and Clarke 2000. Kant presents his argument from incongruent counterparts in his pre-critical essay, Kant 1968, and in 1997: §13. The difference in kind between sensible intuition and the concepts of the understanding is essential to Deleuze's project, and is outlined in Kant 1929: A22–6/B37–42.

Chapter 1: Difference in Itself
1.2) The key work Deleuze addresses is Aristotle 1984a, although Aristotle's logic is scattered through the 'Categories', 'De Interpretatione', 'Prior Analytics', 'Posterior Analytics' and 'Topics'. He also references Porphyry 2003, which, while a trifle repetitive, still provides a useful introduction to the relevant portions of Aristotelian logic.

1.3) Aristotle 1984b: Book III and the opening of Book IV, are the focus of this section, although the works cited in 1.2 are still in the background. Pontilis 2004: 90–121, provides a detailed discussion of the problem of the highest genus, and the solution of focal meaning.

1.4) Deleuze provides an easier to follow account of the importance of Scotus' univocity in L 14/01/1974 ('Anti Oedipe Et Mille Plateaux, Cours Vincennes'). Duns Scotus 1978a and 1978b contain Scotus' definition of univocity. Cross 1999 provides a good summary of Scotus' account of univocity and the intensive infinite.

1.5) L 14/01/1974 is again a useful resource for understanding

Deleuze's reading of Spinoza, as is, of course, EPS. Chapter 3 of Hardt 1993 presents the main aspects of Deleuze's reading clearly. The main text is Spinoza 1994.

1.6–1.7) See Nietzsche 2006a: §13, and NP (with a focus on Chapter 2) for the difference between the two distributions. Nietzsche 2001: §341 gives Nietzsche's most famous account of the eternal return.

1.9) In this guide, I have focused on Hegel's dialectic of the finite and infinite (Hegel 1999: 116–56), but to do justice to the Hegel-Deleuze relationship, readers should look at the book-length studies, Adkins 2007, Duffy 2006, or Somers-Hall 2012.

1.10) The key text for Deleuze's reading of Leibniz is 1989a. FLB provides a later and more positive reading.

1.11) Merleau-Ponty's account of the forgetfulness of perspective can be found in Merleau-Ponty 1962: 67–72.

1.12) Myths can be found throughout Plato's work, as can questions of method, but Deleuze focuses on Plato 1997c and Plato 1997d. Moravcsik 1992: Chapter 6, provides an account of the differences between Plato and Aristotle's methods.

Chapter 2: Repetition For Itself

2.2) Kant's transcendental deduction is presented in Kant 1929: A84–130. Most commentaries on the *Critique of Pure Reason* focus on the B-deduction, which Deleuze claims simply covers over the psychologism of the A deduction. Burnham and Young 2007: 76–87, provides an easy to follow account of the three syntheses.

2.3) ES, particularly Chapter 5, provides Deleuze's extended discussion of the difference between Hume and Kant, and discusses the constitutive role of time for subjectivity. Hughes 2009: 86–111 provides a very different reading of the first synthesis (and the chapter as a whole) from a phenomenological perspective. On the nature of synthesis in Chapter 2, see Widder 2008: 86–99.

2.4) Bergson's account of memory can be found in Bergson 1991: Chapter III. Deleuze provides another account of this material in B, particularly Chapter 3.

2.5) The sections of Plato Deleuze is referring to are 1997e: 29d–43a. See also L 14/03/78.

2.6) Kant 1929: A341–405/B399–432 gives Kant's account of the paralogisms.

2.7) Aside from Shakespeare 2003, see Rosenberg 1994, 'Character

Change and Drama'. Somers-Hall 2011 provides a more detailed account than the one found here, contrasting Rosenberg with Aristotle's *Poetics*. Deleuze also makes use of Hölderlin 2009 to argue for a similar structure in Sophocles 2003. Deleuze also sees this structure in Nietzsche 2006b. See 'Of Redemption' for the two forms of time, 'Of the Vision and the Riddle' and 'The Convalescent' for the two false readings of the eternal return, 'Of Involuntary Bliss' for the caesura, and 'The Sign' as the moment of the future.

2.9–2.12) The key text is Freud 2003a, particularly the later speculative sections (IV–VII). Freud 1966 and Freud 2003b are useful background reading.

Chapter 3: The Image of Thought

3.2) Feuerbach 1997 provides Feuerbach's analysis of the Image of Thought. Descartes' critique of objective presuppositions can be found in Descartes 1984b and 1984a: Meditation 2. For Hegel's criticism of Descartes, see Hegel 1999: 75–8, and for his understanding of presuppositions in philosophy, see 67–78.

3.3) See (2.2) and (3.4) for Kant's account of common sense. Descartes' account is presented in Descartes 1984a: Second Meditation.

3.4) For a more detailed discussion of the relationship of Kant's faculties, see KCP 11–27/10–23.

3.5) For the encounter that leads to knowledge of the Ideas, see Plato 1997a: 70a-77a, and Plato 1997b: book VII. For the analogy of the divided line, see Plato 1997b: 509d-513e.

3.6) See Kant 1987: §23–9 for his account of the sublime. Deleuze relates this discussion to Artaud 1968.

3.7) See Descartes 1984a: Meditation 1 for the method of doubt, and meditation 4 for Descartes' theory of error. For Kant on transcendental illusion, see the reading for (4.1).

3.8) See Russell 1940: Chapter XIII. The material presented here is dealt with in greater detail in LS.

3.9) See (4.1).

3.10) See (4.9).

Chapter 4: The Ideal Synthesis of Difference

4.1) Kant discusses Ideas throughout the transcendental dialectic, but in particular in Kant 1929: A310–338/B366–396, and A642–668/B670–696.

4.2) Few of the sources Deleuze refers to, apart from Maimon 2010, are available in English. Boyer 1959 gives a decent account of the history of the calculus, focusing on its conceptual development. Deleuze's approach to the calculus is also heavily influenced by Lautman 2011.

4.4) The two principal sources are Epicurus 1926 and Lucretius 2001. See LS 266–79/303–20 for an extended discussion by Deleuze of ancient atomism.

4.5) Hardly any of Geoffroy or Cuvier's works have been translated into English. Appel 1987 and Coleman 1964 provide good sources for the debate. See also ATP '3. 10,000 B.C.: The Geology of Morals (Who Does the Earth Think It Is?)', for a further account by Deleuze (with Guattari) of the Cuvier–Geoffroy debate.

4.6) See Althusser 2005: Chapter 3, for the difference between Hegelian and Marxist dialectics. See also Althusser and Balibar 2009, particularly Chapter 8.

4.7) For the relation of depth, see Bourbaki 1950.

4.8) Deleuze here relies on Bergson's critique of possibility in Bergson 1992: 73–86, and his analysis of essence in Bergson 1992: 187–216. For Kant on possibility, see Kant 1929: A592–603/B620–631.

4.9) Deleuze relates the difference between knowledge and learning to Plato's analogy of the divided line (Plato 1997b: 509d–513e). Bergson 1998: 192 gives his account of swimming.

4.10) Nietzsche discusses the dice throw in Nietzsche 2006b: 'Before Sunrise'.

4.11) Deleuze here borrows from the discussion of order and disorder in Bergson 1998: Chapter 3.

4.12) The reading for (5.5) covers this section. DeLanda 2002 ties in the dynamic systems approach to Deleuze's work.

Chapter 5: The Asymmetrical Synthesis of the Sensible

5.2) Boltzmann 1964: §87–90, gives Boltzmann's views on the inevitable heat death of the universe. Atkins 2010 provides a relatively accessible account of the development of thermodynamics. Chapter 8 of Stewart and Cohen 2000 gives a good account of its limitations.

5.3) Merleau-Ponty presents his account of depth in 1962: 254–267. This account is reiterated in Merleau-Ponty 1964. See also Kant 1991 and Kant 1968 for Kant's account of the determinations of left and right.

5.4) DeLanda's account of cardinal and ordinal numbers can be found in DeLanda 2002: 73–4. Deleuze interprets this distinction along the lines of Bergson's two multiplicities in Bergson 1910: Chapter 2. L 00/00/70 presents this reading in more depth. Deleuze references Griss's studies in negationless mathematics. While not much is available in English, Heyting 1956: 124–6 provides an outline of Griss's approach and its limitations.

5.5) Deleuze's understanding of the role of cytoplasm in the development of the organism fits well with dynamic systems theory approaches. See Chapter 9 of Stewart and Cohen 2000 for an overview, and Oyama 2000 for a more extensive treatment.

5.6) Deleuze extends his analysis of the Other in his essay on Tournier in LS (301–20/341–58). Deleuze is here engaging with Hegel's analysis of the role of the Other in Hegel 1977: 104–13.

Tips for Writing about Deleuze

1) Deleuze's writing relies on a large technical vocabulary. If you are using it, it is always worth defining your (or Deleuze's) terms. Similarly, be aware of the fact that many of Deleuze's terms also have a non-technical meaning. Do not confuse concepts such as Idea, virtual and identity, with their everyday equivalents.

2) While there are many affinities between *Difference and Repetition* and Deleuze's later collaborations with Guattari, his philosophical views do change. If you are going to use work from both periods, make sure you justify your decision.

3) It is a good idea to use quotations from Deleuze to justify your reading, but make sure you explain any quotations you use, especially when the meaning is obscure.

4) While a certain obscurity of style is an integral part of Deleuze's project, I wouldn't recommend students incorporate this moment into their essays. You need to show the reader that you have understood (or at least made efforts to understand) Deleuze's philosophy itself.

5) Plan the structure of your essay carefully. Because Deleuze refers to so many other thinkers, it is easy to lose focus in your writings.

6) Remember that we are all contractions of elements and passive syntheses: make sure you eat a balanced diet while writing your essays.

Bibliography

Adkins, Brent (2007), *Death and Desire in Hegel, Heidegger and Deleuze*, Edinburgh: Edinburgh University Press.

Althusser, Louis (2005), *For Marx*, trans. Ben Brewster, London: Verso.

Althusser, Louis and Etienne Balibar (2009), *Reading Capital*, trans. Ben Brewster, London: Verso.

Ansell Pearson, Keith (1999), *Germinal Life: The Difference and Repetition of Deleuze*, London: Routledge.

Appel, Toby A. (1987), *The Cuvier-Geoffroy Debate: French Biology in the Decades Before Darwin*, New York: Oxford University Press.

Aristotle (1984a), 'Categories', trans. J. L. Ackrill, in Jonathan Barnes (ed.), *The Complete Works of Aristotle*, Princeton: Princeton University Press, 3–24.

Aristotle (1984b), 'Metaphysics', trans. W. D. Ross, in Jonathan Barnes (ed.), *The Complete Works of Aristotle*, Princeton: Princeton University Press, 1552–1728.

Aristotle (1984c), 'Posterior Analytics', trans. Jonathan Barnes, in Jonathan Barnes (ed.), *The Complete Works of Aristotle*, Princeton: Princeton University Press, 114–66.

Aristotle (1984d), 'Topics', trans. W. A. Pickard-Cambridge, in Jonathan Barnes (ed.), *The Complete Works of Aristotle*, Princeton: Princeton University Press, 167–277.

Arnauld, Antoine (1850), *Logic or the Art of Thinking, being the Port Royal Logic*, trans. Thomas Spencer Baynes, Edinburgh: Sutherland and Knox.

Artaud, Antonin (1968), 'Correspondence with Jacques Rivière', in Victor Corti (ed.), *Collected Works of Antonin Artaud, Vol. 1*, London: John Calder.

Atkins, Peter (2010), *The Laws of Thermodynamics: A Very Short Introduction*, Oxford: Oxford University Press.

Bergson, Henri (1910), *Time and Free Will*, trans. F. L. Pogson, London: Allen and Unwin.

Bergson, Henri (1991), *Matter and Memory*, trans. N. M. Paul and W. S. Palmer, New York: Zone Books.

Bergson, Henri (1992), *The Creative Mind*, trans. Mabelle L. Andison, New York: Carol Publishing.

Bergson, Henri (1998), *Creative Evolution*, trans. Arthur Mitchell, Mineola, NY: Dover Publications.

Boltzmann, Ludwig (1964), *Lectures on Gas Theory*, trans. Stephen G. Brush, Berkeley: California Press.

Bordas-Demoulin (1843), *Le Cartésianisme, ou La Véritable Rénovation des Sciences, vol. 2*, Paris: J. Hetzel.

Bourbaki, Nicholas (1950), 'The Architecture of Mathematics', trans. Arnold Dresden, in *The American Mathematical Monthly*, 57, 221–32.

Boyer, Carl (1959), *The History of the Calculus and its Conceptual Development*, New York: Dover Publications.

Burnham, Douglas and Harvey Young (2007), *Kant's Critique of Pure Reason*, Edinburgh: Edinburgh University Press.

Bryant, Levi (2008), *Difference and Givenness: Deleuze's Transcendental Empiricism and the Ontology of Immanence*, Evanston: Northwestern University Press.

Coleman, William (1964), *Georges Cuvier: Zoologist*, Cambridge, MA: Harvard University Press.

Cross, Richard (1999), *Duns Scotus*, Oxford: Oxford University Press.

DeLanda, Manuel (2002), *Intensive Science and Virtual Philosophy*, London: Continuum.

Descartes, René (1984a), 'Meditations on First Philosophy', trans. John Cottingham, in John Cottingham, Robert Stoothoff and Dugald Murdoch (eds), *The Philosophical Writings of Descartes, Vol. II*, Cambridge: Cambridge University Press, 1–397.

Descartes, René (1984b), 'The Search for Truth', trans. Robert Stoothoff and Dugald Murdoch, in John Cottingham, Robert Stoothoff and Dugald Murdoch (eds), *The Philosophical Writings of Descartes, Vol. II*, Cambridge: Cambridge University Press, 399–420.

Descartes, René (1985a), 'Discourse on Method and Essays', trans. Robert Stoothoff, in John Cottingham, Robert Stoothoff and Dugald Murdoch (eds), *The Philosophical Writings of Descartes, Vol. I*, Cambridge: Cambridge University Press, 111–76.

Descartes, René (1985b), 'Rules for the Direction of the Mind', trans. Dugald Murdoch, in John Cottingham, Robert Stoothoff and Dugald Murdoch (eds), *The Philosophical Writings of Descartes, Vol. I*, Cambridge: Cambridge University Press, 7–78.

Duffy, Simon (2006), *The Logic of Expression: Quality, Quantity and Intensity in Spinoza, Hegel and Deleuze*, Aldershot: Ashgate Publishers.

Duns Scotus, John (1978a), 'Concerning Metaphysics', in Allan Wolter (trans. and ed.), *Philosophical Writings*, Cambridge: Hackett Publishing, 1–12.

Duns Scotus, John (1978b), 'Man's Natural Knowledge of God', in Allan Wolter (trans. and ed.), *Philosophical Writings*, Cambridge: Hackett Publishing, 13–33.

Epicurus (1926), 'Letter to Herodotus', in Cyril Bailey (ed.), *Epicurus: The Extant Remains*, Oxford: Clarendon Press, 18–55.

Feuerbach, Ludwig (1997), 'Towards a Critique of Hegelian Philosophy', in Lawrence S. Stepelevich (ed.), *The Young Hegelians: An Anthology*, Amherst, NY: Humanities Press, 95–128.

Freud, Sigmund (1966), 'Project for a Scientific Psychology', in James Strachey (ed.), *The Standard Edition of the Complete Works of Sigmund Freud vol. 1*, London: Hogarth Press.

Freud, Sigmund (2003a), 'Beyond the Pleasure Principle', in *Beyond the Pleasure Principle and Other Writings*, trans. John Reddick, London: Penguin Books, 43–102.

Freud, Sigmund (2003b), 'Remembering, Repeating, and Working Through', in *Beyond the Pleasure Principle and Other Writings*, trans. John Reddick, London: Penguin Books, 31–42.

Grattin-Guinness, I. (1980) 'The Emergence of Mathematical Analysis and its Foundational Progress, 1780 (1880)', in Ivor Grattin-Guinness (ed.), *From the Calculus to Set Theory, 1630–1910: An Introductory History*, Princeton: Princeton University Press, 94–148.

Guéroult, Martial (1929), *La Philosophie Transcendantale de Salomon Maïmon*, Paris: Librarie Félix Alcan.

Hall, Alex (2007), *Thomas Aquinas and John Duns Scotus: Natural Theology in the High Middle Ages*, London: Continuum.

Hardt, Michael (1993) *Gilles Deleuze: An Apprenticeship in Philosophy*, Minneapolis: Minnesota University Press.

Hegel, Georg Wilhelm Friedrich (1977) *Hegel's Phenomenology of Spirit*, trans. A. W. Miller, Oxford: Oxford University Press.

Hegel, Georg Wilhelm Friedrich (1999), *Science of Logic*, trans. A. V. Miller, Amherst, NY: Humanity Books.

Heyting, A. (1956), *Intuitionism: An Introduction*, London: North-Holland Publishing Company.

Höené Wronski, Józef Maria (1814), *Philosophie de l'Infini*, Paris: P. Diderot L'Ainé.

Hölderlin, Friedrich (2009), 'Notes on the *Oedipus*', trans. Jeremy Adler and Charlie Louth, in *Essays and Letters*, London: Penguin Books, 317–24.

L'Hôpital (1969), 'The Analysis of the Infinitesimally Small', in D. J. Struik (ed.), *A Source Book in Mathematics, 1200–1800*, Cambridge, MA: Harvard University Press, 312–15.

Hughes, Joe (2009), *Deleuze's Difference and Repetition*, London: Continuum.

Hume, David (2000), *A Treatise of Human Nature*, Oxford: Oxford University Press.

Kant, Immanuel (1929), *Critique of Pure Reason*, trans. Norman Kemp Smith, London: St. Martin's Press.

Kant, Immanuel (1968), 'Concerning the Ultimate Foundation for the Differentiation of Regions in Space', in G. B. Kerferd and D. E. Walford (trans. and ed.), *Selected Pre-Critical Writings*, Manchester: Manchester University Press.

Kant, Immanuel (1987), *Critique of Judgment*, trans. Werner S. Pluhar, Indianapolis: Hackett Publishing.

Kant, Immanuel (1991) 'What is Orientation in Thinking?', trans. H. B. Nisbet, in Hans Reiss (ed.), *Kant: Political Writings*, Cambridge: Cambridge University Press, 237–49.

Kant, Immanuel (1997), *Prolegomena to any Future Metaphysics*, trans. Gary Carl Hatfield. Cambridge: Cambridge University Press.

Kant, Immanuel (1998), *Groundwork of the Metaphysics of Morals*, trans. Mary Gregor, Cambridge: Cambridge University Press.

Kant, Immanuel (2005), *Notes and Fragments*, trans. Paul Guyer, Cambridge: Cambridge University Press.

Kierkegaard, Søren (1983), *Fear and Trembling/Repetition*, trans. Howard V. Hong and Edna H. Hong, Princeton: Princeton University Press.

Lautman, Albert (2011), *Mathematics, Ideas and the Physical Real*, trans. Simon Duffy, London: Continuum.

Leibniz, Gottfried Wilhelm (1989a), 'The Principles of Philosophy, or, the Monadology', in Roger Ariew and Daniel Garber (ed. and trans.), *Philosophical Essays*, Cambridge: Hackett Publishing, 213–24.

Leibniz, Gottfried Wilhelm (1989b), 'Samples of the Numerical Characteristic', in Roger Ariew and Daniel Garber (ed. and trans.), *Philosophical Essays*, Cambridge: Hackett Publishing, 10–19.

Leibniz, Gottfried Wilhelm (1997), *New Essays on Understanding*, trans. and ed. Peter Remnant and Jonathan Bennett, Cambridge: Cambridge University Press.

Leibniz, Gottfried Wilhelm and Clarke, Samuel (2000), *Correspondence*, ed. Roger Ariew, Cambridge: Hackett Publishing.

Lucretius (2001), *On the Nature of Things*, trans. Martin Ferguson Smith, Indianapolis: Hackett Publishing Ltd.

Maimon, Salomon (1791), *Philosophisches Wörterbuch, oder Beleuchtung der wichtigsten Gegenstände der Philosophie*, Berlin: Johann Friedrich Unger.

Maimon, Salomon (2010), *Essay on Transcendental Philosophy*, trans. Nick Midgley, Henry Somers-Hall, Alistair Welchman, and Merten Reglitz, London: Continuum Press.

Merleau-Ponty, Maurice (1962), *Phenomenology of Perception*, trans. Colin Smith, London: Routledge & Kegan Paul.

Merleau-Ponty, Maurice (1964), 'Eye and Mind', trans. Carlton Dallery, in *The Primacy of Perception*, Evanston: Northwestern University Press, 159–90.

Moravcsik, Julius (1992), *Plato and Platonism*, Oxford: Blackwell Publishers.

Nietzsche, Friedrich (2001), *The Gay Science*, trans. Josefine Nauckhoff, Cambridge: Cambridge University Press.

Nietzsche, Friedrich (2006a), *On the Genealogy of Morality*, trans. Carol Diethe, Cambridge: Cambridge University Press.

Nietzsche, Friedrich (2006b), *Thus Spoke Zarathustra*, ed. and trans. Adrian Del Caro and Robert Pippin, Cambridge: Cambridge University Press.

Newton, Sir Isaac (1934), *Mathematical Principles of Natural Philosophy and his System of the World*, trans. Felix Cajori, Los Angeles: University of California Press.

Oyama, Susan (2000), *The Ontogeny of Information: Developmental Systems and Evolution*, Durham, NC: Duke University Press.

Plato (1997a), 'Phaedo', trans. G. M. A. Grube, in John M. Cooper (ed.), *Plato: Complete Works*, Indianapolis: Hackett Publishing, 49–100.

Plato (1997b), 'The Republic', trans. rev. C. D. C. Reeve, in John M. Cooper (ed.), *Plato: Complete Works*, Indianapolis: Hackett Publishing, 971–1223.

Plato (1997c), 'The Sophist', trans. Nicholas P. White, in John M. Cooper (ed.), *Plato: Complete Works*, Indianapolis: Hackett Publishing, 235–93.

Plato (1997d), 'The Statesman', trans. C. J. Rowe, in John M. Cooper (ed.), *Plato: Complete Works*, Indianapolis: Hackett Publishing, 294–358.

Plato (1997e), 'Timaeus', trans. Donald J. Zeyl, in John M. Cooper (ed.), *Plato: Complete Works*, Indianapolis: Hackett Publishing, 1224–91.

Pontilis, Vasilis (2004), *Aristotle and the Metaphysics*, London: Routledge.

Porphyry (2003), *Introduction*, trans. Jonathan Barnes, Oxford: Clarendon Press.

Rosenberg, Harold (1994), *The Tradition of the New*, New York: De Capo Press.

Russell, Bertrand (1940), *An Inquiry into Meaning and Truth*, London: George Allen and Unwin.

Ruyer, Raymond (1958), *La Genèse des Formes Vivantes*, Paris: Flammarion.

Shakespeare, William (2003), *Hamlet*, Cambridge: Cambridge University Press.

Somers-Hall, Henry (2011), 'Time Out of Joint: Hamlet and the Pure Form of Time', *Deleuze Studies*, 5.4, 56–76.

Somers-Hall, Henry (2012), *Hegel, Deleuze, and the Critique of Representation*, Albany, NY: SUNY Press.

Sophocles (2003), *Antigone*, trans. David Franklin and John Harrison, Cambridge: Cambridge University Press.

Spinoza (1992), *Ethics*, trans. Samuel Shirley, Indianapolis: Hackett Publishing.

Stewart, Ian, and Jack Cohen (2000), *The Collapse of Chaos: Discovering Simplicity in a Complex World*, London: Penguin Books.

Tomarchio, John (2002), 'Aquinas's Concept of Infinity', in the *Journal of the History of Philosophy*, 40.2, 163–87.

Widder, Nathan (2008), *Reflections on Time and Politics*, University Park, PA: Pennsylvania University Press.

Williams, James (2003), *Gilles Deleuze's* Difference and Repetition: *A Critical Introduction and Guide*, Edinburgh: Edinburgh University Press.

Index